WOMEN IN YORUBA RELIGIONS

WOMEN IN RELIGIONS
Series Editor: Catherine Wessinger

Women in Christian Traditions
Rebecca Moore

Women in New Religions
Laura Vance

Women in Japanese Religions
Barbara R. Ambros

Theory of Women in Religions
Catherine Wessinger

Women in Buddhist Traditions
Karma Lekshe Tsomo

Women in Yoruba Religions
Oyèrónké Oládémọ

Women in Yoruba Religions

Oyèrónké Oládémọ

NEW YORK UNIVERSITY PRESS
New York

NEW YORK UNIVERSITY PRESS
New York
www.nyupress.org

© 2022 by New York University
All rights reserved

References to Internet websites (URLs) were accurate at the time of writing. Neither the author nor New York University Press is responsible for URLs that may have expired or changed since the manuscript was prepared.

Library of Congress Cataloging-in-Publication Data
Names: Oládémọ, Oyèrónké, author.
Title: Women in Yoruba Religions / Oyèrónké Oládémọ.
Description: New York : New York University Press, [2022] | Series: Women in Religions | Includes bibliographical references and index.
Identifiers: LCCN 2021044600 | ISBN 9781479813971 (hardback : acid-free paper) | ISBN 9781479813995 (paperback) | ISBN 9781479814015 (ebook) | ISBN 9781479814022 (ebook other)
Subjects: LCSH: Yoruba (African people)—Religion. | Women and religion. | Women, Yoruba—Religion.
Classification: LCC BL2480.Y6 O46 2022 | DDC 299.6/8333—dc23/eng/20211112
LC record available at https://lccn.loc.gov/2021044600

New York University Press books are printed on acid-free paper, and their binding materials are chosen for strength and durability. We strive to use environmentally responsible suppliers and materials to the greatest extent possible in publishing our books.

Manufactured in the United States of America

10 9 8 7 6 5 4 3 2 1

Also available as an ebook

CONTENTS

Note on the Spelling of Yorùbá Words	vii
Introduction: Why Study Women in Yorùbá Religions?	1
1. Women's Family, Economic, Social, and Political Roles in Yorùbáland	13
2. Women's Leadership in Rituals of the Yorùbá Religion	42
3. Yorùbá Women in Christianity	65
4. Yorùbá Women in Islam	89
5. Women and the Yorùbá Religions in the Diaspora	103
6. Women in the Yorùbá Religion and Globalization	127
Conclusion	137
Acknowledgments	143
Questions for Discussion	145
For Further Reading	149
Notes	151
Bibliography	163
Index	179
About the Author	187

NOTE ON THE SPELLING OF YORÙBÁ WORDS

Yoruba is a tonal language, with the same combination of vowels and consonants having different meanings depending on the pitch of the vowels—whether they are pronounced with a high voice, a middle voice, or a low voice.[1] For example, the word *apa* can mean "hand," "squanderer," or "scar from a wound," depending on the intonation.

In the spelling of Yoruba words using English letters, the high tone is indicated by an acute accent mark (´) over a vowel (á, é, ẹ́, í, ó, ọ́, and ú), the middle tone is indicated by no accent mark over a vowel, and the low tone is indicated by a grave accent mark (`) over a vowel (à, è, ẹ̀, ì, ò, ọ̀, and ù). The *e* with a dot below it is pronounced like the *e* in "hen." The *o* with a dot below it is pronounced like the *o* in "hot."[2] Omniglot: The Online Encyclopedia of Writing Systems and Languages gives the Yoruba alphabet as shown in the figure.

Yoruba Alphabet (Álífábẹ́ẹ̀tì Yorùbá)								
Aa	Bb	Dd	Ee	Ẹẹ	Ff	Gg	Gbgb	Hh
ah	bi	di	e	ẹ	fi	gi	gbi	he
[ä]	[b]	[d]	[e]	[ɛ]	[f]	[g]	[g͡b]	[h]
Ii	Jj	Kk	Ll	Mm	Nn	Oo	Ọọ	Pp
i	ji	ki	li	mi	ni	o	ọ	pi
[i]	[d͡ʒ]	[k]	[l]	[m]	[n/m̩]	[o]	[ɔ]	[k͡p/p]
Rr	Ss	Ṣṣ	Tt	Uu	Ww	Yy		
ri	si	ṣi	ti	u	wi	yi		
[r/ɹ]	[s]	[ʃ]	[t]	[u]	[w]	[j]		

Nasal vowels (Awọn Fawẹli Aranmupe)					Tone marks		
an	ẹn	in	ọn	un	á	a	à
[ã]	[ɛ̃]	[ĩ]	[ɔ̃]	[ũ]	high tone	mid tone	low tone

The Yoruba alphabet (Omniglot; courtesy of Simon Ager)

In this book, the first time a Yoruba word is mentioned in a chapter, it will be in italics with appropriate diacritical marks to indicate how the word is pronounced. When the word is used subsequently in the chapter, it will not be italicized, and it will contain no diacritical marks. The first time a Yoruba word is used in a subsequent chapter, it will again be italicized and contain relevant diacritical marks, but in the subsequent appearances of the word in that same chapter, there will be no italicization and no diacritical marks. This procedure will also be followed the first time a Yoruba deity's name is mentioned in each chapter and for subsequent mentions of the deity's name in the chapter. No diacritical marks or italics will appear in proper nouns, such as names of cities, states in Nigeria, rivers, or personal names. Most names of Yoruba festivals will not be italicized or contain diacritical marks. Many Yoruba titles will omit diacritical marks, except those specifically relating to women.

Introduction

Why Study Women in Yorùbá Religions?

This book considers women's roles and representations within Yorùbá religions, with a particular focus on the dynamics of Yoruba culture in women's experiences in Yoruba, Christian, and Islamic religions. Yoruba women exhibit complex roles and interactions in these three religious traditions. The Yoruba religion is the indigenous religion of the Yoruba people, who are found primarily in southwestern Nigeria. This region, commonly referred to as "Yorubaland," comprises six states in Nigeria today—Lagos, Ogun, Osun, Oyo, Ekiti, and Ondo—with a sizable population of Yoruba people also in the states of Kwara and Kogi. Yorubaland also extends into portions of the countries of Benin and Togo to the west of Nigeria. Though originating in this portion of the African continent, the Yoruba religion has spread across other parts of Africa, and as a result of the transatlantic slave trade, many practitioners were brought to the Caribbean and the Americas. In the twentieth and twenty-first centuries, Yoruba have immigrated to European and other countries throughout the world. Therefore, countries in which Yoruba religion is practiced in diaspora include Cuba, Brazil, Venezuela, the United States, Canada, Germany, and the United Kingdom. Yoruba religion has also provided a foundation for a number of African-based traditions, including Cuban Santería, Brazilian Candomblé, and Haitian Vodou. Also known as "Orisha," Yoruba religion is at the core of Yoruba lived experiences and is intricately bound up in all sectors of daily life in Yorubaland and abroad in the diaspora. Yoruba who are Christians and Muslims frequently also participate in the Yoruba indigenous religion.

Yoruba religion recognizes the existence of a supreme God who is the creator and sustainer of the universe. This supreme being is known as Olódùmarè (owner of the source of creation), Ọlórun (owner of heaven), or Elédàá (creator), among other names. There are many deities, called òrìṣà, who serve as assistants and representatives for Olodumare in the exercise of spiritual power. According to Yoruba oral narratives, orisa are either those who descended from heaven to Earth or famous human beings who became deified. The orisa are divided into two groupings: "The first group includes cool, calm, gentle, temperate gods, denoted symbolically by the color white," and the second "hot" group is "harsh, aggressive, demanding, and quick tempered, denoted symbolically by the colors red or black. However, this classification has nothing to do with issues of good and evil." Each orisa, like a human being, is "made up of positive and negative traits."[1] Both male and female gods are found in the hot and cool groups of orisa. Individual orisa have different responsibilities to exercise divine authority in human affairs and the natural world. For example, Òrúnmìlà is the deity in charge of wisdom known through the Yoruba compendium of oral literature used for divination known as Ifá, Ọya is the goddess in charge of wind and storm, and Ọ̀ṣun is the goddess in charge of femininity, fecundity, and wealth. Interactions between humans and the orisa are accomplished mainly in the ritual space through liturgies, songs, sacrifices, trance, divination, recitations, and dances. Ancestors, represented by masquerades (Egúngún), are also venerated as continuing participants in the family and society.

There are no clear boundaries between a "secular" life and religious life among the Yoruba. In this, the Yoruba are similar to other African peoples. As the scholar of African religions Jacob K. Olupona has noted, "African spiritual experience is one in which the 'divine' or the 'sacred' realm interpenetrates into the daily experience of the human person so much that religion, culture, and society are imperatively interrelated."[2] Social constructions of gender roles in Yoruba culture have been shaped by the division of labor between women and men in the traditional economy based on horticulture and craft and role specialization; these roles are depicted in the religious narratives about the orisa and heroes and heroines.[3] At the same time, gender prescriptions in Yoruba culture are products of the template supplied by Yoruba beliefs and practices.

Yoruba society has structures, institutions, and organizations meant to facilitate the smooth administration of the religious tradition. These structures and organizations manifest a hierarchy among gods, goddesses, and the adherents of different deities. Olodumare, the supreme being, is at the apex of the pyramid, followed by the orisa, who communicate with humans with the help of female and male religious functionaries (priestesses and priests) in ritual spaces. Such spaces include shrines of various types, which may be in a building or a cleared space in the forest, and sacred groves, which are usually situated in serene areas on the outskirts of towns. Secret societies, in addition to different guilds affiliated with the worship of diverse deities, serve to enforce morals and accountability in society. Among the latter are gender-specific groups, including the àjẹ́ society of spiritually powerful women and the society for men who worship the Òrò orisa, whose voice is the "bullroarer" (a strip of wood that is whirled around). Notably, because the Yoruba people embrace principles of interdependency, interconnectedness, and mutual respect between the sexes, female-only or male-only guilds, or worship societies, usually have one or two members of the other sex as members.

The practice of Yoruba religion in diaspora societies is marked by differences in methods and structures due to the various influences of the transatlantic slave trade and different social contexts. However, at the present time there is movement toward more cohesive globalized Yoruba religious practice, due in part to increased communication between practitioners on the African continent and practitioners in the diaspora by means of print and electronic media, as well as adherents' pilgrimages to Yorubaland and training and mentoring by Yoruba religious specialists. Yoruba religion has a strong presence on Facebook, Twitter, and other social media, and there are also websites devoted to different aspects of Yoruba religion and practices. Moreover, there is a vibrant religio-economic network across the continents that focuses on making available religious and cultural items used in rituals or to adorn practitioners, including soaps, creams, jewelry, and traditional clothes of different types.[4]

Women's roles in Yoruba religion are worthy of research as women are the majority of adherents of the religion in both Africa and the diaspora. Hence, they exert considerable influence on the religion, which is largely dependent on Yoruba oral genres. Oral literature constitutes the storehouse of Yoruba religion and philosophy, which informs the people's responses to life experiences, individually and collectively. In addition, oral literature exerts a great influence since it derives a large portion of its content from the Yoruba religious corpus. Examples of genres of Yoruba oral literature are Ifa oracular verses, proverbs, incantations (*ofò, mádàríkàn, àyájó*), praise poetry (*oríkì*), chants of ancestral cults (*ewì/iwì*), and bride lamentation (*Ẹkuń ìyàwó*) sung as a bride leaves her parents' home for life in her husband's family. Women, in their capacity as frequent custodians of Yoruba oral literature, constitute repositories of the people's beliefs, history, and identity. In spite of recent transcriptions of some genres of Yoruba oral literature, the people still generally reenact these genres through recitation and performance rather than through reading.

In addition, precepts and practices of Yoruba religion regarding women's roles have influenced Yoruba women's understanding of their roles in Christianity and Islam as well, helping to shape gender norms in those traditions as they are practiced in Yorubaland and abroad. Therefore, the study of women in Yoruba religion has significant implications for the understanding of the way religious practices in Christianity and Islam have been transformed by Yoruba women with regard to women's status and leadership and the way Yoruba women have been influenced by these religions. As the scholars Jacob K. Olupona and Terry Rey have noted, among the Yoruba, "indigenous religion has in large part shaped or filtered Islam and Christianity."[5]

Women have served as sustainers of Yoruba religious traditions. Not only do they act as key repositories for orally transmitted knowledge, but they are featured as actors in Yoruba cosmological mythic narratives, which emphasize the divine desire for balance to be attained in human relations and activities. Women play active and important roles in Yoruba society and religion, including occupying positions of leadership such as mothers, custodians of tradition, priestesses, medicine women, diviners, and chiefs.

The Yoruba religious tradition contains resources, including goddess figures, religious narratives, and roles for priestesses, that can be used to promote women's equality in Yoruba culture. Yet the Yoruba religious tradition demonstrates men's ambivalence toward women's spiritual power and social and religious authority. Despite powerful resources within the tradition for women's equality, men have historically attempted to control women and keep them subordinated, and Yoruba religion contains resources as well that have been used to subordinate women to men.⁶ Which type of resources (for women's equality or subordination) will be utilized depends on the extent to which women have access to independent economic productivity that promotes a greater social expectation of equality. Education about the religious tradition and economic activity in society also contributes to greater religious and social equality for women.⁷

Yoruba culture has traditionally been male dominated, as evinced by the greater visibility of men in positions of political and religious authority, though evidences of a few female rulers are on record. Also, matrilineal descent and inheritance of ruling position is not unusual in some of the ruling houses among the Yoruba. However, as of 2022 kings (males) rule all communities in Yorubaland, although in a few communities regents may rule pending the coronation of a new king after the death of the previous king. Also, polygyny gives men access to multiple wives in traditional Yoruba culture, whereas women can marry only one man at a time. Children from these marriages bear the husband's name and claim heritage from the paternal line; hence, the mother may appear shortchanged in relation to her children.

Physical and visible resources for the subordination of Yoruba women by male dominance include the kingship system, polygynous marriages, and minimal women's membership in religious councils that enforce social order and carry out punishments, such as the secret Ògbóni group of elders.⁸ However, the nonvisibility of women in the governing institutions of Yoruba society is moderated by the people's concept of dual, interdependent power. The Yoruba conceive of power as both visible/formal and invisible/informal, with males occupying the visible/formal structure of power and females in charge of the invisible/informal structures of power. If an individual assumes that the visible is the whole story, it may be easy to conclude that if women are not visible in formal structures of power, they are oppressed and irrelevant; while this is indeed a common perception among Westerners, for the Yoruba themselves, nothing could be further from the truth.⁹ The invisible/informal conception of power by the Yoruba is within the jurisdiction of the Ìyà Mi, a group of women with tremendous spiritual power and influence across all sectors of Yoruba society and activities. *Ìyá Mi* is a term of respect meaning "my mother," and also "our mothers," but with a slightly different pronunciation. *Ìyà Mi* refers to the powerful mothers. These powerful women, members of the Iya Mi, are usually referred to as àjẹ́. Yoruba have no doubt in the invisible power of women. It is real, they believe, and they have no doubt that the mothers exercise power behind the scenes through their spiritual power. Thus, the issue is not hierarchy, or who is superior. The important thing from the Yoruba worldview is mutual respect, cooperation, and the common good.

Islam arrived in Yorubaland through the activities of itinerant traders around the fifteenth century; the professor of Yoruba history T. G. O. Gbadamosi reports that mention was made of Muslims residing in Yorubaland by the seventeenth century. Christianity arrived in 1842 through the missionaries of the Church Missionary Society (CMS) founded in Britain.[10] The introduction of Christianity and Islam to the region resulted in profound changes to Yoruba religiosity. Today, the majority of Yoruba people are either Christian or Muslim, although many practitioners of indigenous Yoruba religious traditions remain. Some Yoruba people living in Yorubaland combine allegiance to two or more religions. The Yoruba are a religiously diverse ethnic group; adherents of Christianity, Islam, and Yoruba religion may be found in the same family with no acrimony.

The colonial experience, particularly from about 1900, when Nigeria came under the control of the British Empire, to 1960, when Nigeria gained independence, involved the encounter of European Christian missionaries with assertive Yoruba women who challenged subordinate roles for women in Christian institutions because they played significant economic and political roles in their communities. An example is Mrs. Funmilayo Ransome-Kuti (1900–1978), who was educated in Abeokuta, Nigeria, and England. She founded the Abeokuta Ladies Club in 1932, which became the Abeokuta Women's Union (AWU) in 1946, to work and demonstrate for women's representation on governing bodies and to gain relief from a tax that was levied against market women, as well as to promote women's literacy and health. The importance of the AWU grew in promoting women's rights in Nigeria, and it became the Nigerian Women's Union (NWU) in 1949 and the Federation of Nigeria Women's Societies (FNWS) in 1953.[11] Yet with the advent of Christianity and Islam among the Yoruba, women were more pervasively prescribed subordinate roles in the religions. The introduction of Christianity in Yorubaland disrupted traditional Yoruba cultural norms of interdependence and complementarity in gender relations, though women contested this subordination and attempted to assert their spiritual equality in Christian organizations. Similarly, women's prescribed subordinate roles in Islamic culture as it was established in Yorubaland were attenuated by traditional Yoruba gender socialization, which expected economic contributions from daughters and wives.

The Yoruba social construction of gender is reflected in the people's cosmological narratives about male and female orisa, which emphasize complementary gender relations. In these complementary relations, men and women are prescribed different, but both important, roles rather than men and women undertaking the same endeavors.[12] In other religious traditions, concepts of gender "complementarity" have been linked to religious institutions wishing to maintain patriarchal gender roles in contemporary society—with women being assured that their roles are important even as they are barred from any positions of real social or religious power. In contrast to the complementarian Western patriarchal families and societies in which the husband is assumed to be the breadwinner and the wife's work is primarily child rearing and homemaking, Yoruba woman are expected to be economically productive in areas that complement the economic productivity of the men. The work of Yoruba women and men performed in traditional Yoruba families and society is different but complementary to the economic well-being of the children and the entire family.

Additionally, Yoruba gender constructions are fluid and context-bound in social and ritual settings. For instance, in Yoruba patrilineal extended families, sisters are "husbands" to the wives of their brothers. Male priests may be required to dress as women since they are initiated as wives to the orisa. The anthropologist J. Lorand Matory describes the priests of Ṣàngó (a male orisa understood to have been the third king of the Oyo empire) in the city of Oyo as wearing plaits in their hair, like women, and dressing as women because in the ritual setting of Sango worship, they are wives to the deity.[13] As noted by the religious studies scholar Mary Ann Clark, "Within the Orisa-based ritual context, gender ambiguities do not seem to be the result of gender confusion, a search for femininity, or an effort at spiritual play. Neither do they seem to result in either the reinforcing or the calling into question of binary gender schema."[14] These assertions are consistent with my findings that the

Yoruba do have gender constructions, but their gender constructs are fluid, as opposed to the argument of the Nigerian sociologist Oyeronke Oyewumi that gender constructs were nonexistent among the Yoruba in precolonial times.[15]

A contemporary challenge to Yoruba constructions of gender is the issue of same-sex relationships. This is because the legitimization of same-sex relationships challenges complementary (binary and heterosexual) conceptions of gender.[16] Same-sex relationships are controversial among the Yoruba and are presently criminalized under Nigerian law.

For the Yoruba, gender roles and religious beliefs interact and mutually influence each other in complex ways as they also interact with and mirror the dynamics of the culture. Yoruba gender complementarity is based on the notion of balance, so that neither of the sexes could be subsumed in the other; indeed, elements of both the male and female principles are essential in every activity among the Yoruba. As noted by the scholar of African cultures Andrew Apter, in Yoruba society, "female power is openly acclaimed as antithesis and antidote to the destructive power of men. Whereas men are 'hot,' volatile, violent, and tough [male principles], . . . women are 'cool,' subdued, peaceful, and soft [female principles]."[17] Yet the female and male orisa model both hot and cool behavior for both genders. Because Yoruba women have always been economically productive and active in society, including in the marketplace and business in general, the Yoruba concept of gender complementarity does not contribute to the idea that women must be subordinate to men in the world of commerce. However, men remain ambivalent about women's economic and spiritual power, as seen in their view of the aje, women with spiritual power who can and do support constructive endeavors or cause misfortune and death.

Despite Yoruba women's valued economic contributions to their families and societies, Yoruba society is informed by a diffused form of patriarchy that differs from the most extreme expressions of male dominance found, for instance, in northern India, in which women's movement outside the home has been controlled by male relatives and husbands. This type of patriarchy has its origins in intensive agriculture, which involves farming with a plow. Extended families in a society with an intensive agricultural economic base are typically patrilineal (tracing descent through the father), and residence of married couples is patrilocal (they live with the husband's extended family). Farmland and other means of economic productivity are owned and controlled by men, which bestows opportunities for economic and political power to males. Consequently, women are largely deprived of economic and political power and are susceptible to subordination and oppression. Often a male deity is emphasized as sanctioning patriarchy to be right and good, although this does not preclude female deities from being used to support the authority of a male ruler and to emphasize subordinate gender roles for women.[18]

In contrast to this more extreme form of patriarchy, which develops when men till the farmland with a plow and in which women of higher classes are secluded from the public sphere and do not have access to direct economic productivity, in Yorubaland, where the type of agriculture practiced is horticulture (small-scale farming with a hoe), men own the land and pass it to their sons. The farmland is a resource that is owned by the patrilineal family or clan. Men also engage in other professions such as hunting, blacksmithing, or manufacturing. However, Yoruba women are generally socialized to be economically independent through their work as traders and to be creative in wealth management. Though the women leave their natal families at marriage to live with their husbands' families, they maintain close relationships with their families of birth. Yoruba women's economic productivity has a direct impact on their significant religious roles and the ways in which they are viewed in Yoruba religion. Female and male gender constructions—with aggressiveness, violence, and toughness attributed to males and softness, coolness, kindness, and restraint attributed to females—remain crucial to Yoruba lived experiences, with complex male-female interdependency at different levels of family, religion, and society.

Yoruba women's identity construction, as in any society, is based to a significant extent on their placement within the web of social relations. Prominent for the Yoruba in this regard is the role of the mother (*iyá*). To be a mother among the Yoruba is to attain the height of female potential and societal expectation for women. Among the Yoruba, motherhood is perceived as a position of power, both physically and spiritually.[19] The Yoruba also recognize "social motherhood," which though devoid of biological ties, requires emotional, spiritual, and economic investments by the mother in the child throughout their respective life spans.[20] Yoruba appreciate "intervention motherhood," or adoption of children by barren couples, due to the belief that *orí omo lóún pe omo wáyé*: "it is the personality soul of a child that attracts other children to come to the world." Thus, a barren couple is encouraged to bring into their home the child of a sibling of the wife or husband in order to attract their own biological child. Yoruba culture and religion accommodate childless women through the adoption of siblings or children of siblings, because of the conviction that all women are mothers, either through biology or social structures.

In all these cases, motherhood is construed as a position of power. Motherhood among the Yoruba is regarded as being manifest at the level of individual women (who give birth to children) and as an institution in social, political, and spiritual dimensions, but at whichever level it exists, there are spiritual as well as material powers that derive from the mother's procreativity.[21] These views and practices of Yoruba motherhood encompass the roles of mothers in Yoruba religion, Christianity, and Islam. The implication of this position is that procreation, which guarantees collective immortality, is very important to the Yoruba, irrespective of religious affiliations.

The significant roles that women play in Yoruba traditional religion and society on the African continent and in the diaspora have strongly influenced Yoruba women's active participation in Christianity and Islam. Yoruba expressions of Christianity and Islam allow for the creation of alternative spaces for the exercise of women's spiritual power, as female practitioners draw on their Yoruba heritage of women's agency.[22] As a result, Christianity in Yorubaland manifests a strong collective female voice at the decision-making level in congregations, and Muslim women are visible in ways not generally found in Islam in many other areas and among other ethnic-cultural groups, including in northern Nigeria.[23]

Yet historical events, including the introduction of Christianity into Yorubaland, have had profound influences on Yoruba gender constructions in ways that have both tended to empower women and also to diminish their status. For example, as noted earlier, European Christian culture promoted the subordination of women rather than the complementarity in gender relations manifested earlier in Yoruba society, but access to Western education also opened the door to increased financial empowerment for many Yoruba women, which has enhanced their ability to negotiate strong positions within their marriages. The opportunities provided by international travel have offered Yoruba women prospects for experiences across continents, mentorship at various levels, and new economic earning potential. The anthropologist Ernestine Friedl has noted that "jobs that do not give women control over valued resources will do little to advance their general status." She asserts, "Only as controllers of valued resources can women achieve prestige, power, and equality."[24] As Yoruba women have directly acquired valued resources that they can distribute to others, they have gained greater equality in their marriages, families, society, and ultimately their religious traditions. Currently Yoruba gender dynamics are being impacted by globalization, migration, capitalism, and global religious challenges.

This book utilizes historical and phenomenological methods, incorporating data from interviews and participant observation from Ogun and Lagos States and Ilorin in Kwara State, Nigeria. The author is a Yoruba woman born and raised in Yoruba culture in Nigeria who is a practicing Christian. Though the author is not a practitioner or cultic functionary of Yoruba religion, the thin line between Yoruba culture and religion compels considerable knowledge of the religion for every Yoruba person whose process of socialization was through the Yoruba ethos. My training through the past nearly thirty years as a scholar of comparative religion also offers me wide resources on which to draw to understand Yoruba religion. Therefore, I write as an insider in two of the religious traditions discussed in this book and as an outsider to the Islamic tradition, although I have spent the past twenty-five years living in Ilorin, a renowned predominantly Islamic community in Kwara State in Nigeria.

Chapter 1 provides a foundational discussion of the geographic location of Yoruba people in Nigeria, Benin, and Togo; the economic pursuits common in Yorubaland; and the economic, political, and social roles of women therein. It offers insights into how these roles impact the status of Yoruba women in religion and the society at large. Chapter 2 introduces the practice of rituals performed by women in indigenous Yoruba religion and the positions of leadership that they have occupied. This chapter also discusses divination and priesthood in the Yoruba religion, noting women's roles as leaders in worship and the power of the guild of women (aje) rooted in women's roles as mothers. Members of this guild are commonly called Iya Mi (as noted earlier, the powerful mothers). Chapter 3 explores the roles of Yoruba women in Christianity in ritual spaces and ẹgbẹ́ (groups) and as church founders. Chapter 4 examines the status of Yoruba women in Islam as leaders, founders of new prayer movements, and active contributors to decision-making. Chapter 5 focuses on women in Yoruba indigenous religion in the diaspora. It considers the background of transatlantic Yoruba religions, types of innovations in methods of worship, and the contemporary mentoring of women across the African continent and in diaspora societies. Chapter 6 explicates the phenomenon of globalization and its impact on women in Yoruba religion, including the influences of commercialization, the media, and information technology on changing roles of women in Yoruba religion. The conclusion highlights the importance of understanding the impact of culture in Yoruba women's negotiation of power dynamics relating to women's gender roles in religion and society.

This book discusses the roles and status of women in Yoruba religions, placing gender relations in historical and social context and showing how they influence women's place in the religious traditions practiced by Yoruba. Changes in the socioeconomic milieu in Yorubaland, such as British colonialism in Nigeria (1914–60), capitalism, and industrialization, have in recent times promoted increased male dominance and undergirded changes in outlook that have had important implications for Yoruba women, though this has not changed the fact that Yoruba women and men control their individual finances.

The overarching argument of this book is that Yoruba women attain and wield agency through their economic and religious roles. They exercise profound influence on issues of power and gender relations using different mechanisms, as we will see in the following chapters. Whenever Yoruba women have the opportunity, they consistently utilize the resources within their religious traditions that are supportive of women's equality.

1

Women's Family, Economic, Social, and Political Roles in Yorùbáland

In Yorùbá society, women have generally not experienced discrimination in economic ventures or in the opportunity to invest and reap profit from such investments. One example of a prominent and wealthy Yoruba female trader is Efunsetan Aniwura (1790s–1874). She was of Egba origin and had vast business investments in Ibadan, the capital of the Oyo State.[1] She was a landowner, farmer, and producer of food products on a large scale in Yorubaland. She was reported to have controlled as many as two thousand slaves and many farms as part of her vast investments.[2] Yoruba women like Efunsetan Aniwura have historically played active roles in the traditional economy, and this remains true today. In contemporary Nigeria, Yoruba women are generally successful breadwinners, either as professionals or in different types of trading activities.

A 2020 list of the ten richest women in Nigeria includes Yoruba women as numbers one, two, and six. Number one is Mrs. Folorunsho Alakija (b. 1951), a fashion entrepreneur, with interests in printing, real estate development, and oil exploration, worth US$2.5 billion, who in 2014 surpassed Oprah Winfrey as the richest woman of African descent in the world. Number two is Hajia Bola Shagaya (b. 1959), a businesswoman with interests in oil and gas, banking, real estate, communication, and photography, worth US$1 billion. Similarly, number six on the list is Bimbo Alase-Arawole (b. 1966), who is worth US$750 million with investment in furniture. Her company, Leatherworld, is the largest furniture company in Lagos, Nigeria.[3]

These highly successful women demonstrate that Yoruba female gender roles and women's agency allow them to attain success and power in their economic activities. We will see that women's agency in economic productivity in Yoruba society is reflected in women's authority in political and religious endeavors.

Gender Roles and Economic Activity

Gender roles among the Yoruba people have traditionally been regarded as complementary, because males and females occupy distinct but interdependent positions in every facet of Yoruba lived experiences, including the socioeconomic, political, and religious sectors. With few exceptions, economic ventures are gender based. For instance, food processing and the manufacture of cosmetics remain in the domain of women in Yorubaland.[4] Similarly, men specialize in horticultural farming and hunting, although a few women are found in these activities as well. Trading is a key means of creating wealth among the Yoruba. In the traditional Yoruba economy, women have predominated in trading and commercial activities and have constituted the majority of marketers.[5]

A Yoruba woman generally derives economic status by participating in trading with an initial investment or loan from her husband or a relative. Women known as *alájàpà* are long-distance traders. They sell goods in different locations, historically traveling by foot, walking from one town to the other, and in more contemporary times, traveling by vehicles along a trade route. Their trips may last weeks or sometimes months. Other Yoruba women conduct trade in markets closer to their homes. Many Yoruba women are enterprising and economically savvy, and some have become richer than their husbands.

Yoruba People, History, Culture, Women and Religion

Geographically, the majority of the Yoruba ethnic group is located in southwestern Nigeria. However, Yorubaland in West Africa extends west from Nigeria to parts of the Republic of Benin and the Togolese Republic. Yoruba people are found as well as in other locations around the world, spread initially by the transatlantic slave trade and in the late twentieth century through the present by voluntary migration.[6] Yorubaland in Nigeria spans from a savanna region in its north to a region of tropical rain forests in the south. In 2020, Yoruba constituted 15.5 percent of Nigeria's population, comprising more than thirty-three million Yoruba people.[7]

The origins of the Yoruba people are debated, with some people believing that they can trace their roots to such peoples as the Canaanites

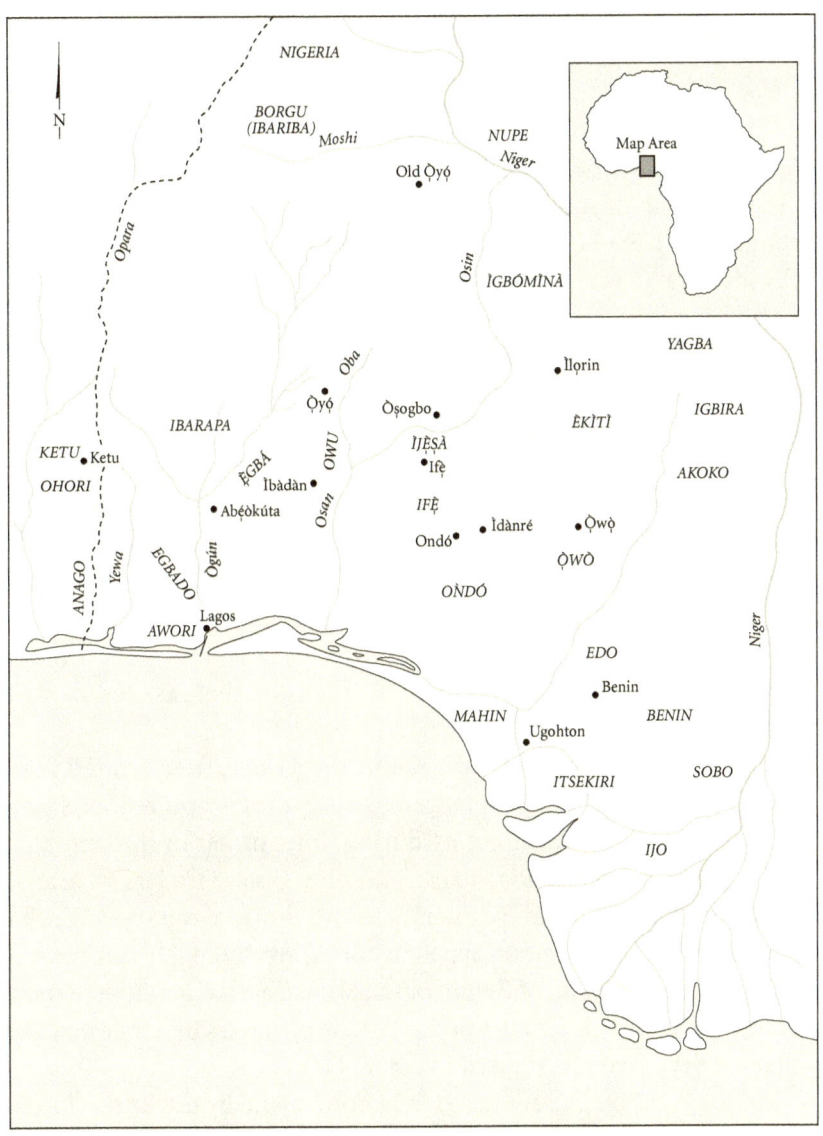

Map of Yorubaland's rivers and major cities in southwestern Nigeria and eastern Republic of Benin. (Jacob K. Olúpònà, *City of 201 Gods: Ilé-Ifẹ̀ in Time, Space and the Imagination* [Berkeley: University of California Press, 2011], xvii; courtesy of Jacob K. Olúpònà, The Regents of the University of California, and University of California Press)

of Palestine, Nimrod, the first king of Mesopotamia, and Sudan.[8] Some believe that the Yoruba are not a single ethnic group but rather a collection of diverse peoples bound together by a common language, history, and culture. Yet genetic studies indicate that the Yoruba of southwestern Nigeria and parts of Benin and Togo, the Ga-Adangbe of Ghana and Togo, the Akan of southern Ghana, and the Igbo of south-central and southeastern Nigeria, all in coastal West Africa, are 99.9 percent genetically identical to each other.[9]

Yoruba wisdom and remembrances of the past have been passed down orally. Yoruba oral genres include myths, cosmological narratives, praise poems known as *oríkì*, tongue twisters, prose narratives, riddles, and proverbs, as well as music, which includes songs of ridicule and praise, lullabies, bridal songs, religious songs, war songs, and work songs.

Yoruba oral tradition holds that all Yoruba people are descended from a hero called Òduà or Odùduwà, the *ọba* (sovereign) of Ilé-Ifẹ̀.[10] Sixteen Yoruba kingdoms are said to have been founded by descendants of Oduduwa. In addition, there are "countless sub-kingdoms and territories that are branches of the original" sixteen kingdoms.[11] These kingdoms sometimes experienced periods of tension that resulted in civil wars during the eighteenth century.

During the period of the transatlantic slave trade, from around 1480 to around 1870, Yoruba people were among those captured, often by members of the same community during times of war or through kidnapping expeditions or brigandage, and sold to slave traders for transport to the New World.[12] By the nineteenth century, captured Yoruba slaves predominated among slaves exported from the African coastal area known as the Bight of Benin, or the Slave Coast. A large percentage of these slaves were a product of the Yoruba civil wars that followed the collapse of the Ọ̀yọ́ kingdom in the 1820s.[13]

The colonization and subjugation of Yorubaland by the British in the late nineteenth century occurred just as the region was beginning to recover from what is known as the Yoruba Civil War (1817–93). The Yoruba experience of colonialism began with the military defeat of the forces of the kingdom of Ijebu at Imagbon in Ogun State by the British colonial army in 1882, which resulted in an initial European settlement in Lagos. British control was gradually expanded by protectorate treaties, which proved crucial in the eventual takeover of the rest of Yorubaland in what became Nigeria.[14] The result was contact between Western and Yoruba cultures and worldviews, which was detrimental to the traditional gender relations of the Yoruba, which were marked by mutual respect between women and men.

Yoruba men were visible in public posts of authority and were assumed by the British to possess power, while women, who were seldom seen in such posts, were assumed to be subordinated. However, that was not an accurate assessment because, as we have seen, the Yoruba subscribe to a concept of visible/formal and invisible/informal power. The visible/formal power is always dependent on the invisible/informal power in the Yoruba conception of power. Thus, the visible is just a part of power and authority and not the full story. Yoruba women continue to be in charge of the invisible/informal power; consequently, it is difficult to discern accurately a clear-cut gender hierarchy among the Yoruba.[15] The Yoruba epistemology of power, like every other concept in the Yoruba worldview, was broad and characterized by negotiations at various levels and mutual respect between the sexes. However, Western Christian cultural expectations for women's subordination to men became assumed for Yoruba women due to colonialism.

Culture

The Yoruba way of life is rooted in the communal living of patrilineal extended families (*ilé*), supported by horticulture, trade, and craft and skill specialization. Until recently, all family members had rights to land, farms, and privileges, though the administration of such resources was usually vested in the eldest male in the family, known as *olórí-ebí* (family head), assisted by the elderly male and female members of the lineage. Furthermore, families live in clusters consisting of a number of ile (house), known as *agbo-ilé* (cluster of a few houses), which may comprise three or four generations. The Yoruba appreciate good character, and every adult in the society has authority to ensure that the young ones imbibe positive moral lessons. Yoruba greet and treat elders with considerable respect; younger males prostrate to greet their elders, while younger females greet them by kneeling on two knees.

Yoruba men are primarily farmers who practice horticulture, but they also engage in hunting and different types of manufacturing.

Deaconess Mrs. Rachel Morawo Oyedeji, a retired hospital Matron on the occasion of her eighty-first birthday, celebrated at Alafia Oluwa Baptist Church, Ikire, Osun State, Nigeria on May 16, 2021. (Courtesy of Oyeronke Olademo)

Yoruba farmers cultivate crops including cocoa, yams, corn, cassava, vegetables like spinach, tomato, and pepper, and fruits such as African cherry (Agbalumo) and oranges; they also hunt antelope, elephants, and lions, among other wild animals. Food preparation is generally done by women. Yoruba cuisine is generally spicy and hot. A meal would normally comprise a carbohydrate (yam or cassava pudding) and a soup containing protein.

Yoruba women hold fashion in high regard, and their attire is often elegant, showcasing a variety of colors. Fashion is regarded as an important component of religious events. For festive occasions, men adorn themselves by wearing *bùbá* and *sòkòtò* (a loose blouse and pants) and *fìlà* (caps of different types), while women wear buba (a blouse), *ìró* (a wrapper skirt that may be tied to stop above or below the knee), and *gèlè* (a head tie). The adorning of family members and/or spouses with clothing made of the same type of cloth (*aso-ebí*, meaning "the cloth of family members") signifies unity, harmony, and different types of ties, which could be blood, marriage, social status, profession, or any other relationship.

MARRIAGE. In Yoruba society, marriage is a union of two families rather than two individuals. Marriage is highly valued due to the importance placed on procreation, which is construed as the major source of collective immortality. Through childbearing, the continuation of the Yoruba is guaranteed.

In the past, Yoruba parents decided on marriage partners for their children after investigating the background of the family of the proposed spouse to rule out cases of illnesses such as mental disorders and epilepsy. Thus, it was possible in traditional Yoruba communities for marriage partners to meet each other for the first time at the wedding ceremony.[16] In contemporary times, the intended marriage partners inform their parents after they have agreed to marry. The parents on both sides try to investigate the family backgrounds, but oftentimes this is of little or no effect, for reasons such as distance and language barriers, especially in interracial or interethnic marriages.

At the engagement party, the bride wealth provided by the husband's family to the bride usually comprises items such as cloth, shoes, and jewelry, in addition to gifts of cash (stipulated by the bride's family) and food items given to the bride's family, like yams, liquor, honey, alligator peppers, sugarcane, water, and a large female goat, among other items, as well as a copy of the Bible or Qur'an, depending on whether the family is Christian or Muslim. Some of the items are utilized as symbols of goodness (water), sweetness (honey, sugarcane), and fertility (alligator pepper, large female goat). These symbols are used to pray for the bride as she leaves her natal home for her marital family. The bride wealth is the seal of the marriage and legalizes the woman's status in her marital home. Bride wealth has been construed by some scholars as the purchase of the woman as chattel, but my respondents (male and female) disagree with such a description. They explain that the bride wealth establishes the right of the marital family to the woman's reproductive capacity, as reflected in the Yoruba saying, *t'orí omo la sé nláya*: "it is because we want children that we marry a wife."[17]

In the past, Yoruba women married between the ages of eighteen and twenty-one and as virgins. Indeed, a white bedsheet stained with the blood from the deflowered bride was publicly displayed and proudly acknowledged by the parents of the bride. Presently, Yoruba brides may be aged between twenty and thirty years old, on average, due to the need to finish school or graduate from training at a vocation. The culture still expects brides to be virgins, but this is rarely the case, with no accruing stigmatization or punishment. Some of my respondents ascribe the change on the requirement of virginity for the bride to the influence of Western education and prevalence of popular culture.

Yoruba marriage is composed of two main ceremonies: the engagement and the wedding. The engagement involves members of both families and is where introductions are made and bride wealth is given to the bride's family by her intended husband. When there is an interreligious engagement such as marriage of a Christian and a Muslim, the religious requirements of the bride's religion are prioritized. The engagement ceremony ends with prayers for the couple, feasting, and dancing. The wedding ceremony may be held the same day or the next day, and its location may be in a church (Christian), mosque (Muslim), or family compound (Yoruba religion). Whichever location is applicable, the wedding ceremony involves the joining of the couple with exchanged vows of fidelity and love. Scriptures about marriage are read to the couple to ensure the success of the union.

The Yoruba practiced polygyny extensively in the past and still do today to a lesser degree. In the past, a man with the ambition of having many wives usually married one wife after the other with or without the consent of the previous wife or wives. A first wife may also acquire younger wives for her husband and then act as the mother of the house. The man with multiple wives was well respected in society. Because of the expense of maintaining a large family, he was perceived as having abundant capital and human resources. A man's wives and children worked on his farm as laborers. The polygynous marriage sometimes created family settings in which wives tried to outwit each other as they sought the favor of their husband. Women's agency to negotiate sexual intercourse in such a marriage was near nonexistent, as the husband had a timetable for the distribution of his attention, with each wife taking her turn per day or week, depending on the number of wives. Polygyny is still practiced among the Yoruba, but it is not as prevalent as it was in traditional Yoruba communities due to influences from Christianity, Islam, and Western education and culture.

The Yoruba gender ideology plays out in the polygynous family at different levels. Whereas the man is the head of the home, rarely will he make decisions without consultation (directly and indirectly) with his wives. In addition, the wives possess different tactics that are used individually or jointly to make the husband's decisions favor them. These tactics include physical means, such as good food, sex, or financial assistance, or metaphysical powers exercised by means of membership in the Ìyà Mi society of powerful mothers (àjẹ́), if occasion demands such. Thus, the template for gender relations in Yoruba polygynous families remains one of negotiation and mutual respect. The appreciation of different spheres of power for males and females undergirds mutual negotiations and respect because men recognize metaphysical powers as being the women's domain and women acknowledge physical power as the men's domain. Monogamy was not an ideal in traditional Yoruba marriage, though evidence suggests that each wife desired that the husband pay her more attention than the other wives. In addition, the wives needed other wives' help in child care since the wives were of different ages and practiced diverse professions. While some women were long-distance traders, others practiced subsistence farming, and some sold food and snacks in the market.[18]

Yoruba expect the husband to provide food, housing, and clothing for each of his wives and the children. The husband is expected not to molest or beat his wives just as the wives should maintain decorum among themselves. The culture provides interventions such as elders warning the erring person when these expectations are violated, which is known to happen. In extreme cases of violence and beatings, there can be divorce, especially when the woman's life is judged to be in danger. Yoruba women can initiate divorce by following these steps: at the first instance of violence, reporting the husband to the elders of the marital family; if no change happens, then reporting to elders of her natal family; and divorce as the last resort. Such a divorced woman may return to her natal home (*dálémosú*) or remarry. If a woman remarries, her new husband will not have to provide as much bride wealth to her family.

Yoruba gender ideology in contemporary society has changed from the situation in the past due to various factors, including the influence of Arab and Western cultures through Islam and Christianity, women holding paid jobs, changing values in popular culture, and the economic effects of globalization. Presently, monogamy is the norm. Yoruba women are flourishing in all professions and are economically successful; thus, they generally are able to negotiate power effectively in their marriages and relationships.

MOTHERHOOD. Yoruba people assume that children will be born in every marriage, and when this does not occur after a year or more, there is cause for worry. Motherhood is prioritized, and every woman is socialized to aspire to be a mother. A Yoruba woman's status hinges on her social roles, mostly as mother but other times as sister, daughter, or wife. Yoruba women are appreciated and idolized as mothers because, as noted, procreation, without which the community cannot continue, is a paramount concern for the people.[19] Consequently, barrenness is a serious matter, and the woman is usually blamed and seen as a failure if no children are conceived. According to the medical sociologist Tola Olu Pearce, "in most developing societies women are more likely to be blamed" for infertility. The Yoruba expect a bride to get pregnant within months after the wedding, and insinuations such as "she only consumes the food of the family without producing any child" are made during conversations if she does not. The infertile wife is called *àgòn*, meaning "to hold in contempt or despised," and thus infertility is cause for distress. This is mainly because a wife's "reproductive impairment" is not only a concern of the husband and wife but a concern of the extended family, which depends on the couple's procreation for their group immortality.[20]

Although Yoruba culture offers interventions to shield the infertile person (female and male), with wives protecting the reputation of an impotent or infertile husband, the stigma of being infertile affects the female more. Generally the ridicule and taunting directed at the infertile woman is by other women rather than by men.[21] In traditional Yoruba culture, all women are mothers, biologically or socially, but in contemporary society, Yoruba women navigate infertility through adoption, in vitro fertilization (IVF), and existing traditional methods. Traditional methods include consultations with a male or female diviner, a *babaláwo* ("father of secrets," a male specialist in Ifá divination) or *ìyánífá* ("mother who has Ifá," or "mother in the work of Ifa"),[22] or a priest or priestess of different orisa who practice Ẹ̀rìndínlógún divination (use of cowries). The babalawo utilizes the memorized Ifa corpus of oral texts, and his proposed solutions may include the offering of sacrifice and/or the suggestion that the barren woman adopt the child of a sibling or other relative of hers, because, as we saw earlier, it is believed that a woman's care for an adopted child will encourage her natural children to come into the world. Moreover, stigmatization of women for infertility is at a minimum now because there are other areas of fulfillment for the modern Yoruba woman, such as professional excellence and financial success.

Mothers are esteemed in Yoruba society because they give and nurture life but also because a mother has ultimate loyalty to her child in all circumstances. Hence, the Yoruba say, *Òrìṣàbìỉyá kò sí*, meaning "Mother is like a deity." The mother sustains the well-being of her husband and children through regular prayers, offerings, and observance of prescribed taboos. Indeed, a babalawo always demands the name of the client's mother before consultation and rarely that of the father. The mother is considered to be the authentic source of the child, as it is possible to contest paternity but not the maternity of a child.

The sociologist Oyeronke Oyewumi acknowledges the socio-spiritual category of Ìyá (Mother) as a social institution that symbolizes a "matripotent principle" that manifests "the powers, spiritual and material, deriving from the *Ìyá*'s procreative role."[23] The position of the mother among the Yoruba does not construe Yoruba women as being weak, socially marginalized, or subordinate. However, Oyewumi's assessment of the institution of motherhood derives from her thesis that gender is a colonial category, because according to her, the Yoruba did not have gender constructions in precolonial times. The data I have gathered in Yorubaland do not agree with her position. Yoruba had gender constructions prior to colonialism, but as noted earlier, the gender categories were fluid, as exemplified in cross-dressing in ritual spaces, records in the oral genres, and the sociological phenomenon of females (daughters) being considered to be husbands to wives who have married into their husband's families (the ile, the extended patrilineal family). Moreover, seniority shapes Yoruba gender classifications on certain occasions, for instance, during the sharing of meals in a family, especially meat, with the most senior family members, whether female or male, receiving the largest portion.[24]

Thus, for the Yoruba, motherhood is a clear pointer to women's agency in power relations. This point is corroborated by the religious studies scholar Mary Ann Clark's assertion that in Yoruba culture, "the female body, particularly in its most exposed form, serves as a metonym of women's childbearing function and extraordinary powers." Therefore, "there is no understanding in Yoruba cosmology that bodies, particularly women's bodies, are inferior, dirty, or unspiritual."[25]

Yoruba prescribe taboos for pregnant women that include restrictions on movement, posture, and diet. For instance, pregnant women are not to walk around in the hot sun (around 1:00 p.m.) or at night. The hot sun and the late night are understood as being periods in which malevolent spirits roam about. In some Yoruba communities, pregnant women may not eat specific food items such as eggs, salt, oil, or okra. Such prohibitions usually hinge on the historical experiences of that family. Traditionally, birth attendants took charge of the delivery of babies in Yoruba communities, and there were no male birth attendants; thus, women were the specialists in this area, and this status reflected mutual gender respect in the community. In the present day, hospitals, clinics, and rural health centers attend to deliveries of babies.[26]

INHERITANCE. Customary law and tradition regarding inheritance rights among the Yoruba dictate clearly that a wife cannot inherit immovable properties such as land and houses from her husband or even movable property, all of which goes to a man's children—and, in the past, also to his brothers and sisters—but a wife could inherit from her brother and sister and her natal lineage. Distribution of inheritance from the father to his children can occur in one of two manners. *Ìdí Igi* ("under each tree," with the tree here representing the mother) succession refers to property distribution *per stirpes* ("by branch" of the family), that is, according to the number of wives of the deceased man who dies without a valid will. If he has five wives, all movable properties will be divided into five portions and then distributed to the children of each wife. Conversely, *Orí Òju Orí* ("heads are equal") succession makes distribution of movable properties directly to each child, irrespective of gender and the mother of each child.[27] The position of the first son, called *Dáwóduù* ("the prime heir"), is an exception to these two forms of inheritance because he is invested with the responsibility of acting as the trustee of all family immovable properties that may not be distributed or sold, including the family house, farms, and land. When there is no son, the eldest daughter can become the Dawoduu.[28] In this system, the wife does not inherit from her deceased husband, because according to Yoruba custom, the inheritance "follows the blood," so the movable property goes to a man's children.[29] A widow may remain living in the husband's family home unless she marries a man outside that patrilineal family. When a woman needs land for farming, the Dawoduu of either her natal family or her husband's family may allocate some land to her; but she can only grow vegetables and crops that mature in less than a year, and she may not plant tree crops, such as cocoa trees, fruit trees, kola trees, and palm trees. The reason for this is to show that whatever use she makes of the portion of land is temporary; the land remains the property of the patrilineal family.[30] If the wife acquired immovable property during her lifetime, at her death the inheritance of her property also "follows the blood" and is distributed to her children. If she has no children, then it goes to her natal family. Her husband only has the right to inherit movable items that she brought into their marital home.[31]

In the practice of Yoruba inheritance customs, daughters have typically received a lesser distribution of movable property than that received by sons, and widows frequently experience a decline in their standard of living after the deaths of their husbands. Scholars have shown that Yoruba customary laws of inheritance contribute directly to women's poverty.[32] In contemporary Yoruba cultures, there are societies where the old system of inheritance continues and other societies where daughters and sons inherit movable property equally. Equal inheritance of movable property for daughters and sons is upheld by the customary Law of Nigeria, as evinced in many examples of court rulings to this effect among the Yoruba since 1924.[33] Consequently, presently the Nigerian judicial system accepts that Yoruba people's movable property transfers as inheritance and goes equally to all children, irrespective of sex.

Religion

As has already been noted, Yoruba religion is based on oral tradition. Although some significant documentation has occurred in recent times, orality remains basic to the religious tradition. These oral narratives, especially the cosmological accounts, often provide models for social stratification among the Yoruba. Yoruba cosmological narratives address topics such as the creation of the Earth, Yoruba society, and the respective roles of men and women. They exert tremendous influence on Yoruba gender constructions and prioritize the complementarity of males and females. Brave, strong, and resourceful goddesses provide models for women to display these same qualities in social interactions.[34]

WOMEN AND ORAL GENRES. One narrative contained in the oral Ifa divination corpus recounts that Olódùmarè sent seventeen deities (orisa) to Earth at the beginning of time. Òṣun, known as "Ṣèègèsí, the preeminent hair-plaiter with the coral-beaded comb," was the only female.[35] The other orisa did not know she was an aje, a woman possessing spiritual power (àṣẹ). When they got to Earth, the male deities did not include her in the planning or execution of any project. After some time, the male deities noticed that their efforts failed at everything they attempted. They approached Olodumare to give a report of the situation. Olodumare inquired about Osun, and the male orisa told him that they never collaborated with her. Olodumare then directed the sixteen deities to go and plead with Osun for forgiveness and henceforth to include her in all plans. Once the male deities reconciled with Osun and included her in all plans, all of their efforts became successful. Thus, mutual respect between males and females was established as essential among the Yoruba for all undertakings.[36] According to the scholar of Yoruba culture and art Rowland Abiudun, the presence of Osun and the Iya Mi (the powerful mothers) "must be acknowledged at all major events, festivals, and celebrations of new seasons and the new year. Virtually all greetings on these occasions end with the prayer Ọ̀dún á yabo which is a wish for a 'feminine, productive, harmonious and successful year, season, or celebration.' This verbal invocation not only acknowledges the spiritual attributes and vital force (àṣẹ) of womanhood which is epitomized in Ọ̀ṣun, but is also a practical acceptance of the superior powers of 'our mothers' in helping the community to cope with all the challenges of a new season, year, or millennium."[37]

Women are noteworthy custodians of Yoruba tradition, especially as reciters of the many oral genres that constitute the storehouse of Yoruba religious narratives. The knowledge and dissemination of these oral genres bestows tremendous power on women, for with it comes the privilege to modify and prioritize which recitation is to be heard in any setting.[38] Women feature prominently in the creation and recitation of certain Yoruba oral genres, including Bridal Crying (Ẹkuń ìyàwó) and Lineage Praise Poetry (Oríkì ìdílé). Bridal Crying is a recitation performed by the bride on the wedding night enumerating the goodness of her parents to her during her growing-up years as well as her trepidation about moving to her new marital home. The term Ẹkuń, "crying," is used for this genre literally and metaphorically.[39] Yoruba women are active reciters of Lineage Praise Poetry—oríkì—which records and recalls the exploits of family heroes and heroines. This is usually to serve as impetus for family members to uphold the lofty models already established by those who lived before them.[40]

Young married Yoruba women learn the oriki of their husband's families from older wives. They become repositories of these oriki as the years pass, and they become part of the group of wives who recite and prioritize which oriki to recite on different occasions. Women seek solace from the orisa of the family as they encounter challenges daily, including the need for financial breakthroughs in business, academic favors for their children in school, and protection from malevolent spirits in society. Women make offerings and pray at the family's shrines when it is required to facilitate the orisa's favors on their requests. In addition, women sing and dance at the shrine when any of these favors are granted by the orisa, which is another occasion to recite the oriki of the orisa. Some of Yoruba oral genres, including oriki, are now in print and on YouTube.

Evidence of mutual interdependency and respect in gender relations abounds in the people's oral genres. The creation of the recitations may be by females or males; in either case, composition of oral genres is a complex phenomenon that follows specified structures. There are two modes of composition: rehearsed and spontaneous. The rehearsed mode involves preparation of materials to be recited and practice of moves and music to go with the recitations, while the spontaneous mode is performed impromptu. These oral genres are passed down from one generation to the next by word of mouth in the traditional mode of education.[41]

The ritual space, which can be any place designated for worship in a home, family compound, or a cleared space in the forest or on the bank of a river, is the location of interaction between humans and orisa. This interaction is accomplished through activities such as divination, sacrifices, liturgies, recitations, songs, dances, and trance.

RITES OF PASSAGE. The Yoruba also celebrate rites of passage including birth, marriage, and burial.[42] Women play important roles during rites of passage. The mother and baby are the focus of attention during the Yoruba naming ceremony. For instance, while the baby is named, the items used during prayers—including water, honey, and salt—are touched to the baby's mouth, but it is the mother who ingests these items. The bride is the focus during the marriage ceremony. Elderly women of the bride's family instruct the bride on her required duties to keep a happy home, like cooking good food, respecting her husband and members of his extended family, and being economically resourceful. Female friends of the bride sing and dance during the wedding ceremony. However, a widow plays no leading role during the burial of her husband and the feasting and gathering of relatives and friends to celebrate his life. She is required to mourn, keep a somber disposition, and remain indoors for a varying number of days depending on the family, but not less than forty days. However, modernity has modulated the traditional expectation of a forty-day stay indoors for the widow, due to the demands of workplaces. Hence, widows resume work at the expiration of the special leave period granted for the burial of their husbands, which oftentimes lasts two weeks.

Rites of passage involving male circumcision and "female circumcision," which is called "female genital mutilation" or "female genital cutting" by Nigerian and international activists seeking to eradicate it, have religious components such as preparations and items used during the procedure. Prayers are recited before the cutting, and fluid from a broken snail, which symbolizes ease (èèrò), is used in ritual recitation before the cutting. The herbal mixture applied on the cut to facilitate healing is produced with prayers recited on it. Whereas male circumcision among the Yoruba involves the cutting of the tip of the foreskin of the penis and is now usually done in the hospital a day or two after the birth of the baby, female genital cutting has generated a great deal of debate. Yoruba have practiced female circumcision in various ways, from nicking to excising the clitoris, as a means of restricting a woman's sexual appetite. Some Yoruba families traditionally have not had the operation performed on daughters.

Female genital mutilation continues to be practiced in Nigeria on girls between birth and fifteen years of age, but since 2015, it is illegal. A girl, usually between the ages of seven and twelve, is given concoctions of herbs to relax her during the operation. Female and male members of specific families, known as oólòlà (operators), perform the operation, which involves the excision of the clitoris.[43] It is a private occasion, and participants are usually a few female members of the girl's family and the oolola. While the practice was formerly widespread, it is discouraged in contemporary Yoruba society, especially as the Violence Against Persons (Prohibition) Act in 2015 banned female circumcision in Nigeria.[44] Nevertheless, statistical studies indicate that there is more educational work to be done to eliminate female genital cutting completely in Nigeria, including in the predominantly Yoruba states.

Surveys conducted in Nigeria indicate that the prevalence of women ages fifteen to forty-nine having had female genital cutting done at some point in their lives in the South West Zone of Nigeria, containing the predominantly Yoruba states of Ekiti, Lagos, Ogun, Ondo, Osun, and Oyo, decreased from 56.9 percent overall in 2003 to 41.2 percent in 2016–17. The percentages vary by state, with Osun State having the highest prevalence of 85.6 percent in 2003, which by 2016–17 dropped to 67.8 percent, and with Lagos State having the lowest prevalence of 40.3 percent in 2003, which by 2016–17 had dropped 25 percent. In 2016–17, Ogun State had the lowest prevalence between ages fifteen and forty-nine, at 18.8 percent, in the South West Zone.[45]

Statistics for the prevalence of female genital cutting among girls from birth to age fourteen indicate that the practice is continuing to decline. The decline in prevalence between 2003 and 2016–17 in Oyo State was from 68.9 percent in 2003 to 22.8 percent in 2016–17; in Osun State from 62.3 percent in 2003 to 25.1 percent in 2016–17; in Ondo State from 68.2 percent in 2003 to 18.2 percent in 2016–17; and in Lagos State from 15.9 percent in 2003 to 8.5 percent in 2016–17.[46]

A survey of female genital cutting in Nigeria among all ethnic and religious groups found that mothers' decisions were driving the continuance of the practice.

> The majority of cut women and girls reported Christian religious affiliation. Lower prevalence rates were observed among Muslims.... Girls whose mothers were in polygamous unions had a higher likelihood of being cut than those whose mothers were in monogamous unions....
>
> Girls were more likely to undergo FGM/C [female genital mutilation/cutting] when their mothers supported continuation of the practice; were the sole decisionmaker regarding household purchases, own health care, and expenditure; and believed that the practice was a religious requirement and prevented girls from having premarital sex. However, the likelihood of girls being cut was low when the decisions were not made by the mother but by her husband, partner, or someone else.[47]

The ban on female genital cutting in Nigeria was achieved in 2015 by a combination of efforts from Nigerian women at the local level; Christian and Muslim groups; wives of government officials, including the wife of the Nigerian president, Mrs. Aisha Buhari, at the national level; and global entities such as the World Health Organization and UNICEF. Their work will continue until female genital cutting is eliminated.

According to the Yoruba worldview, life never ends; hence, the dead are perceived as the living-dead/the ancestors. Funeral ceremonies for elders are celebrations to appreciate the life of the deceased. For a person who has lived a long and productive life, the funeral is an occasion for feasting, singing, and dancing. The format of a funeral is often prescribed by the profession and social status of the deceased person. In contrast, funerals are solemn when the deceased person died at a young age. In the past, a corpse of a deceased elder was buried in the house under the floor or within the compound of the deceased, but this is rarely done now. Burial now takes place at Christian or Muslim cemeteries.

Yoruba believe in reincarnation, but there is no notion of karma or caste determined by actions in previous lives, as in Hinduism. A person's deeds have nothing to do with their life form when reincarnated in another life. The Yoruba belief in reincarnation is intertwined with the qualifications for ancestors. Qualifications to become an ancestor include procreation, a fulfilled life with meaningful contributions to the community, a good death (dying at a ripe old age), and an appropriate burial. Ancestors are considered to be the living-dead, and there is constant interaction between the living and the ancestors through prayers, sacrifice, and reincarnation. Yoruba believe that an ancestor may be born as a member of the family; hence, names given to such children include Babatunde (father has come back again) and Yetunde (mother has come back again). A family member who is regarded as an ancestor is believed to have reincarnated within the family lineage. It is possible for a woman's child to be the reincarnation of an ancestor from her family lineage or her husband's family lineage. The Yoruba cyclic worldview has the same implication for women and men with regard to encouragement to be persons of integrity who offer mutual respect in the community.

Ancestors (male and female), called *eégún* in Yorubaland, remain part of the family, and there are interactions between them and members of the family. Each extended family or a town may venerate their ancestors at designated periods by offering prayers and supplications for help and direction from the ancestors. One such interaction occurs in visits of the ancestors in the form of masquerades (Egúngún). The Egungun masquerades are masked human figures who represent the ancestors. Women and men kneel before the Egungun to request diverse blessings including for children and financial progress. Usually, women's roles during these rituals include singing, dancing, cooking food, and serving food. However, as is true of other Yoruba religious groups, women may play leadership roles during the eegun festival, for example, as the *Ìyá àgan*, who is usually an old woman who leads the Egungun into the arena of performance with a long cane in her hands.

The most senior masquerade, representing the oldest ancestor, is the chief masquerade, which is known by different names in each

The Egungun masquerade represents all of the male and female ancestors of a family. Only men wear the Egungun masquerade. Women are prohibited from touching the Egungun. (Courtesy of ABORISADEADETONA in Wikimedia Commons)

community. The chief masquerade is perceived as possessing highly potent magical charms as he moves along the streets during outings. Only men may see the most senior masquerade.

ORISA WORSHIP AND POSSESSION BY INITIATED PRIESTESSES. Initiated priestesses and priests of different orisa lead worship by giving messages from the deity to the adherents, especially through possession, where applicable. Women possessed by orisa during rituals are primarily those who have been initiated into the worship of that orisa, but possession may also be a means by which the orisa calls a woman to become initiated into their worship. Examples of female spirit possession include the initiated Òfósí, priestesses who are considered to be the wives of the orisa named Ebora, among the Owe people of Kwara State, and who sing and dance to honor Ebora at festivals, and the initiated priestesses of the orisa Olúsarùn, the deified founder of the town of Iṣarun in Ondo State, who are considered to be Olusarun's wives. On festival occasions, the priestess called Aya Olua (Olua's spouse) speaks while possessed by the orisa to give his messages to the town's citizens. The priestesses of Olusarun sing songs that call out and name people who have acted in ways that are contrary to customs that maintain order and morality.[48] According to the scholar of Yoruba culture and religion Joseph Akinyele Omoyajowo, initiated priestesses' "special contribution to the general welfare and cohesion of the society can really be indispensable to the deity."[49]

As described by the anthropologist J. Lorand Matory, during rituals in Yorubaland involving dancing, drumming, and singing, initiates become possessed by their orisa. Through their initiation period, during which the person drinks libations containing herbal mixtures, is given herbal baths, and has plant substances rubbed into the top of the head, perhaps into an incision, a male or female person becomes a "bride" (ìyàwó) of the orisa. The male or female orisa is viewed as being in the relationship of a husband and lord (oko) who "mounts" (gùn) the bride.

In the Yoruba language, the verb gùn has several meanings. It can refer to sudden and violent penetration such as rape. Gùn is also the verb that refers to a rider mounting and controlling a horse. An experienced initiated priest or priestess (olórìṣà, "owner of orisa") is also called esin (horse) and elégùn (mount) of the deity. Thus, the orisa is the rider, and the initiated priest/priestess is the horse or mount of the deity, in addition to the orisa being the husband and the initiated priest/priestess the bride and wife. The priest or priestess is reported not to be conscious of happenings while being possessed by the orisa.[50]

In Yoruba religion in Yorubaland, the possessed priest/priestess is construed as being the wife to the orisa with regard to authority and control. In possession (gùn), the orisa takes over the faculties of the priest or priestess. Sometimes the takeover of faculties by the orisa can be sudden and violent, again similar to rape. Matory suggests that this may be particularly true of the warrior orisa Ṣàngó, a former king of Oyo and identified with lightning, who is known for his aggressiveness. However, Matory relates no definite report given by a Yoruba priest or priestess of Sango that spiritual possession equals sexual penetration. Instead, Matory interprets the possibility of sexual connotations in possession (gùn) based on the features of Sango.[51] In the interviews I have conducted with initiated priestesses of Ọbàtálá, Erinlè, and Osun, there is no attribution of a sexual connotation to *gùn*. *Gùn* refers to the takeover and control of the consciousness by the orisa of the elegun (mount). All instructions pronounced by the possessed person are construed as being direct instructions from the orisa that must be obeyed.

DIVINATION. Divination is another ritual practice among the Yoruba. There are three main types of divination that exist among the Yoruba: Ifa, Eerindinlogun, and Obì. Female diviners engage in each.[52] Each of the 256 oral Ifa narratives or chapters (*odù Ifá*) contain "poems or cantos" (*ẹsẹ̀ Ifá*) that express Yoruba philosophy and worldview in "cosmogonic stories," "details of time-honored rituals," and "quasi-historical accounts and philosophical commentaries."[53] These are passed down orally to persons training to become babalawo (male Ifa diviners) and iyanifa (female Ifa diviners). Iyanifa are fewer in number than babalawo among the Yoruba because of women's domestic responsibilities and their work outside the home, as well as the rigorous and time-consuming nature of memorization of the oral Ifa corpus.[54]

The scholar of Ifa Iyanifa M. Ajisebo McElwaine Abimbola points out that the wisdom contained in the Ifa corpus and the orisa Ifa (Ọ̀rúnmìlà) derives from his wife, Odù. The woman Odu is described as "someone who has died and yet is still living on earth; therefore she must be kept secret and her privacy respected." Of the two types of babalawo—*babaláwo elégán* (babalawo without Odu) and *babaláwo olódù* (babalawo with Odu)—only the babalawo oludu may see the woman Odu, who is kept hidden in a cavity in the babalawo's shrine, which is a metaphor for the womb. Iyanifa have the status of elegan and must not see the woman Odu, but Iyanifa Abimbola reports, "Ìyánífá around the world huddle together sometimes and meditate upon the fact that this cavity is a metaphor for the womb, the uterus, and that although women cannot see Odù, to some extent Ìyánífá *are* Odù."[55] She also states that "Odù the woman can be considered the embodiment of *odù* the literature."[56] Hence, Odu the woman is the source of the odu Ifa, the "chapters," in the oral Ifa corpus.

The "centrality of women in Yorùbá life in general and particularly in the Ifá priesthood" is demonstrated by the fact that there can be no initiation ceremony into the Ifa priesthood for a man or woman without the participation of an iyanifa. "The procession to the sacred grove of Ifá, the *igbodu*, is always led by an Ìyánífá who is carrying an image of Èsù on her head. The recession as the new initiate emerges from the *igbodu* is also led by an Ìyánífá carrying an image of Èsù."[57] Èṣù is the "deity who interprets and delivers messages between heaven and earth."[58] According to Rowland Abiodun, "Èṣù is the òrìṣà most crucial to the maintenance of the precarious balance between malevolent and benevolent powers in the universe. He is the major link between Ọṣun—his mother, who happens to represent the power of 'our mothers'—and the sixteen major òrìṣà, all male, who were sent to the world at the time of Creation."[59]

Divination through the Ifa oracular system requires that the iyanifa or babalawo has memorized and can interpret the Ifa verses in addition to possessing knowledge of the technical protocol for divination. There are eight components to each ese (verse) of Ifa: the names of the Ifa priests involved in the account; the name of the client; the reason for the consultation; the instruction of the Ifa priest to the client after divination; whether the client complied; what happens to the client who complies or refuses; reactions of the client to joy or sorrow from the process; and a fitting moral from the story as a whole. Ifa verses link historical recollection with divinatory contexts. Ifa chapters are dynamic and continue to be shaped by varied influences.[60]

In a typical example of Ifa divination, a client approaches the iyanifa or babalawo for consultation on a problem. The diviner uses sixteen palm nuts (*ikin*) or the divination chain (*òpèlè*) on a wooden divination tray (*ọpọ́n-Ifá*), carved with an image of Esu on its border, containing camwood dust in which the odu Ifa marks are noted as the result of the inquiry. The depiction of Esu on the outer edge of the divination tray indicates his position as an intermediary between "the physical world and the otherworld of spiritual beings." His cooperation is needed for a successful Ifa divination, and his "*àṣẹ* (catalytic life force and sanction) is always necessary in making Ifá's utterances and predictions come to pass."[61] After making inquiries from Ifa, the babalawo or iyanifa settles on an ese Ifa, which he or she recites. The eight components should be present in the recitation by the diviner. At the end of the recitation, the moral of the story serves as the platform for the prescribed solution to the client's problem. Thus, there are usually similarities between the predicament of the client and the protagonist in the ese Ifa recited by the diviner. Hence, the response of the protagonist in the recitation is instructive for the client.

Ifa constitutes the storehouse of the Yoruba philosophy and thought system. It provides the framework that undergirds Yoruba cultural practices and social organization. Ifa may be described as the encyclopedia of Yoruba life and customs. Moreover, the orisa Ifa, who is also known as Orunmila, is construed as *eléri-ìpín*, "the witness of human destiny." That the orisa Ifa/Orunmila witnesses human destiny is a view derived from Yoruba cosmological narratives that posit that he was present at the point when each individual made a choice of destiny before being born on Earth.[62] Important decisions require Ifa consultation among the Yoruba.

The Eerindinlogun divination system has extensive verses and requires long apprenticeships. In addition, it has a similar process but uses sixteen cowries for consultation before the recitation of Ifa verses by the diviner. A Yoruba oral narrative recounts that Osun received the sixteen cowries and the Eerindinlogun divination system from her (then) husband Orunmila, and she became a popular diviner, though the professor of Yoruba language and literature Wande Abimbola argues that it was Orunmila who learned divination from Osun. Osun's method of divination received approval from Olodumare, the supreme divinity.[63] According to the scholar of religion David O. Ogungbile, "The Ẹẹ̀rìndínlógún system today is the most popular, reliable, and commonly used form of divination among Òrìṣà devotees," and this form of divination is "woman-centered."[64] Women who are either devotees or priestesses of orisa such as Osun, Obatala, and Sango become Eerindinlogun diviners after training with an experienced Eerindinlogun, often a biological parent, for about five years, during which they learn verses. An orisa priest or priestess who uses Eerindinlogun is called by the title Olórìṣà, and a person who practices this form of divination to earn a livelihood is called an Eerindinlogun. Eerindinlogun is performed with sixteen cowrie shells, a cloth sack that contains the cowries, and a small tray that is made of wood or is woven. The diviner may also use *ibó*, pieces of broken bones or stone shells that can be thrown to get a simple yes or no answer.[65]

Female and male diviners may also use the Obi divination system, which in Yorubaland employs a four-lobe kola nut split into four pieces or, in the diaspora, a coconut split into four pieces; two pieces are considered to be male, and two pieces are considered to be female. The four pieces are cast onto a clean surface, and the pattern into which they fall determines the answer.[66]

SPIRITUAL POWER AND WOMEN. *Spiritual* power among the Yoruba is called ase, "that which makes all things possible." This is to be differentiated from *agbára*, which refers to physical power. Ase is an attribute bestowed on humans and nature by the supreme being (Olodumare), who has the final say concerning any issue. Prayers in Yoruba religion always end with the statement "ase," meaning "So let it be" or "May it be sanctioned," which expresses the people's petition that Olodumare will approve that which has been uttered by the person praying.[67] Yoruba also assume that there is power in spoken words when used according to stipulated principles, hence the use of command language (incantations of different types) for healing among the people.

The Yoruba people construe a strong link between ase and female procreative potential, especially menstrual blood. This is because menstrual blood is considered a conveyor of power because of its potential to produce life through pregnancy. Hence, there is always a prohibition of menstruating women coming in contact with "spaces of power" in Yoruba religion, such as rooms where warriors keep their charms (*oògùn*) or medicine-soaked shawls (*ibànté-agbára*); however, as is typical of the Yoruba stance of no absolutism, some exceptions do occur. The prohibition of menstruating women coming into contact with a man's charms and other spiritual objects is because the ase of menstrual blood is believed to nullify any other power. Thus, the menstruating wife has the power to nullify all preparations and plans of her husband. The Yoruba model of negotiation and mutual respect in gender relations is thus expressed through the management of ase.

MORALITY AND ACCOUNTABILITY. Yoruba place tremendous emphasis on the notion of continuity in all spheres of life. The conviction that the world operates in cycles rather than in a linear manner underlies the people's sense of accountability and responsibility in daily encounters with each other and with Olodumare. It encourages their belief in the need for high moral standards, especially integrity, which is known as *omolúàbí* (self-actualization and community responsibility, good behavior).[68] It is believed that an individual will reap whatever is sown, whether good or bad. Indeed, the Yoruba conviction is that the results of a person's actions or inactions will also affect their children through the generations.

Yoruba place a high value on respect for both persons and the divine. Valuing respect lies beneath the people's concepts of seclusion and secrecy. In this view, common things are not valued, while uncommon things are; hence, that which is valued and respected is secluded. This worldview undergirds the restriction of movement and visibility for traditional rulers, so that historically in Yoruba communities, the king was seen in his regalia by citizens only once a year, and it also supports the observance of secrecy by worship societies devoted to particular orisa. The Ooni (king) of Ile-Ife, a town considered as the birthplace of the Yoruba, wears his crown in procession around the town only once a year during the Olojo festival, which is an occasion to honor past rulers.[69]

The Yoruba notion of respect also serves as a foundation for gender constructions that emphasize complementarity between women and men rather than competition. Women have particular roles, and so do men; but both sexes must cooperate with each other for success to be attained. Complementarity assumes appreciation for the different gender roles as crucial to the common good.

Gender and Politics

Politically, the public domain was not construed as a predominantly male sphere but as a place where gender interdependence was encouraged. Yoruba rulers are usually from specific families that have been instrumental as founders of a community. The choice of ruler involves consultation with an Ifa diviner and then the decision of the council of kingmakers in every community. Yoruba rulers are construed as being very powerful; they represent the orisa among the people, hence the title *aláse èkejì òrìṣà*, "the one with authority second only to the orisa." Formerly, the sovereign occupied a high position in Yorubaland; the ruler's ase was unchallenged, and the ruler's will was a command on all matters. In present-day Nigeria, some political matters are outside the rulers' jurisdiction in democratic governance.

Interestingly, the Yoruba have oral records of female sovereigns. These include Eye Aro (1339–1419), Eye Mohin (1705–35), and Amaro (1850–51), who were the thirteenth, twenty-sixth, and thirty-sixth Deji (rulers) of Akure. There have also been three female Awujale (rulers) of Ijebu-Ode: Ore-Yeye, Ore Geje, and Rubakoya, who were the twenty-third, thirty-first, and thirty-seventh Awujale; and as many as three female Ajalorun (rulers) of Ijebu-Ife are on record. Similarly, one listing of thirty-nine Oba (rulers) in Ilesa in the order of their reign includes six who were females: Owa Obokun Yeye-Ladega (eighth), Owa Obokun Yeyegunrogbo (ninth), Owa Obokun Yeyewaji (thirteenth), Owa Obokun Yeyewaye (fifteenth), Owa Obokun Yeyewayero (sixteenth), and Owa Obokun Yeyeori (eighteenth). There are other records of female rulers from the past, such as Owaluse, who reigned in Ilesa; Oluawo, the female Ooni (ruler) of Ile-Ife, who is credited with the construction of pavements made of potsherds in Ile-Ife; and the female twin rulers of Ondo.[70]

Moreover, in precolonial times, parallel chieftaincies, in which a man and a woman held a chieftain position at the same time, were common. The female chief attended to the needs and concerns of women in the community and served as an intermediary between the women and the king, and the male chief did the same for the men in the community. Women held formal leadership roles and were influential in policy making. Consequently, Yoruba gender relations manifested notions of mutual respect between the sexes and cooperation and interdependence in the political realm.

Apart from rulers, there are positions for chiefs and leaders (advisers to the ruler) who continue to play crucial roles in the Yoruba polity, for example, the Egba ethnic group in Ogun and Lagos States of Nigeria, who make use of titles of respect for leaders, such as Òtúnba, the right-hand person to the king. The Otunba is well respected and expected to provide leadership in both social and financial relations in the society. The Otunba title in the states of Ogun and Lagos is bestowed on men and women. Similarly, the position of the family head, known as Olórí-ebí, is open to both men and women in these two states. Thus, women have held formal leadership roles and have been influential in policy making.

Women have participated in the structures of governance among the Yoruba. While historical change has attenuated the position of Yoruba women as rulers in contemporary society, their roles as participants in politics remain viable. Yoruba women exercise political influence in social organizations (ẹgbẹ́, groups), which usually have a governing structure. For example, the women of a town have as their head a successful businesswoman known as the Ìyálóde ("mother of the open space," the market), who is a chief in her own right and is a member of the Ògbóni society. The Ogboni is a traditional council of elderly men and women, who in the past held the power of life and death over those whom they judged to be guilty of wrongdoing. They enforced executive orders of the king and his council on offenders who violated the regulations of society, which sometimes involved the execution of murderers. In contemporary society, they are custodians of the norms and values of the Yoruba, and members of the Ogboni council provide leadership roles in society. The Ogboni council ensures social control in contemporary Yoruba societies.[71]

The Iyalode is the only woman who can see the most senior Egungun masquerade, and she has the privilege of gaining audience with the Oba (ruler) without following the normal protocol, as an expression of the role's importance.[72] In general, every political group includes women as members to ensure equity and women's representation in accordance with the Yoruba emphasis on gender balance; thus, every council in any Yoruba polity includes the office of Iyalode.

Conclusion

As we have seen, Yoruba women exercise agency in key ways in the economy, especially in the market, which avails them the opportunity for financial success. In the Yoruba concept of power as being visible/formal and invisible/informal, women control the invisible/informal power structures. Women assert power individually or jointly in polygynous marriages through diverse processes of negotiation. Yoruba conceive of motherhood as highly valued, and the culture blames the infertile woman, although provisions are made to ameliorate the plight of childless women.

Yoruba women have significant religious and social roles as custodians of tradition, because they exercise agency through prioritization and recitation of oral genres for every setting. With the exception of female genital cutting of young girls, which is now illegal in Nigeria and is the object of efforts to eliminate its practice, Yoruba women exercise agency through their roles in rites of passage, trance, and divination. Formerly, Yoruba women held political positions such as rulers, and they continue to have status as chiefs, initiated priestesses, and iyanifa in contemporary society, reflecting women's significant contributions to society. Women remain active economic participants in contemporary Yoruba societies, although their participation in the political sphere has diminished. There are no female Yoruba rulers today, except regents, but there are female chiefs and custodians of tradition. Priestesses and iyanifa in Yoruba religion continue to render valuable services in contemporary society, and women reciters of Yoruba oral genres abound. In sum, women are viewed by both men and women as stakeholders and actors in the Yoruba culture, religion, and polity.

2

Women's Leadership in Rituals of the Yorùbá Religion

The leadership roles of women in Yorùbá religion are significant and are often integrated with their socialization as economically independent actors in society whose work is complementary to that of their husbands. This feature of Yoruba society and religion is manifested in the life experiences of Madam Ajiun Funke Adisa, a seventy-nine-year-old initiated priestess of Erinlè in Abeokuta, who, when she was younger, was an active trader in kola nuts in the markets. In Adisa's worship society, Erinle is a goddess of fertility, elegance, and wealth. Worshiping Erinle guarantees giving birth to children and achieving wealth in business endeavors for the women who constitute the majority of her worshippers. Adisa was born into the Erinle òrìṣà tradition and is currently a leader in the rituals of Erinle. She is a mother and one of the wives in a polygynous marriage. Ajiun is a name meaning "that which one wakes up to admire"; however, theologically, the name is one of the panegyrics in the *oríkì* oral genre for the *àwọn Ìyà Mi*, the spiritually powerful mothers who are *àjẹ́* and who travel out of their bodies at night to eat the intestines, liver, arms, and legs of their victims.[1] The aje have *ẹyẹ*, "bird power," which various narratives in the Ifá corpus attribute to primordial females such as Ọṣun and Odù.[2] *Ajíún afínjú eye tí njí jeun lóru* means "Ajiun, the beautiful bird that wakes up to eat in the midnight." Adisa related that her initiation into priesthood took place at Erinle's shrine at midnight, during which she was instructed in her duties and taboos to observe. The duties include prayers, giving offering items to the orisa, and initiating aspiring priestesses. Her taboos are to avoid eating pawpaw fruit and *okro* (okra), and she should not place any item on her head. A typical day for Adisa begins with prayer and giving offerings to Erinle, including roasted beans, alcoholic drinks (libation), and kola nut. She repeats this ritual again at dusk.[3] She is a religious and social leader in her community and a manifestation of women's agency among the Yoruba, for whom the supernatural is a daily reality.

The reality of the supernatural is a basic assumption among the Yoruba; hence, leadership bestows both religious and social responsibilities. Initiated priests and priestesses in the Yoruba religion are not only religious leaders but also important social figures among the Yoruba. Their conduct, speech, and mode of dress are dictated by the demands of their roles, which necessitate their acting as models of social conduct and etiquette.

One of the crucial characteristics of a leader is charisma. Here the term "charisma" refers to extraordinary qualities displayed by a leader that are construed as stemming from divine endowment rather than personal achievement.[4] Charisma is signified in the Yoruba word *akíkanjú*, which indicates a popular, strong leader, usually an orator. It is the ability to convince and mobilize others to action to achieve set goals. While the ruler is at the apex of leadership among the Yoruba, there are other leaders at different levels in the polity who are akikanju. It is difficult to abuse charisma in Yoruba religion, as leadership is seen as a trust guided by divine prescriptions, such as the requirement of integrity, love, and faithfulness in human relations by Olódùmarè, the supreme being. Violations of these prescriptions attract the wrath of Olodumare, which may become manifest as drought, sicknesses, or premature death.

The charisma of the leader sustains the attention of followers, especially in rituals. For example, the loyalty and respect that is accorded to the priest or priestess in Yoruba religion is dependent on the conviction that they embody the orisa. Leaders in Yoruba religion may be designated by orisa through dreams, visions, strange illnesses, a mark on the body at birth, or Ifa or Ẹẹ̀rìndínlógún divination. No matter the mode of selection, the person is expected to dedicate themselves to the service of the particular orisa through initiation, sometimes after much reluctance and consequent suffering.

Initiation varies from one worship group to another in Yoruba religion, but there are generally three stages, which the ethnographer Arnold van Gennep (1873–1957) has identified as separation, transition/liminal, and incorporation.[5] Within the Yoruba religious tradition, different procedures of initiation into orisa cults consist of periods of seclusion and making different types of sacrifices. Generally the initiation ritual called *rárí* consists of separating from daily life and going through a liminal period in which the orisa is installed in the initiate's head. After coming out of that transition period and being incorporated back into daily life, the initiate must worship the orisa diligently and live under the orisa's instructions. From that point on, the initiate is obliged to serve the orisa through making animal sacrifices, food offerings, and the performance of rituals in which spirit possession sometimes occurs. Through such possession, the orisa communicates with the community through the body and voice of the initiate. When this happens, the orisa takes over the faculties of the person possessed, as, for example, when an aggressive male orisa like Ṣàngó possesses a soft-spoken woman, making the woman speak in a deep guttural voice and take giant strides.

Different analysis has been proffered for the possession of the adherent by the orisa. The American anthropologist J. Lorand Matory describes that during possession among Yoruba in Oyo, "not only do supplicants recognize the presence of a god with every gesture of obeisance, but the possessed declare the absence of their personal subjectivity and agency through [subsequent] reports of amnesia during possession."[6] As we saw earlier, the use of the verb *gùn*, meaning "to mount," is construed by Yoruba as referring to the orisa taking over the faculties of the possessed person. Although some initiated men in specific worship societies wear women's clothing to indicate that they are the wife of the orisa, including kings and male chiefs on special religious occasions, and it is true that the initiate is perceived and described as wife to the orisa irrespective of their sex, this is not to be construed as referring to heterosexual or homosexual relations between the initiate and the orisa.[7]

In Yoruba religion, the various relationships between worshippers and the orisa are described and named in terms of the relationships between different members of a Yoruba extended family. People who feel called to become initiated into the worship of an orisa are called *omo-òrìṣà*, the "child of the orisa." For example, among the initiated worshippers of Osun, there are *omo-Ọ̀ṣun*, males and females, who are "children of Osun," either by heredity or by a specific special calling of Osun on the individual's life. Families who have worshipped Osun for many generations are children of Osun, but also certain individuals, irrespective of their religious affiliations, who display certain characteristics are children of Osun. These include dreaming of Osun's appearances, intense attraction to bodies of water, or unexplainable sicknesses that oracular consultation interprets as showing the necessity for the individual to worship Osun for a lifetime. The orisa can signal that a person is selected as an omo-orisa by suddenly taking over the faculties of an individual at any time or setting, including active group worship of the orisa, which is characterized by singing, dancing, and making offerings by initiated priests and/or priestesses of the orisa. After initiation, the initiate may become possessed by the orisa to sing, dance, eat and drink, and speak in worship sessions and also at other times.

Orisa possession connotes a husband-wife relationship between the orisa and the initiate. Initiation into the worship of the orisa, including possession, constitutes the marriage of the orisa and the initiate. A new male or female initiate into the worship of the orisa is termed the *ìyàwó*, "bride" of the orisa. After one year as an iyawo, experienced initiated priestesses and priests are considered to be the wife of the orisa. Because senior priestesses and priests mentor omo-orisa and initiate them into the priesthood of the orisa, they are respectfully called *ìyá-òrìṣà* (or *ìyálóòsà*, "mother of orisa") and *baba-òrìṣà* (or *baba-òòsà*, "father of orisa"), respectively.

The orisa is always present with the initiate, even when not possessed, and the initiate takes on the characteristics of the male or female orisa in their daily life. Once initiated, the priest or priestess is recognized as a leader in both religious and social settings. Some orisa, such as Osun, Sango, and Ifa, have priests and priestesses, but among the people of Ogun State in Nigeria, Ọbàtálá (king in white clothing) and Erinle (a goddess, although construed as male in some Yoruba communities) have only priestesses. It is worthy of note that Obatala in some Yoruba communities is also construed as a female orisa.

Priestesses in Worship Sessions

In a typical worship session, which may be devoted to one or more orisa, there are two groups of people: the officiating priests and/or priestesses and the congregation. Some congregations have only priestesses who officiate during the worship sessions. On such occasion, a priestess leads prayers, the liturgy, and a sequence of necessary body movements like dancing or kneeling. In addition, the priestess conveys messages from the orisa to adherents, sometimes through possession.[8] The priestess may recite the praise names (oriki) of the orisa, which is believed to put the deity in the mood to bless the worshippers. Thereafter, the intent for the worship session is stated—ranging from thanksgiving for a blessing received to petition for help on a challenge—followed by singing, dancing, offering/sacrifice, and feasting. It should be noted that some worship sessions may be solemn, during which feasting is prohibited.

The priestess for a particular orisa must observe all of the taboos of that deity (e.g., palm kernel oil is prohibited at Èṣù's shrine, while initiates of Osun, goddess of the Osun River, must not eat fish, though variation of this taboo has been reported in other Yoruba societies) and ensure regular daily private and annual public worship of the orisa with whom she is in constant communication. As each orisa is responsible for different aspects of life, such as gynecology (Osun), pediatrics (Obatala), environment (Sango, Ọya), transportation (Ògún), general health (Ọsanyìn), and finances (Ajé, Osun), a priestess may be consulted by clients who need the assistance of that deity. Anyone in the community may consult the priestess of the relevant orisa for help and instruction on the existential concern at hand, because the priestess represents and brings messages from the orisa. When the priestess prescribes that certain items be offered to the orisa, this must be adhered to for any positive outcome to emerge.

Obatala Priestesses

According to Yoruba cosmological narratives, Olodumare (the supreme God and ruler of the heavens) gave Obatala the duty of creating the Earth with some elements (dirt, a hen, and a pigeon) and the responsibility of molding the physical form of humans. According to one version of the Yoruba creation story, after descending from heaven to the waters below by a chain, Obatala (also known as Òrìṣà Nla, "Great Orisa") poured the dirt to make the location known as Ifẹ̀ ("that which is wide," later known as Ilé-Ifẹ̀, "the home that is wide") and released the hen and pigeon, who spread the dirt by means of their scratching to make the Earth. After the completion of the task of creating the Earth, Olodumare sent Obatala back to plant the Earth with trees and plants. Olodumare then sent rain so the plants and trees would grow. Olodumare gave Obatala the task of molding human forms from the earth, and life was breathed into them by Olodumare. Therefore, Obatala is known as the orisa who creates the form of a baby in the womb.[9]

The Yoruba regard Obatala as the most senior orisa below Olodumare. Obatala is the god of whiteness (in relation to the color white, purity, and holiness, rather than a racial term). All people with disabilities and with albinism are special children of Obatala. Obatala is offered worship to attain prosperity, peace, progress, and longevity. Worshippers dress in all white, wear white beads on the neck and the wrist, and are expected to maintain high moral standards. Worship is accorded to Obatala every seven, seventeen, and thirty-three days. Obatala is worshipped between 6:00 and 7:30 a.m. or at sundown yet not when it is dark. Palm wine and palm oil are taboo to Obatala and are not to be brought near the shrine containing Obatala's altar or touched by adherents. Historically, Obatala has also been regarded as a sovereign ruler who reigned at Ile-Ife, the birthplace of the Yoruba.[10] Obatala was deposed by Odùduwà and his supporters. This incident is reenacted yearly in Ile-Ife at the rituals of the Itapa festival.

Obatala has no priests, only priestesses. This acceptance of solely female initiates in the worship of Obatala helps to provide societal models for the importance and legitimacy of female leadership. Obatala calls a woman to become a priestess through an experience of spirit possession or through a dream or vision. When this occurs, the custodians of Obatala worship—all women—are notified. They in turn inquire of the sacrificial items needed from Obatala through divination. These usually include Obatala's preferred foods: shea butter, snail, yam, solid pap/corn-starch pudding, she-goat, and pigeon. Obatala will also choose a location (e.g., the shrine or the house of the candidate) where Obatala will "sit and eat" with the chosen one. This is a meal to seal Obatala's special relationship with the initiate, during which Obatala is represented by the chief priestess. In prior times, this initiation usually lasted ninety days, but the ritual is now compressed to a few days because of the demands of office employment. The meal is prepared by women who bore children after making a vow to Obatala, and a meal is eaten by Obatala and the initiate. Mentoring is encouraged between older priestesses and new initiates to ensure effective learning of the etiquette of the orisa.

Every priestess of Obatala has her own shrine containing an altar, which may be located in her home or in a designated section of the family compound.¹¹ Within the shrine, Obatala is worshipped by *iyá-oómo*, women who married into a family that worships Obatala and who made a vow to Obatala in order to bear children, and male initiates. Male initiates known as *asògún* in the worship of Obatala have the role of slaughtering sacrificial animals and carrying the priestesses when they are under possession by Obatala. A male initiate may adhere to the worship of Obatala and own a shrine but cannot offer worship to the deity; rather, he must seek the services of an Obatala priestess to officiate. Any male who dares to officiate at an Obatala shrine stands the chance of becoming a woman through penalties such as impotency, hunchback, or hydrocele (a condition in which the scrotum is enlarged due to fluid accumulation).

The various Obatala priestesses are under the jurisdiction of the head priestess of Obatala, the Ìyá Ajé, the mother of commerce. She is held in high esteem and receives different gifts from the priestesses, and the omo-orisa who aspire to initiation, under her jurisdiction. For example, during the Ẹla-isu (dividing yam) festival around September of each year, the new yam is eaten for the first time, but only after certain rituals have been performed. On this occasion, all initiated priestesses (iyaloosa) bring gifts to the Iya Aje as a mark of homage and love to a worthy leader.¹²

A major challenge for an Obatala priestess is how to balance her home life, especially her conjugal duties, with her religious commitment to the orisa. It is believed that the closer she is to Obatala, the less she will cherish her wifely duties. Until recently, this was not a common problem, as priestesses were sixty years old or older, but there is a more recent trend toward priestesses being below forty years of age.¹³ Thus, many iyaloosa (initiated priestesses) who prosper acquire younger wives for their husbands and then act as the mother of the house. Women's agency is apparent in the decision to marry a new wife for the husband, just as the cooperation of the priestess and the new wife confirm women's solidarity, yet the husband cooperates with the arrangement. The ultimate aim of all participants is to ensure the continuous favor of the orisa.

Dignity and integrity are of paramount importance to an Obatala priestess. These two elements are crucial to her functioning as a problem solver and model in society. She should at all times have a clean conscience and be fair. Marital infidelity is highly abhorred for the iyaloosa, and the consequences are grave, including losing all connections with Obatala, lying unconscious for days at the Obatala shrine, and spiritual decline. Consequently, the Iya Aje of the iyaloosa always intervenes in marital conflicts involving priestesses under her jurisdiction to nip trouble in the bud.

Obatala priestesses cannot officiate a ritual while menstruating but must solicit the help of another priestess who is not menstruating. As noted earlier, menstrual blood in the Yoruba worldview is not viewed as a contaminant but rather as a conveyor of life, and it thus connotes power (àṣẹ).[14] The banning of menstruating women from sacred space in Yoruba religion emanates from the conviction that menstruation is a conveyor of power just as sacred space is. If the two were to meet, there would be a clash of powers that is best avoided. This conceptualization offers a distinct approach compared to attitudes toward menstruation as being impure in more patriarchal religious cultures. The scholar of Yoruba religion Iyanifa M. Ajisebo McElwaine Abimbola avers that "many women and some men contend that it is at this time when women are at their most powerful to effect spiritual work."[15] The management strategy in the Obatala worship society prioritizes female solidarity and mutual interdependence in gender relations rather than exclusion.

Erinle Priestesses

Erinle, whose name means "earth elephant" or "elephant who flourishes on the earth," is an orisa who has been described in various stories as being a hunter, a farmer, or an herbalist who was nicknamed "Elephant." A story states that he sank into the earth and turned into a river. As a consequence, he lives under the water, and there he is the king of a city named Kobaye.[16] A nineteenth-century account of Erinle suggests that the deity was worshipped as a male orisa in Lagos but as a goddess in Ota, a town in Ogun State.[17] Erinle is said to have sunk into the earth near the town of Ilobu in present-day Osun State and to have become a river because of a loss suffered while fighting or because children needed to be provided with water due to drought. Erinle is widely worshipped for prosperity, children, and well-being in Yorubaland, including in towns such as Ilesa and Ilobu in Osun State and Ijebu, Egbado and Remo in Ogun State.[18] Erinle is regarded as inhabiting both water and earth. "Erinle heals with water [from the river] and with leaves and herbs from the forest; he [or she] hunts on land for animals and for fishes in the water."[19] While Erinle has in some places been regarded as male, we will focus on Erinle's female depiction.

Erinle is a goddess widely worshipped in Abeokuta and other parts of Ogun State. Her main shrine is located at the river previously known as *odò èyìn odi* (the river at the outskirts), but now known as *asodò Ìjàyè* (the Ijaye river). Erinle has only priestesses; no male can officiate at her worship. Men are seldom initiated because male roles are minimal in her worship. Duties for initiated males in Erinle worship include carrying to the shrine women who are possessed by Erinle and who have fallen down during trance, the slaughtering of sacrificial animals, and carrying the load of orisa (*erù-òòsà*), that is, the items of sacrifice in a large calabash, which is usually heavy, on the way to the river, where the sacrificial worship is performed by the priestesses. All male initiates of Erinle are called *asògún*, and they are usually from families with a long history of worshiping Erinle. They are chosen by Erinle through Ifa consultation. They openly confess their allegiance to Erinle but do not undergo priestly initiation.[20]

The goddess selects her priestesses from the female children of families that have worshipped her for many generations, also regarded as her descendants. She calls them through dreams, visions, or prolonged illness. Usually, her worship is hereditary, passed down from generation to generation, hence the saying *Erinlè lo nbo Erinlè*, meaning "It is Erinle who worships Erinle." Such chosen ones undergo training through observation and being mentored. The goddess Erinle continually instructs the initiate-in-training through rituals until she eventually becomes an *ìyálóòsà Erinlè* (Erinle priestess). The goddess endows her priestesses with special abilities, including healing, wisdom, and other benefits. The duties of the priestess encompass regular worship and officiating at the annual festival.

Erinle's annual worship takes place by the Erinle river bank every February; it is a festival involving all priestesses and adherents. It is elaborate and colorful and has been compared to the festival for Osun in Osogbo next to the Osun River.[21] Each priestess has attending initiates who carry very heavily adorned images of the orisa and the eru-oosa (the load of the deity), which are decorated with jewels and flowers. The priestess and initiates are accompanied by drummers as they move in procession to the river, where sacrifice is offered. Some of the items used as offerings to the goddess are fowl, kola nut, bitter kola, and roasted beans. Roasted beans are very important in the worship of Erinle, and this food is to be found in all shrines (*ojúbà*) of the goddess. The roasted beans are put in bottles and placed at her shrine, as it is believed that the beans perform wonders such as healing diseases that Western medicine could not cure and achieving victory over attacks from malevolent spirits.

Homage is paid to Erinle in other ojuba located on the way to the river by touching the shrine with the right leg three times.[22] There is competition between different shrines to outshine each other in the adornment of Erinle figures. This is interpreted by the worshippers as a manifestation of the measure to which Erinle has blessed each ojuba. A single phrase is recited as the different teams approach the central shrine, *ódi odó ìjàyè*, meaning "Onto the Ijaye River."

The teams arrive at the central shrine amid much fanfare, touch the shrine with the right leg three times, and head for a pit three feet in circumference and four feet deep, into which they pour the roasted beans from the eru-oosa. Every attendee of the festival struggles to get a scoop of the beans, and as they eat, prayers are offered for each person's heart's desire. The belief is that the roasted beans eaten at the central shrine of Erinle at this time will bring solutions to every existential problem that worshippers may be experiencing. Priestesses of Erinle can officiate while menstruating but should maintain good hygiene;[23] this shows the inclusiveness of Yoruba gender principles. The Yoruba do not subscribe to absolutism in any setting or form.

Women Worship Leaders

Within the Yoruba worldview, the female principle is conceptualized as involving coolness, gentleness, and peace, while the male principle reflects toughness, volatility, and aggressiveness.[24] These principles—male and female—are sought in religious rituals to attain balance.[25] Women's religious leadership roles include diviners, priestesses, *arugbá* (calabash-carrying virgin girls dedicated to the orisa), and custodians of tradition. As diviners, women consult deities through Ifa or Eerindinlogun to address diverse issues on which clients require direction in making decisions. Hence the *iyánífá* and eerindinlogun, just as the *babaláwo*, provides crucial direction for the sustenance of social harmony in Yoruba societies.[26]

As votary maids (arugba), virgin girls serve as embodiments of an orisa. Arugba can be found in the worship of some deities among the Yoruba, including Osun and Òbà—goddesses of the rivers Osun and Oba in Osun State. While in some communities the arugba may be married, in these states arugba are virgins aged between twelve and eighteen years old who live with chief priestesses of the orisa but have a normal social life with regard to schooling. The arugba is restricted in social outings and relationships with men. For example, the term of the arugba of Osun in Osogbo, the capital of Osun State, terminates with her marriage. An arugba carries offerings for the deity on her head during festival processions. Worship on such occasions would be impossible without the arugba.

While some priestesses officiate at the shrine of a single deity and observe all prescribed taboos of that deity, other priestesses own shrines devoted to various deities, officiate in the regular worship of these deities, and train novices (omo-orisa) who aspire to initiation. The novices serve and train under the deity that rules their *orí* ("head," personality-soul) under the tutelage of the priestess.

One such priestess is Iya-Oloya, Iya Agan Idayat Irele Oke-Ipa, who lives in Lagos, Nigeria. She is involved in the worship of Osun, Awoopa, and Ògbóni and holds senior positions in the worship societies for these orisa. She feeds the deities Oya, Esu, Obatala, and Osun every Friday with each deity's favorite food and observes the taboos for each.[27] She oversees the worship of many deities within her shrine regularly throughout the year and every year on August 20 celebrates Odun Isese, which is a festival involving singing, dancing, and eating food offerings to honor the deities and appreciate their benevolence to the adherents.[28] In addition, she consults with clients who may need the intervention of these deities in tackling various challenges of life, such as childbearing, prosperity in business, and illness. Most of her clients are women. Priestesses serving multiple orisa are rare among the Oyo-Yoruba in Oyo and Osun States, where a priestess usually serves no more than one or two deities, but the practice is common among priestesses in and between Lagos and Abeokuta.

The arugba dedicated to Osun leads a procession to the Osun River, Osogbo, Nigeria, January 28, 2017. (Photo by Bappah, available from Wikimedia Commons)

Iya-Oloya, Iya Agan Idayat Irele's high position in the Ogboni society shows that she is a custodian of tradition. Hence, there is no exclusion of women from the status of *awo*, a male or female who possesses vast knowledge of mystical powers and functions in Yoruba religion.[29] Awo include hunters, diviners, midwives, artists, and cultic functionaries who possess mystical knowledge. Mystical knowledge consists of spiritual powers to utilize the laws of nature and to commune with spirit beings.

The awo is respected by the Yoruba because of their knowledge of spiritual laws and endowments. Thus, Iya-Oloya, Iya Agan Idayat Irele is representative of effective women's agency in rituals in Yoruba religion and the new face of women religious leaders because she serves multiple deities.

Àjẹ́, Women with Spiritual Power

As we have seen, Yoruba assert that there is a link between motherhood and spiritual power. A female adult may be an aje, a woman "with special powers that can be used for good or evil."[30] The Yoruba word àjẹ́ is "often incorrectly translated as 'witches.'"[31] A senior orisa priestess believed to be an aje will be addressed respectfully as Iya Mi (powerful mother); the same term is used, as noted earlier, for the collective of powerful elder women.[32] Generally, all women are potential mothers and are therefore endowed with the mysteries of bloodshed in menstruation and childbirth. Yoruba construe aje as groups of women with special spiritual endowments that may be employed for positive or negative agendas. In Yoruba religion, aje are symbolized by birds and possess ase, "that which makes all things possible," that is, "power." There is always a bird depicted on a Yoruba king's staff of authority or throne, which represents the mothers and women's agency, on whose powers he can draw "for the public good."[33] For example, Oba (ruler) William Adetona Ayeni of the kingdom of Ila-Orangun is reported as having said in reference to the birds on his crown, "Without 'the mothers,' I could not rule."[34]

Yoruba cosmological narratives provide the explanation for the origin of the Iya Mi group as a reaction to the ignoring of Osun by the male primordial deities at the beginning of time, which resulted in failed projects and chaos. As we have seen, the situation was resolved when Olodumare instructed the male deities to acknowledge the importance of Osun in order for peace to be restored. Another cosmological narrative is found in Odù Ọ̀sá Meji in Ifa, which tells how after the Earth was created, Olodumare sent Obatala (called Ọbàìṣà), Ogun, and Odù to administer the Earth. Obaisa was given ase to make things do his bidding by his command, and Ogun was given the power of "iron, hunting, and warfare." Odu was not given a specific power, so she returned to Oludumare with a request for ase. Oludumare told her, "You will be their mother forever.... You will sustain the physical world," and he gave her a calabash containing a bird as her ase. Odu told Olodumare that "she would use [the power] to fight those who insult or disrespect her, but would not hesitate to use it to help those who adore her." According to the art historian Babatunde Lawal, "This partly explains the popular belief that the àjẹ́ are capable of both good and evil."[35]

The Yoruba recount different cosmological narratives on the origins of suffering, sickness, and death, but no narrative solely blames women. The Iya Mi group are sometimes perceived as malevolent spirits, who should be avoided at all cost by appeasement and sacrifice.

Until recently, aje were usually considered to be old women (over seventy years old) who displayed characteristics that are considered wicked by society, including fraud, cheating, stealing, and murder through the use of charms or incantations. For instance, Yoruba advise moderation in lifestyle to avoid attracting the attention of the Iya Mi, which may bring evil occurrences. However, in the past forty years, younger women, some still of childbearing age, have been considered to be members of the Iya Mi group.

Aje are associated with mysteries, out-of-body travels, and spells. Everything about the group is shrouded in secrecy, including their gathering venues and rituals, but the effect of their actions in the community is beyond debate for the people. Aje have been known to promote the advancement of their children in polygynous families and aid their children in economic ventures but also to cause harm at the individual, family, and community levels. The anthropologist Peter Morton-Williams posited that women with spiritual power were more likely to be feared in the context of the Yoruba patrilineal and polygynous extended family (ilé), into which women from other families were married, frequently as co-wives.[36]

The central position of this group of women in Yoruba consciousness is manifest at every important occasion, where the powerful mothers are always acknowledged and their support solicited for the venture to succeed. Yoruba construe aje to be females who utilize their spiritual powers for evil as well as good; hence, there are àjẹ́ funfun (white witches: positive) and àjẹ́ dúdú or àjẹ́ pupa (black or red witches: negative). Women known in contemporary Yoruba society to possess riches, boldness, and knowledge and to be generally nonconformist in relation to patriarchal prescriptions for women's domesticity and deference to male authority may be labeled as witches.

An elderly priestess of the goddess Odua, Egbado-Yoruba, Nigeria, 1975. (Photo courtesy of Henry John Drewal)

Aje as a phenomenon is real for Yoruba.[37] The Yoruba view of the aje is negative or positive for women depending on the agenda for which it is believed that their ase is utilized. The aje are the highest and last court of appeal in Yoruba society; when any issue defies administrative and political solutions, it is referred to the Iya Mi and resolved. (The matter is reported to the leader of the Iya Mi group by the king, since she is known to only a few people in the community.) The Iya Mi are custodians of power that is informal and invisible but potent and indispensable. They are the powerful mothers of the community and serve interests that guarantee peace and prosperity.

Despite the empowering effect of the Iya Mi group for women in Yoruba polity, however, the aje as an individual, when identified in society, is labeled as an antisocial person and may be despised and deprived of her fundamental human rights. According to the sociologist Friday A. Eboiyehi, "In rural Nigeria," women who are "childless, the farmers, those aged women living alone, those with certain physical abnormalities such as having red eyes, a common feature of older women who spend their lifetime cooking for their families over smoky, inefficient stoves using poor quality fuel," may be accused of being malevolent aje.[38]

Eboiyehi describes how in 1989 in the case of *Ezekiel Adekunle versus the State*, the Supreme Court of Nigeria upheld the murder conviction and death sentence of Ezekiel Adekunle "for orchestrating and spearheading the murder of . . . Felicia Ejide, a seventy-year-old woman whom the appellant accused of being a witch": "Witnesses described how Adekunle jeered at the victim by calling her a witch before jostling her and causing her to fall while she was being carried home on her daughter's back. When the elderly woman fell, the appellant raised a public alarm about a witch being transported away. This action led a converging crowd to pelt the elderly woman to death with large pieces of cement block while chanting, 'Kill the witch with stones.'"[39]

Eboiyehi concludes that in Nigeria the accusation of "witchcraft is a form of control and dominance over women."[40] Moreover, among the Yoruba of southwestern Nigeria, many elderly women in villages who have been accused of witchcraft flee to cities where they are frequently destitute.[41] Scholars such as Eboiyehi confirm that belief in witchcraft is a social disability for women who are accused of being aje. Thus, belief in aje, women who wield spiritual power (ase), can empower women, especially the initiated priestesses, in contemporary Yoruba society, but it can also be used to scapegoat elderly women with no protection from abuse. Negative attitudes toward women identified as witches can be promoted by Christianity. An elderly wife living in a marital patrilineage without children to speak up for her can be at risk for abuse related to accusations of witchcraft.

Gẹ̀lẹ̀dẹ́

Various oral historical accounts connect the origin of the Gẹ̀lẹ̀dẹ́ festival to honor the powerful mothers, the aje, to a succession dispute between two princes (twins) of the Ketu kingdom, with the elder prince leaving Ketu and establishing a smaller kingdom at Ilobi, perhaps in the early nineteenth century. Subsequent to ruling Ilobi, the elder brother returned to Ketu and became its king. Alaketu Adebiya has been identified as the older prince who was the ruler of Ketu from 1816 to 1853.[42] When the art historian Babatunde Lawal visited Ilobi in 1971, elders there told him that when the prince fled to Ilobi from Ketu, he brought with him the sacred symbols of Ketu kingship to prevent his brother from being installed fully as king. The brother in Ilobi had a masquerade with metal anklets made and sent it to Ketu, where the jingling of the anklets in the night frightened the inhabitants. A reconciliation between the brothers took place that was mandated by divination, but the brother in Ilobi remained there as king. Later the people in Ilobi taught the people in Ketu the secrets of the masquerade with the jingling anklets, which was later known as "Gelede." The exiled brother eventually returned to Ketu to become its king. Today the town of Ketu remains known for its Gelede festivals.[43] Lawal concludes that the focus of the Gelede festival on placating the aje and Ìyá Nlá (Great Mother) to ensure the birth of healthy children indicates that the festival has origins prior to the dispute between the twin brothers who became kings of Ketu and Ilobi.[44]

A narrative in the *Odù Ìwòrì Méjì* of the Ifa corpus recounts the origin of the Gelede festival as the consequence of the inability of Yemọja, "the mother of all the òrìṣà and all living things," to conceive a child after she married a man of Ketu.[45] Ifa was consulted, and Yemoja was advised to perform a ritual in which mashed corn and clay dishes were offered as a sacrifice and to dance with "wooden images on her head and metal anklets (*aro*) on her feet."[46] After she performed this ritual, Yemoja's first child was a son nicknamed Ẹ̀fẹ̀ (the humorist), and her second child, a girl, was nicknamed Gẹ̀lẹ̀dẹ́.

The Gelede festival, in which men masquerade as women and dance, honors Iya Nla and "her earthly disciples, the 'powerful mothers,'" the aje (the Iya Mi).[47] According to Lawal, Iya Nla is identified as "the wife of the artist deity Ọbàtálá." She is the epitome of "the maternal principle in the Yoruba cosmos," and she combines "in her nature the attributes of all the principle female deities—Yemọja (mother of all waters), Olókun (sea goddess), Ọ̀ṣun (goddess of the Ọ̀ṣun River), Òdù (founder of witchcraft), Oòduà (Earth goddess), Ilẹ̀ (Earth goddess), and Ọya (goddess of Niger River)."[48]

> As Olókun (spirit of the sea) and Yemọja (mother of all waters), Ìyá Nlá was the primeval sea out of which habitable land emerged at Ilé-Ifẹ̀, the cradle of Yoruba civilization. As Ilẹ̀ (the Earth), venerated by the Ògbóni, she sustains life, humanity, and culture. As an embodiment of the good and evil of the physical world, she is Olúwayé (ruler of the world), and Ìyámi Òṣòròngà, the first female to whom the Supreme Being gave a special power (àṣẹ) in the form of a bird enclosed in a calabash, copies of which she presented to her disciples, the "powerful mothers." In her popular aspect as Yemọja, she is the generous and the dangerous mother.[49]

The onomatopoeia in the Yoruba word Gẹ̀lẹ̀dẹ́ calls to mind "the leisurely and relaxed gait of an obese woman," which refers to the description of Iya Nla as "the plentiful, pot-breasted mother; the nursing mother with the rolling buttocks," and the masquerades created and worn by the men as they dance in the festival emphasize women's "big breasts and buttocks that rock voluptuously with each step."[50] The name Gelede also refers to indulgence and "something that cools and relaxes." According to Lawal, the name Gelede indicates the purpose of the festival: "the use of poetic humor to pacify the Great Mother and the àjẹ́, on the one hand, and to dissolve social tension, on the other."[51]

The Gelede festival as it is practiced in the Omida, Ijeja, and Idi Isin areas of Abeokuta in Ogun State is known as Ìyá Gẹ̀lẹ̀dẹ́ (Mother Gelede) among the worshippers. The name Gelede refers to a goddess and a festival at once, both geared toward giving honor to the Iya Nla and the aje. The goddess Gelede is the physical manifestation of the aje—the Iya Mi, who are represented in the festival by masquerades with female features such as painted faces and breasts. By carving the masks, wearing the masquerades, and dancing at the festival, male worshippers acknowledge that they derive all their powers from the aje and make all supplications to the Iya Mi. No worshipper of Gelede is expected to be infertile, for she gives children to all who offer her worship.[52] Hence, the goddess Iya Gelede is called "deity of children" (*nítorí omo ni, Òrìṣà olómo ni*). She promotes birth and protects children.

The purpose of the Gelede festival is to appease Iya Nla and the Iya Mi in order to acquire children and well-being in society. Adherents testify that at least four days before the Gelede festival—which lasts seven days—and the corresponding nightly festival named Èfè, they will be financially blessed. According to one respondent, "Prosperity, good health and fertility are normal in our lives. The whole religion is about aje."[53]

A costume (mask) for the festival is financially sponsored by a man or woman chosen by the goddess through Ifa consultation. *Gelede* refers to the mask and the person wearing it. The different costumes and masks in vibrant colors depict different aspects of the Iya Mi. Men carve and wear elaborate masks made from wood for the Gelede festival. The wooden masks of Gelede worn by the men in the Gelede (daytime) and the Efe (nighttime) performances are kept in the worship center and are the property of the shrine, although they are produced by individual worshippers as prescribed by spiritual consultations with Ifa. Although males put on the masks and dance during the Gelede festival, all characteristics of the masks and symbols are feminine. The Gelede festival displays rich aesthetic features such as dance, songs, a variety of colors, and recitations performed by the men, but beneath all of these is the fundamental power of the Iya Mi.

Adherents come for worship in the Gelede shrine as occasion demands throughout the year;[54] but at the seven-day Gelede festival, dancing, singing, and feasting occur, and the shrine containing the mask of Iya Nla is decorated with an array of colors. The festival occurs three days after Ileya, that is, Id el Kabir (the Nigerian name for Eid al-Adha, the Islamic festival that commemorates the willingness of Ibrahim [Abraham] to sacrifice his son Ismail [Ishmael] at Allah's command) in Abeokuta in Ogun State, Nigeria.

The Efe ensemble performs in a nightly vigil during the Gelede festival. The Efe ensemble is composed of male mask wearers. The Efe ensemble is a group of elaborately decorated male masked performers (maybe four, five, six, or more) who sing and dance in celebration of women's sacred powers. Efe performances are opportunities to ridicule evildoers in the community, no matter how highly placed. The identity

Gelede of a mat seller, Egbado-Yoruba, Nigeria, 1977. (Courtesy of Henry John Drewal)

of the persons performing in the Efe ensemble are known to the unmasked Gelede initiates, who may be male or female. (The Gelede mask performers are all males.) The Efe ensemble honors the "mothers," the aje, who are also known as *àwọn ẹyẹ òru*, "the midnight birds."

Although no woman leads prayers or offers libations at the daytime Gelede festival or the nighttime Efe festival, all men who officiate do so on behalf of the women, the mothers, the aje. A man I interviewed stated, "We got all our power from the aje. If you don't have a better way to describe us, you may describe us as worshippers of aje."[55] According to Lawal, "The prominence given to the female image in Gèlèdé, coupled with the fact that the maskers are men, apparently bespeaks an attempt by the 'male establishment' to appease women in general, and the 'powerful mothers' in particular. It is a public acknowledgment of the vital contribution of the female sex to the community; for as mothers, they embody the procreative power of àṣẹ, on which depends the survival of organized society as well as the human race."[56]

The aje that Gelede represents are construed as capable of killing and shedding the blood of the human victims of their wrath. One form of the Iya Nla mask is in the shape of a bird with a red beak, designating blood. Another form of the mask for Iya Nla is a large face with "bulging eyes" with a "long flat board-like extension below the chin" that represents her beard, indicating that she has power. Sometimes a snake may encircle the head, or a carved bird will be perched on top of the mask. Ears may be absent from the mask, or the ears may be "small pointed animal-like ears placed high on the temples."[57] According to the art historian Henry John Drewal, during the Efe nighttime gathering, the mask of Iya Nla makes her appearance after all lights are extinguished. She wears a white cloth and the mask, is bent over like an old woman, and dances slowly surrounded by the elders of her worship society. During her appearance, songs are sung in her praise. Then she returns to the shrine, where her mask is "the focus of worship."[58]

Thus, the Iya Mi are one with Iya Nla and are perceived as women of vast knowledge with great mystical powers that they may employ for either negative or positive agendas. They are powerful women who are highly respected among the Yoruba. The roles played by men during the Gelede festival may be understood as the men's acknowledgment and appreciation of women's agency and productive activities. It is an attempt to maintain balanced gender relations wherein both men and women cooperate for the common good. The extensive reference to mothers and motherhood in the Gelede festival highlights the Yoruba priority for procreation to sustain the collective immortality of the Yoruba.

Conclusion

Women play crucial roles in rituals in Yoruba religion. The existence of an important male deity—Obatala—who accepts only priestesses to serve him shows clearly that women can hold positions of high esteem in Yoruba religion. The Gelede festival that honors Iya Nla (the Great Mother) and the aje, the elder powerful women in the community, also indicates that initiated priestesses are regarded as powerful and must be shown respect. These religious expressions and others in Yoruba religion provide the basis for harmonious gender relations and reciprocal respect between women and men, as well as models for social relations. Women are perceived to be able to take on leadership roles in society because they serve as leaders in ritual spaces. This embrace of women's leadership and mutual gender respect in the Yoruba religion has influenced women's participation in Christianity and Islam in Yorubaland, affording them more opportunities for religious leadership than in other parts of the world.

Changes have become apparent recently in the requirements for becoming a female leader in Yoruba religion. While earlier, postmenopausal women were primarily the ones who received a calling to be orisa priestesses, younger women now lead and serve as priestesses in ritual settings. This shift has been attributed to the influence of Western education and social changes such as women working in the civil service and factories. The instance of the priestess of Erinle who can officiate while menstruating, contrary to taboos in other orisa worship societies that prevent menstruating women from entering sacred spaces, highlights the dynamism of Yoruba religion, which is never static. Women's leadership in ritual spaces has been a significant feature of religious traditions among the Yoruba and by all indications will continue. Indeed, according to the scholar Iyanifa M. Ajisebo McElwaine Abimbola, the "very nature of Yorùbá religion is inclusive, leaving space for difference while not excluding anyone from participating in the group or groups of their choice and calling."[59] Gender relations in Yoruba religion attempt to strike a balance rather than the oppression of one sex by the other. The exception is the negative attitudes and suspicion toward aje, women with spiritual power, that are often prevalent in Yoruba popular culture and disseminated in popular media such as movies.

Overall, complementarity and respect has marked relations between Yoruba women and men in indigenous Yoruba society. However, the situation has changed since there has been contact between the Yoruba and Western and Arab cultures through Christianity and Islam. Since these religious cultures have prescribed subordinate roles for women, how have Yoruba women challenged the received subservient roles of women in Christianity and Islam? This question is examined in chapters 3 and 4.

3

Yorùbá Women in Christianity

Yorùbá women play significant roles within Christian denominations but are seldom given the overall leadership of a church, province, or ministry. When this occurs, it oftentimes hinges on prophetic instructions and pronouncements from the woman that are accepted by a congregation and even denominational leadership. A woman's prophetic dreams and visions may lead her to found a new religious organization or movement.

An example is Pastor Mrs. Busola Olotu, who was born in Lagos, Nigeria, on October 23, 1957. Her parents are the late Justice Adegboyega Edward Ademola and Mrs. Odulate (née Agusto); her mother was from Brazil. Her parents separated shortly after her birth. Her maternal family was Muslim, and thus the first religion she knew was Islam. Indeed, her maternal grandfather was the founder of Jamatu Islamiyah in Lagos, Nigeria. According to her, she had a hunger for God from a young age, and she often yearned to know more of God. She had early religious experiences during her secondary-school days at Saint Louis Grammar school, Ibadan. Mrs. Olotu trained as a lawyer at the University of Ife, Nigeria, in 1974–78 and in the Nigerian Law School in 1979. She was a Catholic until she gave her life to Christ on June 14, 1983, and became Pentecostal and shortly after experienced a vision with angels moving around in the heavens; she described it this way: "the heavens opened up as I was walking on the street."

Mrs. Busola Olotu's spiritual training and mentorship began when she joined the Full Gospel Businessmen Fellowship through an invitation from a friend in 1985. Here she was mentored by the Reverend Emmanuel Oset of Canaan Ministries, aka Champions' Church, and the Reverend George Adegboye of Rhema Chapel International Churches (RCIC), both in Ilorin.[1] In 1992, she joined and worshipped at a Pentecostal church called the Redeemed Christian Church of God (RCCG), Sabo-Oke, Ilorin. RCCG is a Pentecostal megachurch in Lagos that has established many congregations in Nigeria and exists in other countries.[2] Mrs. Busola Olotu continued to worship in the RCCG church in Sabo-Oke, Ilorin, until March 26, 1995, when Pastor Ore gave her words of the Lord that she had been raised up to comfort many people from all nations at the RCCG congregation on Oro Road, Ilorin. She eventually became a minister in charge of the Sunday school at this Redeemed church. In 2000, her area pastor, the Reverend (Professor) Folu Ologe, told her of the instruction of General Overseer Enoch Adeboye (b. 1942) that a woman pastor be nominated to start a model parish in Ilorin and that she was chosen for the position. She sought the face of the Lord in fasting and prayers and was instructed to read the book of Joshua and the Acts of the Apostles. She founded the City of Refuge Adewole, a branch of the Redeemed Christian Church of God, in Ilorin. In the face of great challenges concerning accommodation, finances, and membership, the church was initiated and prospered. Two years after planting the church, she became the first woman area pastor of the Redeemed Christian Church of God in Kwara State.

Pastor Mrs. Busola Olotu recounts how God kept reminding her that her stay in the Redeemed Christian Church of God was for training and was temporary. God told her that she was to operate a ministry for women and gave her the name of the ministry: Daughters of Deborah International Ministry (DODIM).[3] On November 4, 2006, around 5:00 a.m., the Lord woke her up and requested that she write down the mandate, vision, purpose, and mission of the Daughters of Deborah International Ministry. She wrote down everything, and after reading it over, she became frightened because it was a huge vision. She was plagued with many questions about whether she was capable of achieving such a great mandate, especially as she was doing fine as a woman pastor at the Redeemed church. This fearful attitude initially prevented her from doing anything about the mission and vision of DODIM. By June 2007, she started receiving a series of warnings through dreams and spiritual counsel from other servants of God. She wept a lot during this period because of her struggle within herself to obey the instructions of God to start the ministry. On July 1, 2007, she entered into a covenant of preservation with God (agreeing with God's promises in the Bible on the preservation of a believer and prayers)

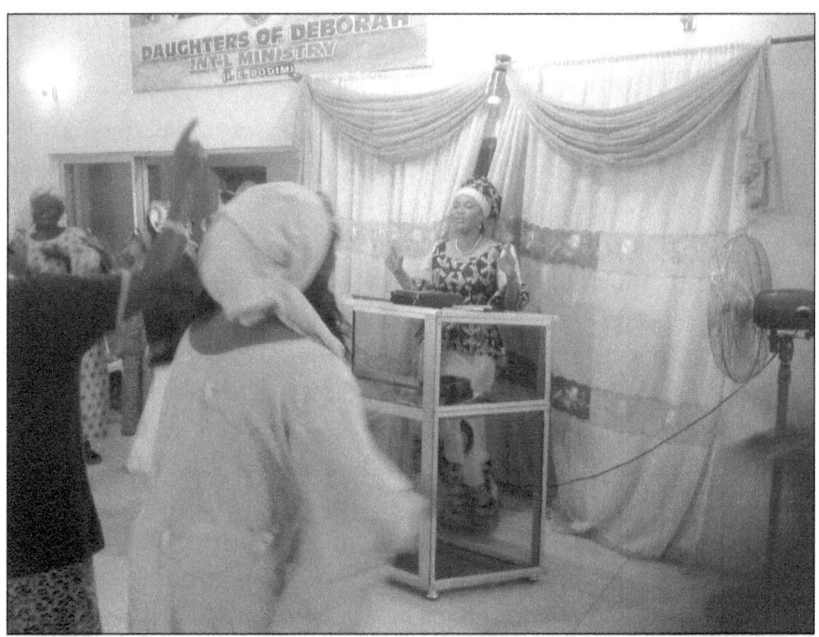

Pastor Mrs. Busola Olotu leading a meeting of Daughters of Deborah International Ministry in 2014. (Courtesy of Pastor Mrs. Busola Olotu)

to start the Daughters of Deborah International Ministry. DODIM, located at Fate Road, Ilorin, was founded in October 2008.[4]

Pastor Mrs. Busola Olotu's experiences illuminate certain features of women's roles in Christianity among the Yoruba. Women are leaders in Christianity in Yorubaland, and some women are church founders. Further, there exists a positive relationship between adherents of Christianity and Islam among the Yoruba. Christianity and Islam are the two major religions in contemporary Yoruba society. Although statistics for Christians and Muslims in Yorubaland are not currently available, it is rare to find an entire extended family among the Yoruba in which everyone adheres to only one religion. The norm is to have Christians, Muslims, and adherents of Yoruba religion in the same family living peacefully together. In addition, most Yoruba people—with just a few exceptions—participate in varying degrees in Yoruba religion through involvement in festivals like the Egúngún or Òṣun, even if only to enjoy the music, dance, and feasting on such occasions.

The influence of Yoruba culture on the practice of Christianity by Yoruba people is undeniable. These include liberal use of Yoruba language and oral literary genres such as proverbs and praise poems describing the attributes of God in worship, the use of traditional musical instruments like Bàtá drums and rattles (sèkèrè), and active participation by members of congregations in worship through song and dance. As we will see, the prescribed subordinate roles for women in various Christian denominations are a challenge because, as has been discussed, Yoruba traditional gender roles for women and men are complementary; hence, Yoruba Christian women attempt to negotiate their status by drawing on Yoruba customs and constructions of gender.

Christianity arrived in Yorubaland in 1842 through the port of Badagry, Nigeria, with the arrival of the Reverend Henry Townsend (1815–86), a missionary of the Church Missionary Society affiliated with the Anglican Church. The involvement of missionaries who were formerly enslaved and the use of the Yoruba language aided the spread of the Christian message in Yorubaland.[5] Christian missionaries provided Western education and health facilities, among other social services, to the Yoruba. Christian missionaries condemned Yoruba culture in its entirety and advocated for its total rejection by converts. Christian converts were to practice monogamy, and men in polygynous marriages were expected to discard all other wives except the first one.[6]

The coming of Christianity brought fundamental changes to the Yoruba way of life; indeed, Christianity has been described as being a "catalyst for social change in Yorubaland."[7] One significant change was the disempowerment of women in the practice of religion. The Christianity brought to Yorubaland prescribed the "Victorian" gender role for women, who were to be seen but not heard; this approach was in sharp contrast to the traditional leadership roles of women in Yoruba religion. Thus, Christianity coming from England disempowered Yoruba women by depriving them of the opportunities to be active participants and leaders in religious affairs, as is the case in Yoruba religion.

There are economic and social implications to the large population of women in Yoruba Christian churches and denominations. The monetary contributions of women are likely to be proportionate with their large population in the religious organization and thus considerable. Women have been described as the sustainers of religion because of their dedication to religious tenets, though they frequently are engaged in mundane upkeep such as daily cleaning of the places of worship as well.[8] However, there are little or no corresponding political benefits to women in Christianity among the Yoruba despite their large numbers, because women are barred from leadership positions and decision-making in the mission Christian churches. It is noteworthy that the interpretation of passages from the Bible plays a formidable role in prohibiting women from leadership roles in a number of Christian denominations. Other arguments that have been proposed to support the prohibition of women's religious leadership include women's alleged weak emotional disposition, the necessity of breastfeeding after childbirth, domestic responsibilities, and menstruation. These reasons have been analyzed and debunked by feminist scholars (female and male) in Yorubaland as well as in Western contemporary society.[9]

Yoruba women have generally rejected the second-class status given to them by patriarchal expressions of Christianity that were brought to Yorubaland, and they continue to draw on Yoruba concepts of gender and cultural customs to improve their status in their Christian affiliations. In Yoruba culture, women's leadership is recognized and appreciated, especially in religious settings. Thus, Yoruba women in Christianity have created alternative spaces for spiritual relevance by using the importance in Yoruba culture of associations (egbẹ́) to negotiate authority in the churches. Yoruba Christian women have founded churches and formed prayer groups in which women's spiritual leadership is exercised outside the structures of patriarchal churches. Consequently, Yoruba women in Christianity have been able to gain access to authority in formal and informal structures of their religious tradition.

Yoruba women have also reinterpreted scriptures from feminist perspectives to provide a balanced picture of divine authorization of women's leadership in Christianity. They have particularly drawn on Christian scriptural interpretations that prioritize depictions of God as a mother, for instance, in Isaiah 49:15: "Can a woman forget her nursing child, or show no compassion for the child of her womb? Even these may forget, yet I will not forget you" (New Revised Standard Version). The motherly qualities of God are emphasized to show the femaleness of the divine.[10] In the same vein, the contributions of women to the successful spread of the Gospel in Yorubaland and establishment of churches are brought to the fore.

Globalization provides the context for access to Western education and economic empowerment for Yoruba women in Christianity. Thus, in addition to Yoruba culture's female leadership heritage, globalization is a salient contributing factor to women's efforts to better their status within the religion. Because of the education and economic achievements of Yoruba Christian women, they are able to negotiate power in churches and ask questions about the lack of female voices in leadership. Consequently, the continual efforts by Yoruba women to contest their secondary status in churches and Christian denominations clearly indicate that the social construction of gender roles that Christianity presented at its advent in Yorubaland is no longer tenable. In the following sections, we will explore specific examples of how these negotiations and resulting empowerment of Yoruba women in Christianity are ongoing.

Roles of Yoruba Women in Christianity

There are three overarching expressions of Christianity among the Yoruba: mission churches, African independent churches, and Pentecostal/charismatic churches. Each of these three types of Christianity exhibits specific features relating to the roles of women.

Mission churches began in Nigeria under the influence of churches in Europe and the United States. The mission churches adhere to the types of Christianity introduced by missionaries, whose influence prescribed a strong, hierarchical, and male-dominated clergy, adoption of Western culture, and rejection of an African worldview. The Christian denominations that were introduced into Yorubaland by missionaries include the Anglican Church (Church of Nigeria), the Methodist Church Nigeria, the Roman Catholic Church, the Nigerian Baptist Convention, the Evangelical Church of West Africa (ECWA; now known as Evangelical Church Winning All), and the Southern Interior Mission (SIM). Women in mission churches play a number of roles, including as members of the choir, Sunday-school teachers, ushers, deaconesses, and members of church councils. In 1997, the Nigerian Baptist Convention began to ordain women as ministers and in this regard is an exception among the mission churches in Yorubaland.

The African independent churches (also termed African-initiated churches) began in Yorubaland in 1925 with the Apostle Joseph Ayo Babalola (1904-59) and the Aladura (Christ Apostolic Church) movement. These churches prioritize African cultural perspectives in the propagation and practice of the Christian message. African independent churches originated in Africa; hence, they utilize African languages and symbols in worship, and they prioritize an African worldview. In addition, it was in the African independent churches that the spiritual gifts of women were recognized for the first time in Christianity in Nigeria. Consequently, women play roles such as prophetesses and church founders in these churches. An example is the case of Captain Christiana Abiodun Akinsowon Emanuel (1907-94), who cofounded the Eternal Sacred Order of Cherubim and Seraphim with Moses Orimolade Tunolase (1879-1933) in 1925. After the death of Tunolase in 1933, Emanuel went to court over her claim that she was the leader of the Cherubim and Seraphim organization. The court case was finally resolved in favor of Captain Christiana Abiodun Akinsowon Emanuel in 1986.[11]

Pentecostal or charismatic churches arrived in Yorubaland at different times beginning in 1962 with the establishment of the Church of God Mission International by Archbishop Benson Andrew Idahosa (1938-98). These churches emphasize the manifestation of the Holy Spirit through speaking in tongues, divine healing, charismatic leadership, and belief in the prosperity gospel, which emphasizes the conviction that God has provided prosperity for every Christian who follows his instructions and that, consequently, wealth symbolizes God's blessings. Yoruba Pentecostals are greatly influenced by the global Pentecostal movement.[12] Women's roles in the Pentecostal churches span the membership and leadership cadres, and hence women are able to manifest expressions of the Holy Spirit in the Pentecostal or charismatic congregational worship in their churches at various levels.

Yoruba Women in Mission Churches

At the beginning of Christian mission churches in Yorubaland, the worship in church was solemn and nonparticipatory for the Yoruba people. Prayers were read by the clergy, and worshippers responded to a fixed format rather than participating in worship marked by dancing, singing, and clapping, which is the norm in African worship in indigenous religions such as Yoruba. Religious leadership and organization in the mission churches were patriarchal; consequently, women were subordinated in the churches, and only men were ordained as ministers. Bible passages cited to support this stance on women include 1 Timothy 2:11–15, which states, "Let a woman learn in silence with full submission. I permit no woman to teach or to have authority over a man; she is to keep silent. For Adam was formed first, then Eve; and Adam was not deceived, but the woman was deceived and became a transgressor. Yet she will be saved through childbearing, provided they continue in faith and love and holiness, with modesty"; 1 Corinthians 14:34, which states, "Women should be silent in the churches. For they are not permitted to speak, but should be subordinate, as the law also says"; and Genesis 3:16, which states, "To the women he said, 'I will greatly increase your pangs in childbearing; in pain you shall bring forth children, yet your desire shall be for your husband, and he shall rule over you'" (NRSV). Many works by scholars have proffered diverse interpretations of these and similar biblical passages to show the error of barring women from sacred space as active participants and leaders.[13] Today women in the mission churches among the Yoruba play many roles such as choir leaders and choir members, Sunday-school teachers, ushers, members of church committees, members of the parochial committee (Governing Council), deaconesses, and in some denominations, ordained priests and ministers.

The major difference between Yoruba women's practice of Christianity when compared to women elsewhere has been Yoruba women's culture and process of socialization, which encourages self-assertiveness and innovation. The Roman Catholic and Baptist Churches are examined here as case studies for Yoruba women's roles in Christian mission denominations.

YORUBA WOMEN IN THE ROMAN CATHOLIC CHURCH. The Roman Catholic Church arrived in Yorubaland in 1846 and prescribed subordinate roles for women, by which they were excluded from church leadership roles.[14] Women in the Roman Catholic Church are in two categories: the religious (nuns and sisters) and all other women. Catholic women in both categories are considered to be laywomen, because they are not ordained priests. Although the terms "nun" and "sister" are used interchangeably for women religious who have taken vows of poverty, chastity, and obedience, the term "nun" is used especially to refer to those who live a life of prayer in a cloistered monastic community, while "sister" is used, especially after the Second Vatican Council (1962–65), to refer to a vowed woman religious who is committed to a ministry that brings her into an active role in society, including teaching, ministering to health and social needs, and working for social change to bring justice to the poor. Sisters' orders that serve society are termed Institutes of Apostolic Life.[15]

Changes in canon law after Vatican II opened the positions of "diocesan chancellors, . . . judges of diocesan courts, members of diocesan synods and financial administrative councils, professors, and board members of seminaries" to women.[16] A woman can serve as a lector, reading the Word of God in scripture, during the Mass. A woman may be a minister of the Eucharist, distributing the bread and wine that has been blessed by a priest. After the Second Vatican Council, women in North America and Europe were admitted to Catholic seminaries, where they could earn master's degrees in theology or pastoral studies. With these earned degrees, more religious sisters and other laywomen and laymen in the United States began to be appointed to serve as "parish administrators" of parishes that did not have a full-time priest due to the decline in the number of men entering the priesthood.[17]

In 1967, Pope Paul VI (papacy, 1963–78) reestablished the "permanent diaconate" as an ordained role for married men who do not intend to become ordained as priests.[18] Priests in the Roman Catholic Church take a vow of celibacy. As Catholic women influenced by feminism began to request ordination to the priesthood for women, the Vatican's department known as the Congregation for the Doctrine of the Faith issued on October 15, 1976, a "Declaration on the Question of Admission of Women to the Ministerial Priesthood" (*Inter insigniores*), stating that women cannot be ordained priests for two primary reasons: first, that the biblical "nuptial analogy" of Christ's relation to the Church is parallel to a bridegroom's relation to a bride and, therefore, the priest has to be male to act in the person of Christ (*in persona Christi*) when celebrating the Eucharist; second, that Christ had indicated his intent to have only males as priests in his church by selecting men to be his apostles. Both of these rationales have been criticized by Catholic theologians and Bible scholars, who have argued that an analogy is not supposed to be taken literally, that the Gospels show no evidence that Jesus Christ intended to establish a church, and that the term "apostle" ("one who is sent out") was understood in the early Christian movement to apply also to women. In 1994, Pope John Paul II (papacy, 1978–2005) gave official permission for girls to be altar servers during the Mass. He followed that up in 1994 by issuing an apostolic letter titled "On Reserving Priestly Ordination to Men Alone" (*Ordinatio sacerdotalis*), which states, "the Church has no authority whatsoever to confer priestly ordination on women," and adds that this view is "to be definitively held by all the Church's faithful." In 1998, Pope John Paul II published an apostolic letter titled "To Protect the Faith" (*Ad tuendam fidem*), stating that anyone "who rejects those propositions which are to be held definitively is opposed to the doctrine of the Catholic Church" and that anyone who rejects a "definitive" doctrine will "no longer be in full communion with the Catholic Church"; in other words, they are excommunicated.[19] In May 2016, Pope Francis (papacy, 2013 to present) promised the heads of women's religious congregations who are members of the International Union of Superiors General that he would set up a commission to study the question of ordaining women as deacons; but the members of the commission could not come to an agreement by January 2019, so the commission was dissolved by the pope.[20] Ordaining women as deacons is controversial because a man being ordained as a "transitional deacon" in the Catholic Church is preliminary to ordination to the priesthood. A second commission to study the question of ordaining women as deacons was created by Pope Francis in April 2020, but there are no guarantees that this commission will conclude that women were deacons in early Christianity so that there is a precedent for reestablishing the diaconate for women in the present day, although Romans 16:1 in the New Testament refers to Phoebe as a deacon (*diakonos*, "minister").[21] Pope Francis has stated that it is important that the Catholic Church include more women in governance and advising roles.[22] On May 11, 2021, Pope Francis formally instituted a new ministry of laypersons titled "catechist," thus acknowledging service that many laywomen and laymen were already performing in the parishes.[23]

My interviews with a priest and two sisters of the Catholic Church among the Yoruba reveal that women in the Catholic Church in Nigeria can be sponsors during baptism and confirmation, especially if the infant concerned is a female. However, the norm presently is for sponsors to be married couples in order for the child to enjoy the combined efforts of sponsors as they grow up. In addition, women serve as members of committees and the parish councils. Women rarely serve as parish administrators in place of a priest because such roles require advanced theological education, which only few women in Nigeria have. However, according to the Reverend Father Lawrence Abiona, a Catholic priest in Ilorin, and Mrs. Dupe Folashade Omole, who serves as a catechist, a few women have been teaching catechism classes for about ten years in the Yorubaland area of Nigeria.[24] During my visit to a Catholic church, I observed six young girls decorating the altar and was informed by the sisters that this role serves as an avenue to educate the girls about the liturgical colors and calendar of the church, which they hope will be transmitted to the next generation of children when these girls marry.

There are controversies among members of Catholic local parishes concerning women as ministers of the Eucharist. The Reverend Father Patrick Nwosu explained to me that innovations, even when approved by the pope or the Vatican, have to be evaluated by the local priest as to whether they benefit or impede the "faith of the people."[25] Consequently, although the 1983 Code of Canon Law of the Catholic Church has authorized laypersons to serve as "extraordinary ministers of the Holy Communion," that is, Eucharistic ministers, the implementation in relation to women is selective, so long as whatever is practiced agrees with the faith of the people. However, women function in every capacity needed to conduct Mass, other than consecrating the bread and the wine, which has to be done by a priest, when Mothering Sunday, or Mother's Day, is celebrated once a year.[26]

My interactions with the respondents indicate that there are few women in the Catholic Church in Yorubaland with the required theological training to serve in pastoral leadership. To rectify this deficiency, the bishops of the Catholic Church are planning a degree program to train laity, including women, who wish to acquire theological training at the Catholic Institute of West Africa in Port Harcourt in Rivers State, Nigeria.[27]

Yoruba women have negotiated power in the ritual spaces of Catholic churches in Yorubaland, in tune with their cultural socialization as active participants in religious settings, and the church management team consults with leaders of the women's groups before salient decisions are taken. As in other mission churches, Yoruba women sing in the choir. During the Mass in some Catholic churches in Yorubaland, a woman along with a man will carry the Eucharist elements (the bread and the wine) to the altar. In addition, Yoruba Catholic women find alternative spaces for authority by means of the Yoruba emphasis on associations (egbe), which serve as the basis on which to negotiate authority in the Catholic Church. The overarching group for Roman Catholic women in Nigeria is the National Council of Catholic Women Organizations (NCCWO). In Yorubaland, women in this group are often responsible for providing for the needs of the parish priest; they also engage in social solidarity by giving support to members during celebrations or mourning periods. The NCCWO provides avenues for economic empowerment through the training of women in vocational skills and providing loans in some cases.

Just as is true of women in the broader Yoruba culture, women chiefs exist in the Catholic churches in Yorubaland. The Catholic woman chief serves as head and spokeswoman for all women in the church and is usually known as Ìyá Ìjo, mother of the church.[28] The occupant of this office is usually an elderly woman who is well respected by all members of the congregation, and her opinion is sought on issues in the church. Her voice on all matters represents the aspirations of the women in the congregation, and therefore her opinion is crucial to any meaningful decision. Thus, the Roman Catholic Church in Yorubaland has measures in place to countenance women's voices in decision-making, although the official status quo remains patriarchal.

YORUBA WOMEN IN BAPTIST CHURCHES. The Baptist Church arrived in Yorubaland in 1850 through the activities of the Reverend Thomas Jefferson Bowen (1814–75) of the Southern Baptist Convention, which was formed in 1845 in the United States when it split with white Baptists in the North over the issue of slavery.[29] At the advent of Baptist churches among the Yoruba, women were excluded from leadership roles. Women served as choristers, ushers, Sunday-school teachers, youth leaders, and deaconesses. The Women Missionary Union (WMU) of Nigeria is the umbrella body for women in the Nigerian Baptist Convention.[30] The Women Missionary Union of Nigeria was founded in 1919 in Ogbomoso in Oyo State. It was formerly called the Baptist Women's Missionary League and then the Women's Missionary Society. The WMU of Nigeria was given auxiliary status by the Nigerian Baptist Convention in 1925.[31] It is a fellowship of Baptist women organized with a focus and involvement in missions. The WMU is committed to the practice of visitation, which can be described as a systematic and persistent mode of visitation that targets women who are absent from attending church and others for the purpose of evangelism. The WMU is committed to the establishment and flourishing of churches, sometimes by holding open-air services to make new converts to Christianity. For example, in 1926, the church report stated the commitment of women to the newly founded Baptist church in Igbajo, Osun State: "Every Sunday, the elderly women (mothers of the church) hold open-air services and several women and girls have been converted through their teachings. One of these mothers—Mary Bolatan—ever since she became a Christian has never failed to sweep the place of worship and its surroundings every day before she goes to her work."[32]

The WMU provides substantial financial support to the Nigerian Baptist Convention through six different types of offerings: the WMU weekly offering (or Convention Fund); the Mother's Day offering; the Baptist Women's Day of Prayer offering; the Home Mission offering; the Foreign Mission offering; and the Young Memorial Scholarship fund. These offerings by the women show that they are stakeholders in the denomination who are committed to the progress of their Christian faith. In addition, the WMU is known to execute building projects, as well as to purchase vehicles for the churches. The organization pioneered the Adult Literacy Program in the Nigerian Baptist Convention in 1942 and operates many scholarship programs to assist students at various levels of educational development.[33] In addition, members share mutual support and theological reflections at the regular weekly meetings of WMU chapters and during social gatherings of celebrations (naming a newborn, graduation, marriage) or mourning periods. In spite of these valuable contributions to the Nigerian Baptist Convention, however, women were barred from ordained ministry until 1997. Although the wife of the pastor plays leadership roles, she is limited to the activities of women in the church.

When the Baptist churches arrived in Yorubaland, hospitals and schools were established, including seminaries. The seminaries began to admit female students in the 1990s, and after graduation, these women worked in the Baptist churches in positions other than as ordained minister/pastors. Once there were qualified and trained women graduates from the seminaries, with the same training as the ordained men, the women began to struggle for the approval of women's ordination by sensitizing church members and leaders to the necessity. In 1997, the Nigerian Baptist Convention approved the ordination of women as ministers.[34] The first female minister to be ordained was the Reverend Mrs. Bosun Adegboyega in May 1997, and a month later, a second woman was ordained in the person of the Reverend Mrs. Olusola Ayo-Obiremi. Thus, women can now be ordained and serve as the pastor of a church without any male supervision. For example, the Reverend Mrs. Olayemi Titilope Aderibigbe was the presiding reverend at the Ijero Baptist Church in Ebutte-Meta, Lagos, until March 15, 2016, when she retired.[35] However, as of 2016, less than 1 percent of Baptist churches were headed by women with no male supervision. Rather, ordained female Baptist ministers typically serve as associate pastors, deaconesses, members of church councils, church secretaries, and treasurers.

Ordained women ministers encounter challenges including sexism from members of their congregation as well as male clergy, who because of the prevailing patriarchal norms find it difficult to submit to female leadership. Domestic and maternal demands may produce tremendous pressures that are difficult to manage by an ordained woman of childbearing age. Also, women ministers may experience a lack of support and encouragement from their family members. However, as one of the few Baptist ordained women stated, "The gift of a person makes way for him or her. When people know you have something to offer, they would not have a problem accepting you as their leader. This made my relationship with men very cordial, and they all gave me their full cooperation."[36] Thus, the women ministers in Baptist churches in Yorubaland are not despondent despite being in the minority among ordained Baptist ministers. Some have recently observed a new trend in theological training in the Baptist seminaries, which is to encourage couples to receive seminary education together and then for both to serve the same congregation. While the husband preaches the Gospel from the pulpit, the wife propagates the Gospel through other avenues such as teaching children and teen groups. There is also a dynamic in which an ordained woman pastor preaches the Gospel from the pulpit on Sundays but operates under the supervision of a male senior pastor, who could be, but also may not be, married to her.[37] The situation in relation to women's ordination in the Nigerian Baptist Convention is unfolding, and the percentage of ordained women may increase in the future.

Yoruba Women in African Independent Churches

Throughout Africa, the many African independent churches were founded by Africans with the ambition to contextualize the Christian message within African cultural beliefs and worship practices. For instance, African views on witchcraft and spirits are taken seriously rather than explained away as superstitions, as is the case in the Christian mission denominations. African culture and worldviews are accepted by African independent churches, but not to the detriment of the Gospel. Examples of these churches among the Yoruba include the Christ Apostolic Church (CAC), founded by Apostle Joseph Ayo Babalola (1904–59) in 1941; the Celestial Church of Christ (CCC or Cele), founded by the Reverend Samuel Bilewu Joseph Oshoffa (1909–85) in 1947; and the Eternal Sacred Order of Cherubim and Seraphim (C&S), founded by Moses Orimolade Tunolase and Christiana Abiodun Akinsowon Emanuel in 1925.[38] Women play active roles in these churches as ushers, choir members, deaconesses, scripture readers, and prophetesses. The office of the prophetess does not exist in the Christ Apostolic Church but is prominent in the Celestial Church of Christ and the Eternal Sacred Order of Cherubim and Seraphim.

A prophetess in the Celestial Church of Christ and the Eternal Sacred Order of Cherubim and Seraphim occupies a position of authority, which negates the view that God is male and can only be represented by a man.[39] The prophetess is construed as a conveyor of messages from God to the members of the church, and these messages should be obeyed. Often the prophetess goes into a trance filled with the Holy Spirit and delivers messages from God during church services in an atmosphere of singing, clapping, and dancing. She also delivers messages from God during prayer sessions.

In addition, women's authority is found in women's groups (egbe) in these churches, as well as in the office of the Iya Ijo, or mother of the church. It is interesting to note the close affinity between the roles of the Iya Ijo and the Ìyálóde, "mother of the market space," in Yoruba culture, especially in relation to their lieutenants. The Yoruba worldview operates with binary categories, with the constant aim to attain a balance; hence, the right side goes with the left side. Moreover, there are convictions that absolutism or extremism, in the sense of taking one position only on an issue as opposed to flexibility and openness to negotiation, is to be avoided in all circumstances. Therefore, there are provisions for assistance in different settings. For instance, the Iyalode in Yoruba governance structure is assisted by the Òtún Ìyálóde, another woman (chief) official, and the same is true in the African independent churches, where there is the office of the Òtún Ìyá Ìjo. The Iya Ijo and her assistant, Otun Iya Ijo, provide leadership to the women members and represent them in the decision-making council of the church.

Some women have founded churches in the Celestial Church of Christ, the Cherubim and Seraphim, and the Christ Apostolic Church denominations. These women-founded churches operate with male and female leadership and clergy, but the overall supervisor is the woman founder. Examples of women-founded churches in Ilorin include the Christ the Messiah Church, founded by Prophetess Aimela in 1968 (CAC), and the Way of Truth Gospel Church, founded by the Reverend (Mrs.) Ailara in 1993 (CAC).

Within African independent churches, women are barred from entering a church and participating in a worship ritual while they are menstruating, and they are required to undergo a cleansing process after their menstruation is concluded so that they can reenter the church. The same is required of women who wish to resume worship in church after childbirth. The cleansing ritual occurs after a woman's menstruation or a set number of days after childbirth for the new mother, forty or eighty days after the birth of a boy or a girl, respectively (see Leviticus 12:1–8 for these time periods). The priest prays for the woman at the entrance of the church to cleanse her, then she enters the sanctuary. In addition, at the appropriate time during worship, the new baby and mother are

Choir members in a Celestial Church of Christ performing at a pilgrimage at Seme, Benin, December 25, 2013. (Courtesy of Live.philips and Wikimedia Commons)

called to the front of the congregation, prayed for, and welcomed back to the sanctuary. Thereafter, the woman may resume regular church attendance.[40] However, my interactions with women in Cherubim and Seraphim churches indicate that while there is not strict compliance with the prescription of cleansing after menstruation, ritual cleansing after the birth of a baby is strictly enforced.

While women play important roles in the African independent churches in Yorubaland and have access to leadership positions, they are constrained by regulations that periodically bar women from the sacred worship space during menstruation and after childbirth.

Yoruba Women in Pentecostal Churches

Pentecostalism arrived in Yorubaland at different times beginning in 1970, with various methods of propagating the Gospel. However, all Pentecostal churches prioritize the manifestation of the Holy Spirit, using the occurrences recorded in Acts 2 in the New Testament as a model. The statement by Peter after the men and women were filled with the Holy Spirit and went out into the streets of Jerusalem speaking in various languages, quoting the prophet Joel in the Hebrew Bible (Joel 2:28–29), is important in Pentecostal churches for affirming that women may receive the Holy Spirit, as well as men, and therefore proclaim God's words:

> In the last days it will be, God declares,
>   that I will pour out my Spirit upon all flesh,
>   and your sons and your daughters shall prophesy... (Acts 2:17, NRSV).

Consequently, the worship in many Pentecostal churches is characterized by profuse manifestations of the Holy Spirit, such as speaking in unknown tongues, healing miracles, exorcisms, and miraculous financial breakthroughs. There is little structure to the worship, according to the popular adage, "It is the Spirit that directs." However, diversity can be noticed in the operations and areas of emphasis of each of the Pentecostal churches in Nigeria. For instance, some Pentecostal churches emphasize deliverance from evil spirits. For other churches, it is divine healing, which sometimes involves prohibition of the use of medicine. Some churches prioritize the use of media during worship, especially electronic media such as projectors, television broadcast during worship, and online streaming of church services, whereas others condemn the use of such technologies. For some churches, the emphasis is on rules for Christian expressions of sexuality, while for other churches, it is on prosperity and entrepreneurship.

Women play significant roles at all levels in the Pentecostal churches, including as teachers in the Sunday schools, ushers, scripture readers, evangelists, counselors, ordained ministers or pastors (titles used interchangeably whether pastoring a church or not), and church founders. Two groups will provide examples of Yoruba women's participation in Pentecostal churches: the Mountain of Fire and Miracles and the Redeemed Christian Church of God.

WOMEN IN THE MOUNTAIN OF FIRE AND MIRACLES. The Mountain of Fire and Miracles (MFM) was founded by Dr. Daniel

Kolawole Olukoya (b. 1957) in Lagos. Between 1989 and 1994, the group met as a fellowship in informal settings. The first formal worship service was held on April 24, 1994.[41] MFM emphasizes the need to destroy the works of Satan and his agents in the form of spirits and witches, and hence deliverance sessions occur frequently. As noted by the religious studies scholar Deji Ayegboyin, "most deliverance ministries in Africa, including the MFM, explain that evil may gain access to some lives through amulets, charms, incisions, tattoos and swallowed concoctions which parents give to or etch on their children."[42] Dr. Olukoya appeals extensively to Yoruba cosmology to explain the causes of evil, suffering, and misfortune in the lives of members, which liberation through prayers offered in the name of Jesus will rectify. Congregational worship in the MFM consists of prayers, songs, Bible readings, and sermons, which are given by presiding pastors of the congregation.

Every activity that relates to women and women's issues is taken care of by the MFM Women Foundation, which is headed by the wife of the general overseer, Pastor (Dr.) Mrs. Shade Olukoya, who is the international coordinator, while the general overseer himself is the international president of the Women Foundation. The MFM Women Foundation has a Governing Council and a Central Working Committee. Furthermore, there are regional coordinators, zonal coordinators, and branch coordinators in the MFM Women Foundation.[43]

Regional overseers supervise all MFM churches in each region, and they are mostly men; wives of regional overseers automatically become coordinators of MFM women in their husbands' respective regions. Thus, marriage bestows leadership positions on women in the Mountain of Fire and Miracles and other Pentecostal churches, irrespective of individual qualifications and endowments of the woman.

Women are ordained in the Mountain of Fire and Miracles, and a few of them serve as pastors in charge of congregations. One example is Pastor (Mrs.) Bosede Bolaji of the Mountain of Fire and Miracles, Fire Brand Assembly, Sawmill Area, Ilorin, Kwara State, Nigeria. Oftentimes, these ordained female pastors are wives of pastors, and they oversee other sections of church affairs in their husbands' congregations, especially women's affairs.

In sum, women play significant roles in the Mountain of Fire and Miracles at all levels including leadership, although it should be noted that the ordination of women as ministers (they may function as pastors of churches or play administrative roles in church hierarchy) is a recent development, and these women ministers constitute a minority of the ordained clergy. The number of ordained women in MFM is not presently available.

WOMEN IN THE REDEEMED CHRISTIAN CHURCH OF GOD. The Redeemed Christian Church of God (RCCG) was founded by Pa Josiah Olufemi Akindayomi (1909–80) in 1952. He was succeeded by Pastor Enoch Adejare Adeboye (b. 1942). Pastor Adeboye joined the RCCG in 1973 and was ordained in 1975. He is currently the general overseer (the highest office in this church) and chairman of the Governing Council of the RCCG. His wife, Pastor (Mrs.) Folu Adeboye (b. 1948), is next to him in rank in the structural organization of the RCCG.[44] It is reported that the RCCG has 23,880 congregations in Nigeria and almost that number outside Nigeria. It has congregations in 165 countries.[45]

The RCCG is known for its Holy Ghost Service, held every first Friday of the month, with up to about half a million people attending, at the RCCG megachurch at its international headquarters at Kilometer 46, Lagos-Ibadan Expressway, Ogun State, Nigeria.[46] The Holy Ghost Service entails singing of choruses and dancing, prayers, and prophetic messages with instructions for individuals or groups in the congregation. A sample program of the Holy Ghost Service comprises intercessory prayers, praise worship, announcements, songs, sermons, offerings, testimonies, and prayer for the nations. Women participate fully in RCCG worship by offering intercessory prayers and singing in the choir. Women leaders also offer counsel to members with special challenges, such as infertility, failed business, or health issues, who need specific types of prayers.

Pastor (Mrs.) Folu Adeboye leads the prayer for the nations at every Holy Ghost Service. In addition, since 2002, Mrs. Folu Adeboye has organized a very important program named the Feast of Esther for the women who are church leaders in RCCG; the Feast of Esther is an annual program held in February.[47] She is usually the vice president of any arm of the RCCG, for instance, the School of Disciples (SOD), which trains Christians to do the work of Jesus Christ, and the Redeemed

Christian Bible College.⁴⁸ She also coordinates women's issues and the Good Women Fellowship in the RCCG.⁴⁹

Roles played by women in the RCCG include serving as associate pastors, ushers, choir members, Sunday-school teachers, and counselors for people with life challenges, on the basis of what the Bible teaches on different issues such as chastity and truthfulness. Women constitute the majority of worshippers and participants; however, ordained women are few.

Ordination of women began in 1996 with the ordination of Pastor (Mrs.) Folu Adeboye. Women who are ordained ministers may serve as the sole pastor of a congregation, but women ministers make up less than 10 percent of ordained RCCG ministers.⁵⁰

Yoruba Christian Women's Independent Prayer Movements

Prayer is important in Christianity, and adherents appreciate this, especially women. Prayer groups for males and for females exist in churches, including the women's and men's fellowships.⁵¹ A recent development in Yorubaland is the establishment of Christian prayer groups by women who claim to have been called by God to serve in that capacity. These prayer groups meet regularly for prayers and scriptural meditations. The woman leader is also consulted often for special prayers on serious issues. The majority of attendees are women with challenges in their marriages or problems affecting their children. The reaction of the male religious leaders in churches was hostile at the onset of women organizing separate prayer groups, but eventually the men became resigned to accept these women because of the large following that the women's prayer groups enjoy and the varied testimonies of divine interventions in women's areas of need. Prayer groups serve as another avenue for Yoruba women's empowerment in Christianity.

Examples of such prayer groups include the Daughters of Deborah International Ministry (DODIM), discussed earlier, which is a Pentecostal Christian ministry to women by women founded in 2008.⁵² It is a new dimension to the Pentecostal experience of women in Nigeria, with no branch except in Ilorin, Kwara State. It constitutes a different angle to women's assessment of their access to the divine within Christianity. The mission of DODIM is to raise a generation of godly women who, like Deborah, a prophet and judge of the people of Israel (Judges 4–5), will arise as mothers in Israel and take their rightful positions for the current time. To achieve this, many events are held. Activities of the group include Women of Faith Bible classes, women's prayer meetings, meetings where the divine visits worshippers as shown in healing miracles, conferences, special programs for children, and Holy Communion services that are consecrated by a female or male minister. DODIM provides welfare packages of food and clothing to widows, orphans, and the physically challenged. In addition, vocational training is offered to women in fields such as catering and computer science. Cash grants are provided to indigent women to enable them to start small businesses. All activities come after praise worship, prayers, Bible reading, and preaching/teaching of the Bible. Women officiate and lead in the different services, cutting across age groups—youth, middle-aged, and elder.

From my interactions with the founder of the DODIM, Pastor (Mrs.) Busola Olotu, and observations while attending programs, it is clear that the women are the focus of sermons and other activities, especially prayers. Certain concerns are predominantly within the purview of women in Nigeria, including the need to give birth to children, relief from poverty, victory over Satanic forces such as malevolent spirits, and the maintenance of marital peace. Specific prayers on these issues and others like them are offered by attendees at these services. These are prayers said with physical and spiritual strength, with lots of noise if need be. It appears that women enjoy and are convinced of the efficacy of these prayers. Women ministers from different churches are invited to give sermons at these programs. Women from all denominations attend the DODIM programs, but the group is only found in Ilorin, Nigeria, for now.

Conclusion

As we have seen, Yoruba culture exerts considerable influence on practices of Christianity. Such influences include the use of local languages, genres of Yoruba oral literature, and traditional musical instruments in worship. In addition, children's socialization occurs in an atmosphere of positive interreligious interactions, as modeled by family members subscribing to different religions yet living in harmony. Since Christian mission denominations prescribed subordinate roles for women when they arrived in Yorubaland, Yoruba women have found more opportunities to exercise religious leadership in African independent churches and in Pentecostal/charismatic churches, although male dominance typically continues. Yoruba women negotiate their status in forms of Christianity by drawing on Yoruba cultural expectations about the leadership roles of women in religious organizations, women's separate societies (egbe), and women's active economic roles in society and their financial contributions to churches and denominations. Yoruba cultural elements that have proven influential in this regard include the socialization of Yoruba girls and women to be independent and innovative, as well as Yoruba women's experience in forming associations that aid social networking and collective representation of women in decision-making processes. Modest gains have thus far been achieved concerning women's ordination in some Christian denominations in Nigeria; it is likely that this upward trend will continue in the coming years. Moreover, Yoruba women receive divine calling to establish and lead churches and prayer groups, in contrast to the subordinate roles propagated by European missionaries for women at the advent of Christianity in Yorubaland.

Christianity influenced social change among the Yoruba people through the provision of social amenities like schools, hospitals, roads, and clean drinking water, as well as urging the ending of the practice of polygynous marriage. However, the Christian religious tradition disempowered Yoruba women as active participants and leaders in religious affairs. Although women are the sustainers of these religions through their consistent dedication, financial support, and participation, women's inclusion in the governing structures of their religious organizations is restricted. The Bible is frequently interpreted to exclude women from leadership and decision-making roles; but some Christian congregations have the office of Iya Ijo (mother of the church) and her assistant, Otun Iya Ijo, and these voices represent women's views during decision-making.

Women in Christianity in Yorubaland are active participants in worship, and they are shaping the future of the Christian traditions among the Yoruba. Women utilize gender expectations in Yoruba culture as a means by which to create alternative spaces for women's authority within Christianity. Hence, this chapter has highlighted Yoruba women's agency in Christianity through negotiations via Yoruba cultural templates of gender balance in power relations between women and men and the influence of women's organized groups (egbe). Examples of women founders and leaders of churches and a woman leader of a prayer group illustrate this approach. Thus, Yoruba women have utilized the Yoruba culture as a viable tool of negotiation in their quest for religious leadership and equality in Christianity.

4

Yorùbá Women in Islam

Islam is an Abrahamic religion that is frequently embedded in patriarchal cultures with prescribed roles of domesticity and limited public activities for women. The religion recommends that women should marry, dress modestly (e.g., wear a *hijab*/veil), and bear and raise children. Despite the restrictions of imported Islamic culture on women, similar to the Christian denominations and movements discussed in chapter 3, due to being brought up in Yorùbá culture, Yoruba Muslim women exercise agency and leadership in the practice of Islam and in their daily lives.

The life of Dr. (Mrs.) Hassanat Funmilayo Abubakar is an example. Though born in 1977 in Ilorin, a city known for its Islamic culture and philosophy, her parents, Alhaji Abubakar Alarape Salman and Madam Ashyau Abubakar of Eleran compound, Korosayodun Area, Itakudimo, Ilorin, ensured that she had both Islamic and Western educations. She received Islamic primary education from the Qur'anic school at Alaaya compound, Pakata area, Ilorin, and secondary Western education in 1996 at Muhyideen College of Arabic and Islamic Studies, Ilorin. During her school days, she played some leadership roles among women, such as Amirah (a female leader of women in the mosque) in her undergraduate years and as a member of the spiritual committee of the University of Ilorin Ladies Circle. She married in 2003 and subsequently became a mother. Dr. Hassanat is a lecturer at the Department of Arabic, University of Ilorin, Ilorin, Nigeria, an academic who engages in the rigors of research, publication, and teaching in conjunction with domestic duties. She reflected, "Being a Muslim is a source of joy in my life and most divine gift to me by Allah."[1]

Islam is practiced worldwide by people of many ethnicities. Islam is a major religion in contemporary Yoruba society, although accurate statistics for Muslims in Yorubaland are not currently available. As noted earlier, it is rare to find an entire extended family among the Yoruba in which everyone adheres to only one religion. It is very common to have Christians, Muslims, and adherents of Yoruba religion in the same family, living peacefully together. In addition, as has been noted, the majority of Yoruba people participate in varying degrees in Yoruba religion through involvement in festivals like the Egúngún or Òṣun festivals, even if only to enjoy the music, dancing, and feasting on such occasions.

Islam arrived in Yorubaland around the fourteenth century, but large-scale conversion to Islam did not happen until the seventeenth century and is theorized to have been disseminated in Yorubaland through trading activities and scholarship. Hausa and Fulani Muslim traders from the northern part of Nigeria and Muslim scholars (*mallams*) of Hausa origin promoted trading activities and Islamic scholarship among the Yoruba.[2] Islam was propagated as commerce was ongoing between visiting traders and the Yoruba people. The children of Yoruba converts to Islam were taught the Arabic language and Qur'anic verses, oftentimes in a school attached to a mosque (an *ilé-kéwú*, i.e., Arabic school). Mervyn Hiskett, a scholar of Islam in West Africa, has pointed out that to "the north of the Yoruba lay a wide band of Islamic territory that stretched from west to east and included the empires of Mali, Songhay and Borno, as well as the Hausa States," and therefore during the period between 906 to 1500, Muslims "must surely have been entering Yorubaland from several directions at once."[3] According to the comparative religions scholar Dada Adelowo, "the inception of Islam in almost all parts of Yorubaland was 'unplanned' and 'unannounced,'" as it arrived not through overt missionization but through gradual exposure.[4] Islam has enjoyed three centuries of cultural prestige in Yorubaland, from the nineteenth century to the twenty-first century, especially in the northern and central regions.[5]

In the 1930s, the Bamidele movement, which was a conservative Islamic movement founded by Shaykh 'Abd al-Salam Bamidele (1911–69), imposed *purdah* (veiling and seclusion) on some Yoruba women. By 1958, an Ibadan Muslim woman named Alhaja Humuani Alaga (1907–93), the Òtún Ìyálóde (female leader at the right hand of the Ìyálóde of Ibadan), founded the Isabatudeen (band of religious enthusiasts) Society to provide Muslim girls with a sound Muslim and Western education. Members of the group founded the Isabatudeen Girls' Grammar School through the contribution of nine British pounds each on January 24, 1964, with an initial enrollment of thirty girls. It was the first Muslim girls' secondary school in Ibadan. As of 2014, the school had enrollment of over one thousand girls.[6]

Yoruba have adapted words from the Arabic language in reference to religion, such as the terms for a Christian priest (*Alufa*), saint (*woli*), prayer (*adura*), and heathen (*keferi*). Methods utilized for the propagation of Islam have included the accommodation of Islam to African culture and the establishment of mosques. For instance, Ifá oracular consultations were replaced with *salat al-istikhara* (guidance-seeking prayer, which involves recitations by worshippers to God), and celebrations of òrìṣà were replaced with the religious holidays of Eid-el-Fitri (at the end of Ramadan) and Eid-el-Kabir (Festival of Sacrifice, commemorating the willingness of Abraham to sacrifice his son to God). Many festivals to orisa involve sacrifice, prayers, and celebration. The Eid celebrations in Islam, which includes the killing of a ram, were emphasized among Muslims to replace orisa festivals. In the same vein, Yoruba unlimited polygyny was replaced with the Qur'anic permission that a man may have up to four wives at a time, if he can treat them equally (Surah 4:3). Conversely, the influence of Yoruba religion and culture on the practice of Islam by Yoruba people is undeniable. These include profuse use of local language and oral literary genres in worship, the use of traditional Yoruba musical instruments, and active participation by members of congregations, especially women, in worship.

According to the American Qur'an scholar Amina Wadud, the Qur'an, which is Islam's holy book containing God's Word, does not support specific gender roles for female and male believers. At the level of piety (*taqwā*), women will be judged by Allah equally with men. Both women and men are responsible for being "submitters" (Muslims) to Allah. In Islam, a woman is considered to be a member of a social system and an individual who must practice remembrance of Allah constantly.[7] With regard to a relationship with Allah, women and men are the same.

Surah 49:13 in the Qur'an reads, "O mankind, indeed We have created you from male and female and made you peoples and tribes that you may know one another. Indeed, the most noble of you in the sight of Allah is the most righteous of you. Indeed, Allah is Knowing and Acquainted."[8] Surah 33:35 and similar verses in the Qur'an include women equally with men in the duties and heavenly reward of Muslims:

Women praying at the Alanamu Jamuiyat Istijabat Society of Nigeria (AJISON) in Ilorin, August 2, 2020. The women are wearing face masks due to the prevalence of COVID-19. (Courtesy of Wulemat Motunrayo)

Indeed, the Muslim men and Muslim women, the believing men and believing women, the obedient men and obedient women, the truthful men and truthful women, the patient men and patient women, the humble men and humble women, the charitable men and charitable women, the fasting men and fasting women, the men who guard their private parts and the women who do so, and the men who remember Allah often and the women who do so—for them Allah has prepared forgiveness and a great reward.[9]

Muslim women, like Muslim men, are obliged to make the profession of faith (*shahadah*), observe the five daily prayers (*salat*), engage in charity (*zakat*), fast during the daylight hours of the month of Ramadan (*sawm*), if possible make the pilgrimage to Mecca (*hajj*), and participate in Islamic festivals. In addition, women should attend to the needs of their husband and children. Nonetheless, at the level of religious practice in society, women and men play different roles in Islamic settings, and this is also true among Yoruba Muslims.

Although the Islamic culture that began arriving in Yorubaland in the fourteenth century assigned to women the roles of obedient wife and good mother, Yoruba Muslim women have negotiated for inclusiveness in decision-making in mosques on the basis of their economic activities and financial contributions. Within the context of Islam practiced in Yoruba culture, women have taken on leadership roles within groups (*egbẹ́*) of Muslim women, and following Yoruba custom, male leaders consult a senior woman to ascertain that the women's views on practical matters are taken into account.

Yoruba Women and the Practice of Islam

Islam places a high premium on the care of females, as supported by the *hadith* (narratives about the things that the Prophet Muhammad did and said), according to which the Prophet said, "Anybody who has three daughters or three sisters and is beneficent to them (in training) shall enter paradise."[10] Concerning gender roles for women in Islam as practiced by Yoruba, a Muslim woman reported, "The specific role for which women are created is that of bearing, rearing children, and general management of the home." She posited further that "Islam, however, permits them to contribute to the socioeconomic and political development of their nation in such a way that will not affect their primary roles of domesticity."[11]

However, Islamic traditions arrived in Yorubaland with prescribed subordinate roles for women within a patriarchal cultural outlook. Yoruba Muslim women play subsidiary roles in the practice of Islam due to many complex issues that concern Islamic conceptions of and prescriptions for chastity and propriety that are heavily dependent on scriptural interpretations. For instance, though no scriptural passage of the Qur'an bans women from activities outside the home, scriptural interpretations are given to promote the seclusion of women. Surah 4:34 in the Qur'an, for instance, is interpreted to emphasize the obedience of a wife to her husband in conforming to any and every instruction that is given by him, and if a wife is not obedient to her husband, he may strike her. Surah 4:34 has been translated as saying,

Men are in charge of women by [right of] what Allah has given one over the other and what they spend [for maintenance] from their wealth. So righteous women are devoutly obedient, guarding in [the husband's] absence what Allah would have them guard. But those [wives] from whom you fear arrogance—[first] advise them; [then if they persist], forsake them in bed; and [finally], strike them. But if they obey you [once more], seek no means against them. Indeed, Allah is ever Exalted and Grand.[12]

The scholar of women in Islam Fatna A. Sabbah reports that "the ideal of female beauty in Islam is obedience, silence and immobility, that is inertia and passive."[13] Also, the Moroccan sociologist and feminist Fatima Mernissi has noted that "in Islamic cosmogony, the sexes play an important role in symbolizing obedience and authority—in no way can women take the initiative. If they do, the whole order is in jeopardy, since their function and duty is to obey."[14] When women challenge the status quo, they threaten not only patriarchal power (their relation to their father, brother, and husband) but the very existence of the entire system (and more specifically God's claim to obedience). Consequently, the demand for women to remain "obedient" and maintain the status quo constitutes a challenge to female agency in the practice of Islam and to any feminist interpretation of scriptures.

Yet, Yoruba Muslim women, through their Yoruba cultural heritage, negotiate prescriptions that restrict women's roles. They are true Muslims, dressed modestly and wearing their veils, which may be a *hijab* (headscarf) or also include a *niqob* (a face veil). They say their daily prayers but pursue their economically productive work nonetheless, be it in the markets or in offices. Yoruba Muslim women engage in economic activities in the markets and other sectors of the economy and have utilized the Yoruba heritage of women long-distance traders (*alájàpà*) to strike a balance between the Islamic expectations of women's domesticity and their agency in society. Thus, in the practice of Islam among the Yoruba, the influence of Yoruba cultural socialization for women to be self-confident and financially independent is apparent.

Interpretations of the hadith in Islam present diverse opinions on whether it is proper for women to attend mosque to pray. According to the hadith narrated by Abdullah bin Umar, "Allah's messenger said 'the salat in congregation is twenty-seven times superior in degrees to the salat offered by a person alone.'" However, another hadith asserts that the Prophet said, "The best mosque for a woman is the inner part of her house."[15] The reality for Yoruba Muslim women is that they frequently attend mosque on Friday for the midday prayer but pray in a separate section that is meant for women only. The women's section is behind the men's section to avoid distractions to men during prayers. In some parts of Nigeria, the attendance of mosque is compulsory for men but optional for women, although it is considered beneficial for women if they can attend.

Therefore, Muslim women are not given any formal mosque leadership position in Yorubaland. Although no section of the Qur'an specifically bars women from religious leadership of gatherings consisting of women and men, Yoruba Muslim women are restricted from being an *imam* (prayer leader) or *khatib* (one who gives the sermon) during the Friday congregation worship. In Yorubaland, Muslim women's roles in the mosques are mainly informal. Similar to what we saw with Christian women, arguments that have been proposed to support this prohibition of women's religious leadership include women's alleged weak emotional disposition, the temptation and distraction that women's beauty cause for men, domestic responsibilities, and menstruation. These reasons have been severally analyzed and debunked by feminist scholars (female and male) in Islamic contemporary societies.[16]

In contrast to the patriarchal view that women should not exercise leadership in the mosques, Wadud notes,

> The roles of women who have been referred to in the Qur'an fall into one of three categories: 1. A role which represents the social, cultural, and historical context in which that individual woman lived—without compliment or critique from the text. 2. A role which fulfils a universally accepted (i.e. nurturing or caretaking) female function, to which exceptions can be made—and have been made even in the Qur'an itself. Finally, 3. a role which fulfils a non-gender specific function, i.e. the role represents human endeavours on the earth and is cited in the Qur'an to demonstrate this specific function and not the gender of the performer, who happens to be a woman.[17]

As is customary in Yoruba religious associations, to emphasize the complementarity of women and men, Muslim women take chieftancy titles in mosques in Yorubaland. The prominent title among Yoruba Muslims is the Ìyá Àdíní (mother of religious affairs).[18] She is usually a respected woman of faith who is blessed financially; however, her area of jurisdiction in the mosque is limited to the women. The Iya Adini leads other women in Islamic activities, and her opinion matters at the decision-making level in the mosque. Consequently, in any decision on the welfare of worshippers, the male elders of a mosque will seek the opinion of the Iya Adini, who represents the women in that congregation. In addition, she makes considerable financial contributions toward the progress and propagation of Islam and charity. According to Dr. Mrs. Hassanat Abubakar-Hamid, the following statement of Muhammad reported in a hadith includes the support of women in these leadership roles: "Do not be like anyone except in two cases. (The first is) a person, whom Allah has given wealth and he spends it righteously; (the second is) the one who Allah has given wisdom of (Holy Qur'an) and he acts according to it and teaches others."[19]

In Islam, the basic principle concerning menstruation is that "only the blood is impure; a menstruating woman's body is not impure, and she does not contaminate persons or things she touches."[20] However, a menstruating woman should not touch a copy of the Qur'an.[21] According to the Yoruba Muslim women I interviewed, women cannot pray, fast (during Ramadan and other types), circumambulate the Ka'bah during hajj or *umrah* (pilgrimage to Mecca), or have sexual intercourse with their husbands while they are menstruating.[22]

It is apparent from my interviews with Yoruba Muslim women that most of them hold to the conviction that the will of Allah is for them to be good wives and mothers. Indeed, even when they work in the economic sector, every effort should be geared toward ensuring the prioritization of the domestic roles prescribed for women.[23] Yoruba Muslim women expressed their conviction of divine approval for domesticity as the realm for women rather than any other role. Consequently, an ideal Muslim woman is seen as being an obedient, respectful wife and loving mother. She is expected not to challenge male religious leaders and their prescribed roles for women as they are the will of Allah. However, there are indications that some Yoruba Muslim women are challenging the second-class status given to them by patriarchal expressions in Islam that were brought to Yorubaland, and, similar to Yoruba Christian women, they do so by drawing on Yoruba concepts of gender and cultural customs to improve their status in their Islamic affiliations, mainly in separate women's spaces.

As we have seen, in Yoruba culture, women's leadership is recognized and appreciated, especially in religious settings. Accordingly, Yoruba Muslim women have created alternative spaces of power utilizing the Yoruba importance of associations (egbe) to negotiate power in Muslim settings. Muslim women have formed prayer groups in which women's spiritual leadership is exercised outside the structures of formalized Islamic congregational worship in which men participate. Consequently, Yoruba women in Islam have been able to contribute to the exercise of authority in the informal women's areas of Islam. Access to Western education and economic empowerment for Yoruba Muslim women have also been a salient contributing factor. Thus, Yoruba Muslim women are able to put forward initiatives to entrench positive gender relations in many Islamic settings, such as men helping with chores during festivals and the promotion of education for girls at all levels (primary, secondary, and tertiary). However, the possibility of the modification of gender roles in Islam as it is practiced in Yorubaland is debatable, because the opportunities to interpret the Qur'an with feminist sensitivity remain limited and minimal opportunities for leadership roles exist for women in patriarchal Islamic culture in Yorubaland.

Women's Agency and Islam among the Yoruba

Chapter 4 (an-Nisa) of the Qur'an is dedicated to a discussion of women. The Qur'an states that there are no differences in spiritual requirements for men and women to achieve salvation in Paradise on the Judgment Day. In addition, women's social roles, including being wives and mothers, are considered as acts of worship for which rewards are given by God. This is especially true of child upbringing, which is relevant to Yoruba women's concerns since "many Yoruba women are pillars of homes, they coordinate domestic activities and are the first teachers of children—thus, they mold destinies."[24] Also, wifely roles during Ramadan are rewarded by Allah. Women's roles during Ramadan require sacrifice and dedication, because women have to be innovative with scarce resources for the feeding of family members, as well as to wake up between 2:00 and 4:00 a.m. to cook meals for the family to be eaten early in the morning before sunrise and in the evening after the sun has gone down, despite the fact that the women themselves are also fasting. Many women combine these activities with child care and in some cases pregnancy.

Yoruba Muslim women lead other women during all-female group meetings in the mosque, during which songs of praise to Allah are sung, which is known as *asalatu*, during which the women seek blessings on the soul of the noble Prophet and, while doing so, receive blessings too. Asalatu is also a venue in which women can discuss issues bothering them, socialize, and assist the needy. A typical asalatu session begins with the praise of Allah, followed by prayers for Prophet Muhammad and other prophets. These are followed by prayers for members of the group and others and lastly announcements. Women leaders preach (*da'wa*, "invite" or "call" to the faith) and engage in special prayers, for instance, the Tahajjud prayer, a special midnight prayer that is recommended for all Muslims but is not required.[25]

Women leaders include the Muallimaat and the Amirah. The Muallimaat is a female teacher who instructs women in reading the Qur'an, hadith, and other texts in Arabic. She imparts Islamic knowledge to other women. She is knowledgeable in Arabic texts and Islamic injunctions. The Amirah is a female leader who coordinates women's activities in the mosque. Her role includes coordinating and supervising women's affairs, setting meeting times and agendas of women's groups, and providing leadership in crisis situations.

Yoruba women make important financial contributions toward the dissemination of Islam. The impact of this is best appreciated in view of the fact that women are the majority of Yoruba Muslims who attend religious activities regularly. Generally, Yoruba women engage in economic activities in all sectors of Yoruba society, including selling wares in the markets, working in private and public sectors, and working in other industries such as hospitals. These Muslim women utilize their personal income in social and religious enterprises. In addition, Yoruba Muslim women engage in works of charity such as caring for orphans and the less privileged in society. Women propagate the message of Islam in their daily interpersonal relationships, preach in women's prayer groups, and use their financial contributions to organizations that preach the message of Islam in different forums.

Amirah Biliqees Abdullahi at the Alanamu Jamuiyat Istijabat Society of Nigeria (AJISON) in Ilorin, August 2, 2020. (Courtesy of Wulemat Motunrayo)

Yoruba Muslim women are members of organizations that carry out charitable works. An example is the Federation of Muslim Women's Association in Nigeria (FOMWAN), which is a faith-based umbrella organization that has linked Islamic women's groups in Nigeria since it started in 1985. FOMWAN "was established for the purposes among others of promoting education and social development of women through the establishment of classes and institutions for women's education and literacy and the development of Tarbiyya (proper child up-bringing) of

Muslim children."[26] This association has members from all of the thirty-six states in Nigeria, and it has "over six hundred affiliate groups nationwide which spread across villages and towns."[27] FOMWAN works with women's organizations such as "National Council of Women's Societies (NCWS), Women in Nigeria (WIN), Federation of Women Lawyers in Nigeria" on projects such as "HIV/AIDS prevention, . . . reproductive health, women's economic empowerment, and elections."[28]

The effect of Western education on Yoruba Muslim women has been both positive and negative. Many Yoruba Muslim women in contemporary Yorubaland have degrees and postgraduate education, and this has significantly influenced their perceptions of Islam. For instance, Western education has heightened the awareness of younger generations of Yoruba Muslim women of women's rights in Islam, leading to the exercise of women's right to divorce, which they have in Islam but which their elders may regard as being "unnecessary divorce."[29] According to an older Muslim woman I interviewed, Western education "makes women believe they can compete with men in all facets of life," and she considered this to be "un-Islamic."[30] These expressed opinions by Yoruba Muslim women show that the patriarchal status quo is already being challenged by Muslim women due to the influence of Western education. It is also apparent that efforts by Yoruba women to change or amend limited roles for Muslim women occur mainly in women's groups. However, access to Western education enhances Yoruba Muslim women's capacity to propagate Islam with knowledge. For instance, knowledge in religious studies, the Arabic language, philosophy, economics, Islamic law, and the sciences equips Yoruba Muslim women to propagate Islam in contemporary society. One indicator of gradual change to more leadership roles for Yoruba Muslim women is the establishment of independent prayer movements founded and led by women.

Muslim Women's Independent Prayer Movements

Prayer is important in Islam, and adherents of the religion appreciate this, especially the women. Prayer groups for women exist in Islam, and an example is the *ęgbę́ alasalatu* (prayer societies) in Yorubaland.[31] These prayer groups are founded by women who claim to have been called by God through diverse means, including dreams, to serve in that capacity. Similar to what we saw with Yoruba Christian women, Muslim women in prayer groups meet regularly for prayers and scriptural recitations. The woman leader is also consulted often for special prayers on serious issues. The majority of attendees are women with special challenges in their marriages or problems affecting their children, though a few men may be present. As with Christian women's prayer groups, the reactions of the male religious leaders in mosques were hostile at the onset of women organizing separate prayer groups, but, similarly, eventually they became resigned to accept them due to the large following that the women's prayer groups enjoy and the varied testimonies of divine interventions in women's areas of need. Prayer groups serve as another avenue for Yoruba Muslim women's empowerment in Islam.

One example is the Fadillulah Muslim Mission in Osogbo, Osun State, founded by Alhaja Sheidat Mujidat Adeoye in 1997.[32] This women's group engages in prayers, singing, and theological discussions with special attention to women's issues. The majority of members are women for whom prayers targeting infertility and marital strife are major concerns. The leader of the group, Alhaja Adeoye, provides counseling for women on different issues by giving advice that is in line with teachings of Islam. Her clients have testified to healing miracles from her prayers and fasting. Some of her clients are required to go through ritual bathing in a stream near the mosque where she worships. The ritual bath is taken by some clients whose cases require cleansing after Alhaja Adeoye has prayed over a keg of water brought from the home of such a person. Thereafter, the client moves to the side of the stream to bathe and discard the sponge and soap used. The belief is that whatever predicaments were facing the client have been washed away.[33] This type of bathing for healing and cleansing purposes is similar to ritual bathing in Yoruba religion and in Yoruba African independent churches. Alhaja Adeoye attends to clients who are from anywhere and any religious affiliation every day of the week, except Fridays, the Muslim day for congregational prayer in the mosque. Fridays are her days of personal meditation and rest. Alhaja Adeoye is an example of the women leaders in Islam among the Yoruba who are meeting the needs of women in particular.

Conclusion

The profound influence of Yoruba women's active gender roles in economic endeavors and in the religious leadership of Yoruba religion has ameliorated existing Islamic customs for women's subordination in Yorubaland. Yet thus far, women's influences have been mainly informal, except in the few cases where Yoruba Muslim women have founded prayer groups led by women who address the needs of women through prayers, worship, fellowship, and rituals. In these cases, the importance of group meetings (egbe) in Yoruba society and religion has served as a potent tool for women's empowerment and solidarity. Muslim women continue to utilize their Yoruba cultural heritage to support the exercise of their agency in Islam in Yorubaland, especially through chieftancy titles like that of the Iya Adini.

5

Women and the Yorùbá Religions in the Diaspora

The spiritual and academic career of Dr. Funlayo Easter Wood-Menzies exemplifies the attraction of Yorùbá religion to persons who are part of the African diaspora, some of whom travel to Nigeria to receive initiations in Yoruba religion. Wood-Menzies was born in New York City and named Easter Zenovia Wood. She received the name Funlayo when she was initiated into Yoruba religious traditions. Her stepfather, the Reverend Dr. Ralph H. Hoist III (who worked for New York City transit), and her mother, the Reverend Dr. Ellen R. Hoist (a professor of nursing at Bronx Community College), raised her as a Baptist, but she reports that she never embraced Christian theology concerning the doctrine of original sin, needing to be "saved," or Jesus as being the only way to be saved. While growing up, she was fascinated by issues concerning the spirit, the unseen, magic, nature reverence, and components of indigenous spiritualities. She earned her master's degree in history at the City College of New York in 2010, and she earned her PhD in African and African American studies and the study of religion at Harvard University in 2017. In 2008, she traveled to Nigeria to be initiated into Yoruba religious traditions, specifically into the worship of three Yoruba deities. She received Ògún initiation from Chief Oluwole Ifakunle Adetutu Alagbede in New York City in 2009. In 2011, she was initiated into Ifá by Oluwo Efunwape Olatunji and into Ọbàtálá and Ọṣun by Yeye Olasuinbo Olomowewe at Isara Remo, Ogun State, Nigeria. She has received further mentoring from Iya Oyelola Elebuibon at Osun Osogbo. In the diaspora, her mentors include Yeyefini Efunbolade in Ft. Lauderdale, Florida, and Yeye Luisah Teish, from New Orleans, Louisiana, and now in Oakland, California. After her initiations, Funlayo was required to be guided by certain taboos and observances, including avoiding the consumption of palm wine and not wearing any color other than white for two years. After two years, she was required to wear something white at all times. Her duties include conducting divination sessions and wedding and naming ceremonies and offering prayers to the deities and food to the ancestors. In 2018, she founded a religious house named Aṣẹ Ire, and its website is a platform on which she shares teachings on Yoruba religious traditions. Dr. Funlayo Easter Wood-Menzies has been featured in documentaries for the Public Broadcasting Service and the National Geographic Channel speaking about Yoruba traditions.[1]

Yoruba religion is practiced today in many countries in Europe, Latin America, and North America. The prominent roles that women play in the rituals and worship in Yoruba religion in the New World are both dynamic and fascinating. Various factors affect women's involvement in Yoruba religion in the diaspora, including the regulations and laws of the host community, the dominant religion and values of the country, issues relating to sexual orientation, and depictions of African and African-derived religions in the media. Laws in host countries oftentimes compel innovations in ritual practice in òrìṣà worship. For instance, some items needed by priestesses might be banned from import, necessitating substitutions. Yoruba religion in the New World exists also in offshoot religious traditions, including Santería, Candomblé, and other African diaspora religions created by enslaved Yoruba and other African peoples.[2] In recent decades, Yoruba religion as it is practiced in Yorubaland has become known and appreciated by practitioners in the transatlantic diaspora through the efforts of male and female Nigerian Yoruba cultic functionaries of different deities who visit, train, and initiate individuals.

Today, women and men who are adherents of Yoruba religion in European countries (such as Germany, Austria, France, and the United Kingdom) and New World locations (such as North America and Latin America) often travel to Yoruba cities in Nigeria (such as Osogbo, Okuku, Iwo, Ibadan, and Abeokuta) for pilgrimage, mentoring, and initiations. An interesting dimension to these travels is the aim to forge links with lost cultural heritage.[3] Thus, migration in a fluid form is promoted, as some women stay in Yorubaland for extended periods, as well as traveling back and forth between Yoruba cities in Nigeria and their homes in the diaspora. The involvement of practitioners in the diaspora with the Yoruba orisa tradition has been facilitated in significant ways by the internet and social platforms such as Facebook, Twitter, and chat groups.

Dr. Funlayo E. Wood-Menzies. (Courtesy of Dr. Funlayo E. Wood-Menzies)

This chapter examines women's roles primarily in orisa worship in the diaspora, though Yoruba Christian and Muslim women in diaspora are also discussed. The agency, activity, and leadership of Yoruba women in religious, economic, political, and social spheres are manifested clearly in the practices of religion in the diaspora. The starting point of investigation into the presence of Yoruba religion in the diaspora is the slave trade, which resulted in "the Atlantic globalization of Yoruba religious traditions."[4]

The Transatlantic Slave Trade and Yoruba People

It is pertinent to clarify that slavery existed among the Yoruba prior to the transatlantic slave trade; however, the logistics of slavery in Yorubaland and transatlantic slavery were different. The Yoruba structure of slavery consisted of categories of slaves and the terms for eventual release for people in some of these categories. Individuals known as *iwòfà* became slaves through being pawned to pay their debt or the debt of their family head. Their freedom was restored once the debt was settled.[5] The *ìlàrí* were slaves who were captured in warfare and whose descendants continued to serve royal families by performing duties in the political structures of prominent Yoruba kingdoms such as the Ọ̀yọ́ Empire. Even in contemporary Oyo town in Oyo State, Nigeria, members of ilari families still perform specific duties in the palace of the ruler, the Aláàfin.[6] In addition, people captured in defeated territories during warfare were also usually conscripted as slaves (*ẹrú*) who were required to do strenuous jobs in dire conditions, sometimes very far from their place of origin. The afflictions and predicaments of such enslaved persons can be discerned from Yoruba oral sayings such as *ònà ló jìn, erú níbaba*, meaning "The distance may be far, but the slave has a father," an assertion of the slave's humanity. Though there were thus different categories of slaves in Yoruba communities, they did not suffer dehumanizing and excruciating experiences to the extent of persons subjected to the transatlantic slave trade.

Both Europeans and Africans participated in and benefited from the transatlantic slave trade. The transatlantic slave trade was a deplorable period in human history with weighty implications that have influenced perceptions concerning Black persons. The legacy of the transatlantic slave trade diminished the human dignity of every Black person, notwithstanding their inherent qualities. The slave trade disrupted and bled Africa of human and capital resources. Enslavement and uprooting were traumatizing for both the victims who died on the ships and those who survived the transatlantic voyage and arrived in the New World, as well as for their relatives remaining in Africa. Between 1525 and 1866, an estimated 12.5 million enslaved Africans were shipped to the New World, with approximately 10.7 million people surviving the transit. They were taken to Caribbean islands, Central and South America, and North America, with North America receiving about 388,000.[7]

Warfare was the major source of slaves from the Yoruba city-states, especially at the collapse of the Oyo Empire in the 1820s, when Yoruba were dispersed due to the Bariba expansionist wars in 1816.[8] The defeat of the Oyo army led to the dispersal of the civilian population into different non-Yoruba areas in Nigeria.[9] Most Yoruba persons who were enslaved in the nineteenth century were the product of the Yoruba civil

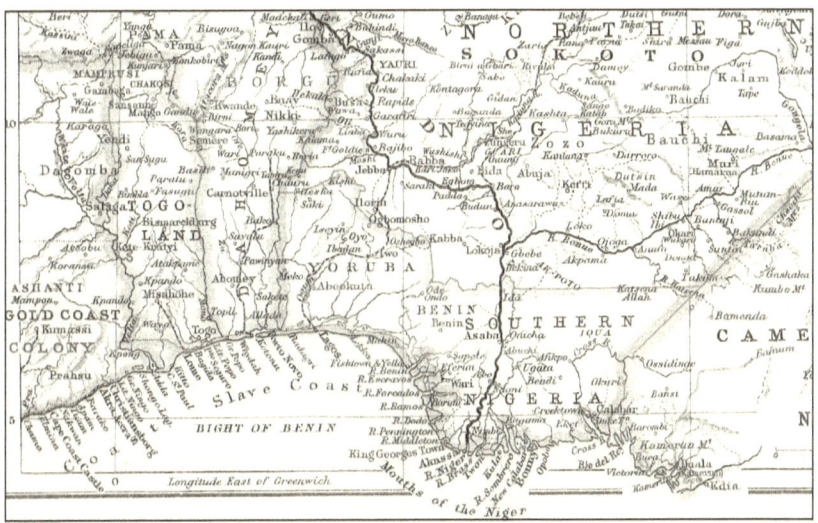

The Slave Coast is marked on a John Bartholomew & Co. map published ca. 1914. (John Bartholomew & Co., Edinburg; Wikimedia Commons)

wars because the winning side sold captured members of the defeated group, though some individuals may have become slaves as punishment for crimes or for committing abominations such as incest or murder.[10] In the nineteenth century, Yoruba speakers came to be predominant in the numbers of enslaved people being shipped from the Slave Coast of West Africa along the Bight of Benin, including the growing port of Lagos in Yorubaland.[11]

The Yoruba enslaved people transported to the New World brought with them their Yoruba culture, although they could not practice their religion openly because slave masters prohibited anything African, including even the people's African names. Consequently, a survival strategy became imperative for Yoruba religion and culture to exist in the white man's land. The slaves taken to Catholic regions found solace in the Catholic saints, with whom they veiled each of the Yoruba deities, resulting in the worship of orisa such as Ṣàngó in the form of Santa Barbara (Saint Barbara), Ogun in the form of Saint Peter, Obatala in the form of Saint Joseph, Ọya in the form of Our Lady of Candlelaria, Osun in the form of the Our Lady of Charity of El Cobre, and Yemọnja in the form of Our Lady of Regla in Santería (which was developed in

Cuba by members of the Lukumí ethnic group among the Yoruba), and similar identifications of orisa with Catholic saints in other parts of the New World.[12]

The Practice of Yoruba Religion in the Diaspora

Yoruba religion exists in two major strands in the present-day Yoruba diaspora: (1) a close replica of the practice of Yoruba religion by recent migrants from Nigeria as well as those who have converted to Yoruba religion; and (2) aspects of the tradition apparent in African diaspora religions, such as Candomblé, Santería, and Haitian Vodou, which resulted from the transatlantic slave trade. Candomblé, originating in Bahía, Brazil; Santería, originating in Cuba; and Haitian Vodou, originating in Haiti, are not Yoruba in their entirety, but Yoruba religion constitutes significant components of these religions. Other West African enslaved persons contributed to these religions as well.

The practice of Yoruba religion in the diaspora is marked by dynamism and boundaries that are ever expanding with regard to membership demography and innovative practices. The anthropologist and global studies scholar Kamari Maxine Clarke has delineated four significant categories of orisa worshippers: (1) orisa devotees in West Africa, especially Nigeria and Benin, among whom there are religious specialists who travel between their countries of origin and places in the diaspora to teach Yoruba religion and culture; (2) practitioners of religions that have significant influences from Yoruba religion, for instance, Santería, Candomblé, Trinidad Orisha, and Haitian Vodou, who live in Cuba, Brazil, Trinidad and Tobago, Haiti, Puerto Rico, the United States, and elsewhere; (3) African descendants who are orisa worshippers in the diaspora with special interest in Black/racial consciousness and heritage; and (4) "òrìṣà modernists, a relatively (post-1980s) group of initiates, led by predominantly white American practitioners," who stress their ties to the orisa not through African ethnic heritage but through their religious ancestral connections via the spiritual parents who initiated them into orisa worship.[13] These four categories constitute overlapping networks of practitioners who continuously adapt and produce orisa practices, resulting in the invention of new orisa worship forms. The types of orisa devotees in categories 1 through 3 are not mutually exclusive.

Practitioners in the Afro-diasporic religions and African descendants who worship the orisa in the diaspora especially mingle and worship with each other.

There are contentions concerning the place of sexuality in Yoruba religion and its practice in the diaspora. In Yoruba culture, every individual is expected to marry and have children, which necessarily assumes heterosexual intercourse. However, the visible participation of LGBTQ persons in Yoruba religion in the diaspora has prompted a discussion of homosexuality in the religious tradition. While some people argue that homosexuality is foreign to Yoruba culture because of its emphasis on procreation and collective familial immortality, others aver that homosexuality exists in some genres of Yoruba oral literature and hence that it is not foreign at all.[14] Some female-gendered LGBTQ persons are priestesses of Yoruba religion in the diaspora. It is generally agreed that heterosexuality prevails among the Yoruba and that other sexual orientations are regarded as obscene and shrouded in secrecy in Yorubaland, and hence documentation is scarce. While the possibility of references to homosexuality in Yoruba oral literature has been explored, it is apparent that most Yoruba consider such practices as shameful and offensive, primarily because they obstruct the possibility of biological procreation, which is of paramount importance to the Yoruba thought system.[15] However, since Yoruba religion is welcoming to all people from every corner of the world, people of different sexual orientations are adherents of the religion.[16]

African Diaspora Religions

African enslaved peoples of many ethnicities brought their religious outlooks to the New World. Thus, the Yoruba religion first came to the New World with Yoruba enslaved people. In French colonial Haiti (then called Saint-Domingue), the religion of the Fon people combined with the religion of Yoruba to produce a unique religion called Haitian Vodou in which Vodou deities are associated with Catholic saints. In Spanish colonial Cuba, the religions of the Yoruba, Fon, and Ewe peoples were synthesized with Catholicism to produce Santería. In Portuguese colonial Brazil, especially in the state of Bahía, Yoruba religion survives with modifications as Candomblé, and its practitioners are also faithful

Catholics. Yoruba deities brought to the New World by enslaved people included Ifa, Osun, Sango, Ogun, and others, in addition to the veneration of ancestors (*eégún*).

Santería

Santería (worship of saints), which is also known as La Regla de Ocha (rule/law/way of the orichá) and Lucumí, is an inclusive religion that respects and worships *orichá* (Yoruba: *òrìṣà*) in forces of nature. There are variants of narratives on the origin of Santería in the United States. One of these is that Santería originated with the religious beliefs and practices of enslaved Yoruba brought to Cuba primarily during the eighteenth and early nineteenth centuries.[17] It is generally accepted that the founding father of Santería in New York City was Babaláwo Pancho Mora, who was called by the Yoruba name Ifá Moroti, who was initiated into Ifá in Cuba in 1944. The name Ifa Moroti means "I stand by Ifa." After visiting New York City in 1946, in 1950 he returned to the city to live there.[18] According to the scholar of Africana religions Tracey E. Hucks, the "early history of African American Yorùbá tradition in the United States is one closely aligned with Cuban migration. As early as the 1940s, Latinos migrating from the Caribbean commenced a process of transplantation, transformation, and expansion of Santería practices into U.S. urban locales."[19]

Women made significant contributions to the early practice of Santería in New York City, including Mama Keke from Barbados, who founded the Moremi Book Store and the African Market. She was a supporter of Efuntola Oseijeman Adelabu Adefunmi (born as Walter Eugene King in Detroit, 1928–2005) in the 1950s when he founded the Order of Damballah Hwedo in 1956 in Greenwich Village in New York City. She was a founding member of the Yorùbá Temple founded by Adefunmi in 1960 in Harlem, New York City, and her ashes rest in the Ọyọ́túnjí African Village in Beaufort County, South Carolina, which Adefunmi founded in 1970.[20] Also, Audley Moore (1898–1997) from New Iberia, Louisiana, known as Queen Mother Moore, was a major figure in the Black nationalist movement. She founded the Reparations Committee for the Descendants of United States Slaves, the African American Cultural Foundation, the Universal Association of Ethiopian

Women, and the Eloise Moore College of African Studies. Although she was attracted primarily to Egyptian and Ethiopian spirituality, she was a leader in the Yorùbá Temple, and Adefunmi gave her a Yoruba name, Iyaluwa (Mother of Our Town or Mother of the People).[21] There was an Afro–Puerto Rican woman named Sunta Serrano (Asunción Rodriguez Serrano) who was another significant figure in the Yoruba religious movement. In August 1958, she underwent full initiation into the Yoruba religion (Santería) by being initiated a priestess of the orisa Obatala in Cuba. During her initiation, Serrano received a divination stating that she was destined to initiate African Americans into the religion. She contributed to building up Shango Temple, which was founded in Harlem in New York City in 1959, along with Adefunmi and Christopher Oliana, also an Afro-Cuban. Sunta Serrano gave spiritual readings at the Yorùbá Temple, which supplanted the Shango Temple.[22]

Santería is an Afro-Cuban religion comprising Yoruba beliefs, rituals assimilated from other African religious practices, Spanish Catholicism, and European Spiritualism. Women play important roles in Santería, especially as priestesses (*santeras*), who are well accepted and represented in Santería's priestly class.[23] Yoruba goddesses that feature in Santería worship sessions include Yemayá (Yoruba: Yemọnja), Ochún (Yoruba: Ọ̀sun), and Oyá (Yoruba: Ọya). Women play prominent roles in the recitations, singing, and especially the dancing, which may occur in private or public worship sessions. The language of worship in Santería is the Lukumí Yoruba dialect, which sounds very much like the Yoruba language but has changed so much when compared to Yoruba language that today an average Yoruba person from Nigeria does not understand it.[24]

The religious studies scholar Mary Ann Clark points out that "unlike many mainstream religions, Santería exists within a female-normative system in which all practitioners are expected to take up female gender roles."[25] Here Clark refers to new initiates who bear the title *iyawo* (Yoruba: *ìyàwó*, meaning "bride" or "new wife"), whether they be male or female, for a year after their initiation.[26] Thus, every initiate is gendered female in relation to their orisa. Initiates are construed as being in a relationship of wife to the orisa (husband), regardless of whether the orisa is male or female. By becoming wives of a deity, both male and female priests are accorded higher status than nonpriestly members of the worship community. These wives of the orisa constitute the avenues through which effective communication between the orisa and worshippers is manifest through possession of the initiated priests and priestesses. The orisa are allowed to possess only the bodies of those whose initiations have prepared them to receive their presence.

As we saw earlier, Yoruba do not construe the relationship of the initiate to the orisa as the orisa having sexual intercourse or penetration of the initiate. Yoruba would be appalled by such assumptions, for it is strange to the Yoruba thought system. The metaphor of husband and wife in Yoruba religion is meant to illustrate the authority and love of the orisa for the initiate, resulting in a close relationship that can be likened to that between a husband and a wife.

Writing about Candomblé in Brazil in comparison to Yoruba religion in Yorubaland, the anthropologist J. Lorand Matory's statement in his *Black Atlantic Religion* is instructive: "In West Africa, Ọ̀yọ́-Yorùbá worshippers employ multiple metaphors to evoke the nature of people's relationships to the gods. Like Brazilian *candomblecistas*, they might call any devotee of an *òrìṣà* the 'child' (*ọmọ* [Yorùbá]; *filho* [Portuguese]) of that god. In both traditions, motherhood and fatherhood are used as metaphors of *leadership* in the worship and activation of the gods."[27] Concerning the relationship between the initiate and the orisa, Matory also writes, "I have never heard any West Africa *òrìṣà* priest speak of himself or his fellow priests as anything like a 'homosexual' or as engaging in same-sex intercourse. I argue simply that the Afro-Brazilians have *reinterpreted* West African metaphors of spirit possession in the light of Brazilian gender categories."[28] Thus, the Yoruba wife-husband metaphor for the relationship between the initiate and the orisa, which is devoid of sexual connotation in Yorubaland, may be reinterpreted in Santería and Candomblé to include people of different sexual orientations.

The anthropologist Aisha M. Beliso-De Jesús argues that all of the *babalao* (Yoruba: *babaláwo*) in Cuba are concerned not to initiate gay men as babalao in Ifa, because gay men may be "penetrated" in sexual intercourse. Gay men who are *orichá* (Yoruba: *òrìṣà*) initiates are understood in Santería as being "penetrated" by the orichá. The Cuban babalao also prohibit women from becoming Ifa priests, *iyanifá* (Yoruba: *ìyánífá*), because women are also "penetrated" in sexual intercourse. According to Beliso-De Jesús, the arguments of the babalao in the debate are aimed at preserving a heteronormative social status, in which the role of babalao is restricted to heterosexual men who are not "penetrated." Thus, in the Santería tradition, women and gay men cannot belong to the priesthood of Orula (Ifá and Òrúnmìlà in Yoruba religion), the orisa of divination.[29]

Worthy of mention is the controversy in Santería that erupted upon the initiation of women as iyanifá in Cuba. In 2004 and 2005, the initiation of women as iyanifá, a practice traditional to Nigerian Ifa, was conducted in Cuba, sparking global diasporic contention. The association of diviners in the Cuban Ifá tradition, the Asociación Cultural Yoruba de Cuba (ACYC; the Yoruba Cultural Association of Cuba), called on Santería practitioners to avoid consulting with the iyanifá and the babalao who initiated them. However, the African-style babalao pointed out that women are initiated as iyanifa in Yoruba religion on the African continent. Therefore, it was argued that in the diaspora, the initiation of iyanifá aligns with the Yoruba thought system, which emphasizes balance between the sexes. Beliso-De Jesús points out that "the Iyanifa debate is primarily a contest over Cuban versus Nigerian global diasporic authority rather than over female initiations." The initiation of iyanifá in Cuba threatened "Cuba's global position as a touristic source of Ifá-Ocha" by "the imposition of African-style religious orthodoxy."[30]

Candomblé

Candomblé emerged in Bahía as a "result of the re-elaboration of diverse African cultures, the product of different affiliations, which actually has resulted in the existence of numerous forms of Candomblé: Angola, Congo, Efan, and so on."[31] In addition, the Jeje-Nagô version of Candomblé is derived from "the Yorùbá and Fon/Ewe cultural language groups, which originated in what is today Nigeria and Benin. A result of the synthesis of these ethnic groups and the Brazilian historical process, *Candomblé jeje-nago*, as it is called, is thus a religion of African origin, but it is specifically Brazilian and is composed of practitioners of all races."[32] It has been described as "an Afro-Brazilian religion of divination, sacrifice, healing, music, dance and spirit possession."[33]

Candomblé has Amerindian and Catholic elements that reflect the influence of multicultural Brazilian society. There are different *ilê* (houses; Yoruba: *ilé*) in Candomblé to which initiates belong, where they are constantly concerned with the maintenance of harmonious relations between themselves and the *orixás* (Yoruba: *òrìṣà*) and the accumulation of sacred life-giving power *axé* (Yoruba: *àṣẹ*), which ensures well-being and freedom from suffering.[34] The ilê in Salvador, Bahía, Brazil, known as Jeje-Nagô Ilê was the main influence on Candomblé from the nineteenth century onward.[35] An ilê's temple may be called a *casa* (Portuguese for "house") or *terreiro* (Portuguese for "yard"). Divination by cowry shells is a significant aspect of worship. The most senior priest (Portuguese: *pai-de-santo*, "father of saint") or most senior priestess (Portuguese: *mãe-de-santo*, "mother of saint") interprets the patterns of the cowry shells to give messages to worshippers. Worship involves offerings and dance consisting of specially choreographed movements and hymns for the orixás in which initiates may become possessed by them.

Women play significant roles in Candomblé; indeed, from the inception of the religion, many of the ilê have been headed by women. Examples include Mãe Stella de Oxossi (1925–2018), whose terreiro was Ilê Axé Opó Afonjá in Salvador; Mãe Filhinha (1904–2014) of Casa de Yemanjá in Cachoeira, Bahía; and Ekedy Sinha, who leads the Casa Branca in Salvador. A head priestess with the title mãe-de-santo or *ialorixá* (Yoruba: *iyá-òrìṣà*, "mother of orisa") leads worship services and trains initiates in Candomblé. The ialorixá is usually the chief authority within a terreiro, and she is assisted by the *iyakekere* or *mãe pequena* (small mother). Below the ialorixá and iyakekere are senior female and male initiates known as *ebomin* (elder sibling). Below them are *iaôs* (wives of the orixás), whose initiation has prepared them to become possessed by orixás while in trance. The iaôs may be women or men, and their orixás may be male or female. The *abiãs* are women or men who have gone through rituals of "spiritual fortification," but they have not yet been fully initiated. The majority of iaôs and abiãs are women. One of the most important roles in any terreiro is the *iabassé* or "mother who cooks." She is the woman responsible for preparing the ceremonial foods offered to the orixás and then shared with the community.[36] The terreiro also includes initiated persons who do not become possessed. *Equedes* are initiated women who serve as ritual assistants to iaôs when they are in trance. Men serve the orixás as *ogãs*, "initiated assistants who advise and protect the community"; *alabês*, who are the drummers; and *axôguns*, who carry out ritual animal sacrifice.[37]

Candomblé initiates participating the the Festa de Iemanjá on the banks of the Paraguaçu River in Cachoeira, Bahia. (Courtesy of Stephen Selka)

The influence of Yoruba religion on Candomblé is apparent in the use of terminologies, names of orisa, and songs and dance patterns during worship sessions. There are two main categories of initiates in Candomblé: ìyàwó (Portuguese: iaôs), people who can be possessed by the orixá; and the ògán (male) and èkejì (female), who cannot be possessed by orixá. The initiation period of iyawo spans twenty-one days; thereafter, the iyawo wears only white clothes for three months, with the head always covered. The iyawo has specific restrictions to observe, such as avoiding consumption of certain foods or going to the beach during one, three, five, and seven years of training before assuming the position of elder. The initiation period and process of the ogan and ekeji vary among the lineages. Duties of the ogan and ekeji include singing, drumming, and dancing, as well as preparation of items for sacrifice. Both ogan and ekeji are considered elders, but they do not perform rituals such as *ebo* (sacrifice) without their babaorixá (father of orisa) or iyalorixá. They do not perform initiations, and therefore they do not have godchildren.[38]

Haitian Vodou

Haitian Vodou was produced by the synthesis of the "social chaos and agony of Haiti's eighteenth-century slave plantations blended with several distinct African religions," such as those of the Fon, Ewe, Kongo, and Yoruba, "with French colonial Catholicism."[39] The central beliefs of Haitian Vodou include belief in a supreme being, who is omnipresent and called Bon Dje, meaning the good/high God in Haitian Kreyól, and in spirit forces known as *lwa*, as well as a belief in ancestor spirits. Haitian Vodou also holds belief in the principles of nature (magic) to affect human destiny. Healing is the core of Haitian Vodou, and it addresses health challenges and existential concerns such as family, work, and romance. There are various spirit forces in Haitian Vodou religion, among which are several female spirits that belong to a group called Ezili. The three most important are Lasyrenn (a mermaid spirit that lives in the ocean), Ezili Danto (a fierce mother figure), and Ezili Freda (representing beauty and romantic love).

In Haitian Vodou, women are held to the same standard as men, and there is no hierarchy that defines one sex as superior to the other. However, in the sociopolitical setting of Haiti, there is massive oppression of women, and often women are treated as second-class citizens. Moreover, "Haitian humor is rife with anti-women jokes, and domestic violence is a frequent occurrence."[40] Hence, in such a patriarchal society, Haitian Vodou empowers women by enabling women's spiritual leadership to be in the public eye, because some Haitian Vodou communities are led by women and women play central roles in the practice of the religion. An example is the role of the priestess known as *mambo*.

The mambo plays important roles in the sustenance of Haitian Vodou. Her three main roles are to serve the spirits; to communicate with spirits and help others do the same; and to bring growth, inspiration, peace, and protection to her community. The mambo and *houngan* (priest) preside over the community's worship ceremonies. There is the *mambo si pwen* (or *mambo sur point*), the junior priestess, and the *houngan sur pwen*, the junior priest. The high priestess is known as *mambo asogwe* and the high priest as *houngan asogwe*. The mambo asogwe, in addition to the houngan asogwe, has the authority to teach and initiate other *serviteurs* (servants) of the lwa. The mambo engages in divination to gain direct guidance from the spirits for her life and others. She communicates directly with spirit forces through signs and presides over rituals and healings for her worship community.[41] "Her divination (consult with spirit) may employ cards, candles, or [cowrie] shells—old and new systems—but a guidance system is used to 'ask the source.'"[42]

Worship in Yoruba Religions in Diaspora

As noted earlier, Yoruba religion exists in two strands in the diaspora. In addition to African religions resulting from the transatlantic slave trade, such as Santería and Candomblé, wherein Yoruba religious tradition is a significant component, there is also a close replica of the practice of Yoruba religion in Yorubaland in Nigeria in the contemporary diaspora. In recent decades, Yoruba religion as it is practiced in Yorubaland has become known and appreciated by practitioners in the diaspora through the efforts of female and male Yoruba cultic functionaries of different deities who travel from Nigeria to visit, train, and initiate individuals into Yoruba religion.

All Yoruba worship—on the African continent and in the diaspora—involves music and performance that correspond with the deity being worshipped. For instance, solemn music marks Ifa worship, while vigorous music characterizes Sango worship. Other features of Yoruba orisa worship are sacrifices or offerings, recitations, particular colors of the clothing worn by worshippers, spirit possession where applicable, and dancing. Worship sessions are feasting times in Yoruba religion, marked by the consumption of varieties of delicious meals, drinks (palm wine and other bottled drinks), kola nuts, and bitter kola. Religious festivals are special occasions to honor deities in Yoruba religion and often serve as venues for social networking as well. Women play significant roles in Yoruba religion at all levels, as priestesses, diviners, healers, reciters of traditional oral genres, and food preparers. Examples of Yoruba worship include weekly worship at altars in individual homes to the deity or deities concerned and annual or special festivals.

Two types of worship can be designated for Yoruba religion in the diaspora: private and public. Private worship (òsè) involves the offering of prayers, songs, dance, and recitations (praise names of the deities and/or command language) at the altar in a home by an adherent of any deity/orisa in Yoruba religion.[43] Such altars display symbols of the orisa, including colors (red for Sango, white for Obatala, blue for Yemanja, gold for Osun, green and brown for Ifa), sculptures, pictures of shrines and sacred groves in Yorubaland, and ornaments of the orisa concerned. The preferred apparel while offering worship is white for both males and females, and there is profuse use of flowers in the decoration of the altars. The worshipper offers praises in songs and recitations to the orisa, followed by prayers and supplications for the well-being of every member of the family. Help is sought from the orisa for any challenges. Each orisa has favorite cooked dishes, and these are offered on small plates or bowls at the altar. The worship ends with praises to the orisa, which the worshipper offers partly in the dominant language of the country and in phrases in the Yoruba language.

In the diaspora, for the purposes of worship, the five days of a week in the traditional Yoruba calendar have been modified to the Western week consisting of seven days. Consequently, private worship in Yoruba religion in the diaspora occurs every seven days, on Saturdays to be precise. For example, adherents of Yoruba religion in Germany offer worship to orisa in their homes weekly every Saturday.[44]

Private worship of the orisa is considered to be very important, because it sustains the link of the worshipper with the deity or deities concerned. Rarely does private worship attendance exceed five people, although one person alone may offer the worship. Priestesses of Yoruba religion constitute a considerable number of people who offer private worship to the orisa of their affiliation.

The need to utilize Yoruba language to varying degrees during worship has necessitated the furtherance of the study of Yoruba language worldwide. Worthy of mention is the increasing number of African Americans who convert to Yoruba religion from different religious affiliations. Many such converts to Yoruba religion in the diaspora have made serious efforts to study, learn, and speak the Yoruba language, and phrases of Yoruba language are utilized for worship regularly. The need to understand Yoruba language and culture in order to worship Yoruba deities effectively has also led to the establishment of schools and study centers. The African Studies Institute at the University of Georgia in Athens, Georgia, in the United States, is an example of a study program of Yoruba language in the diaspora.[45]

Worship sessions in a temple involve the assembly of adherents to honor and interact with the orisa. Worship encompasses recitations of diverse Yoruba oral genres, singing, dancing, supplications, possession of initiated priestesses and priests, and feasting. Cultic functionaries—priests and priestesses—lead during worship sessions. Temples of orisa worship known as ile in the diaspora serve as venues for social networking and the consolidation of harmony among adherents of that particular orisa and of Yoruba religion in general. The worship of orisa in temples constitutes a clear movement toward the institutionalization of Yoruba religion in the diaspora with distinctive administrative structures and functionaries.

Public festivals (*odún*) are held in the diaspora to honor Yoruba orisa. Public worship of Yoruba orisa by immigrant Yoruba people in the diaspora, converts to the Yoruba religion, and friends and admirers (any and all adherents) involve offerings of sacrifice, songs, recitations in a temple/ile, and public processions marked by singing and dancing. Women as well as female orisa play prominent roles during these ceremonies. For example, festivals are held for Osun in New York, Miami, and at the Ọyọ́túnjí African Village in South Carolina; a Yemoja festival is held in Baltimore. The Osun festival held anywhere in the diaspora requires that a river be consecrated as Osun River in Nigeria. According to a Yoruba saying, *omi gbogbo lò'sun*, "all waters are Osun." Indeed, "though the Osogbo festival is the well-known center of Osun devotion, there are significant Osun festivals in other cities of Nigeria and other parts of the world."[46] Once this consecration of the river is done by the performance of the correct rituals by qualified cultic functionaries, adherents are confident that all worship at such rivers is invariably received by the Yoruba goddess Osun. In Trinidad and Tobago, where the Orisha religious tradition (also called Shango) arrived with enslaved people transported across the Atlantic, there are annual festivals for Osun and also for other orisa. An example is the Osun festival that is celebrated in Matura, Trinidad and Tobago, where prayers are made to Osun to request blessings (children, fecundity, prosperity) from the goddess. The celebration is marked with songs and recitations in the Yoruba and English languages.[47] Some of the worshippers wear white dresses and beads, and they dance to drums and the music of Yoruba lyrics in the praise of Osun. Furthermore, regular festivals to different orisa occur at the Oyotunji African Village in South Carolina, founded by Adelabu Adefunmi.[48] For example, the Yemonja festival is celebrated in Oyotunji as the Women's Festival.[49] In another example, the Odun Ifa and Oya festivals are held in New York City.[50]

The Egúngún (Masquerade) festival honors the ancestors who are the living dead and continuing stakeholders in Yoruba societies. These ancestors visit Yoruba people regularly to bless and guide their children in the form of masquerades (*egúngún*, singular *eégún*). On July 27, 2013, the first Yoruba Egungun festival was celebrated in Mexico. The festival involved a procession of adherents of different Yoruba orisa dancing and singing joyfully on the streets of Mexico City. Offerings were made to the ancestors, prayers were offered, and there was general feasting. The general public in Mexico likened the Egungun festival to the Carnaval holiday (before Ash Wednesday, similar to Mardi Gras in New Orleans and Carnival in other countries); hence, there was no tension concerning the event.[51]

Certain controversies arise in relation to the practice of Yoruba religion in the diaspora. The issues include the killing of animals for sacrifice, innovations concerning items of worship that may not be available outside Africa, and clashes with local regulations on religious processions. On the one hand, Yoruba in Nigeria have reservations concerning the efficacy of sacrifices done outside of Yorubaland, and on the other hand, people in the diaspora are concerned about the possibility of violating animal-rights laws. The killing of animals for sacrifice as prescribed by Yoruba orisa has been a contentious issue over the years, as has, in some parts of the world, the substitution of coconuts for kola nuts as items of rituals. The Awise Awo Agbaye (spokesperson of Ifa and Yoruba religion worldwide) and former vice chancellor of Obafemi Awolowo University, Ile-Ife, Professor Wande Abimbola says, "I have performed countless 'sacrifices' all over the world. Which country have I not gone to perform 'sacrifice'? People invite me all over the world to come and do 'sacrifice' for them." He explains that sacrifices performed abroad are not less efficacious when compared to those done in Nigeria. "The materials used for 'sacrifice' differ from clime to clime. *Tí a bà rìà-dan, aó fi odíde se'bo*, meaning 'you improvise when you cannot readily find some materials for 'sacrifice' in a foreign land.'" Such a sacrifice will still be acceptable to the gods.[52]

Commenting on the challenges faced by Ifa worshippers in the United Kingdom and the United States, the renowned Ifa scholar and Araba of Osogbo Ifayemi Elebuibon states, "Ifa worship is efficacious. Ifa is a body of knowledge of Yoruba worldview. We have millions of Ifa believers across the globe. But we encounter some difficulties in the course of worship abroad." Elebuibon explains that animal sacrifice is performed in the United Kingdom and the United States by Ifa priests who are known as babalawo, adding that the choice of the place of sacrifice is determined by Ifa. He says, "We perform 'sacrifice' anywhere the gods direct us. The gods could choose a park, a road, path or an intersection." Speaking of when kola nut was forbidden for importation into the United States (it is now available) along with pigeon and snail, Elebuibon says, "We go to Chinatowns in the USA. You know the Chinese live together and they are permitted by law to have these items. So, we buy from Chinatown. In the absence of kola, which we use for divination, we use coconut which we break into four small pieces."[53] Thus, although challenges exist in the daily activities of adherents of Yoruba religion in the diaspora, these are addressed with innovative provisions.

Religious processions are prescribed in certain types of worship in Yoruba religion, such as the Egungun festival, which, as noted earlier, can be likened to a Carnival celebration. Although some countries allow these processions without tension, there have been occasions when such processions were prohibited for African religion in the diaspora. For example, nineteenth-century "colonial laws in Trinidad restricted specific practices vital to the ritual life of African-derived religions, such as the 'beating of any drum' or 'any dance procession,' and found public assemblies of Africans a threat to colonial social order."[54]

Possible changes and continuities of gender ideology may be identified in the practice of Yoruba religion in the diaspora. As we have seen, Yoruba culture and religion subscribe to complementary gender ideology, with a focus on specific areas of specializations for members of each sex. Yoruba gender ideology does not support absolutism wherein persons of one sex control all resources and authority in any setting. Women have their powers just as men do. These convictions are continued and sustained in the practice of Yoruba religion in the diaspora.

However, the practice of Yoruba religion in the diaspora encounters the reality of complex gender constructions and sexual orientations that are generally not openly expressed among the Yoruba on the African continent, and this has serious implications for Yoruba gender ideology in the diaspora. The reality of LGBTQ adherents of Yoruba religion in the diaspora means that analysis of Yoruba gender ideology must be expanded to include sexual orientation and gender identity. LGBTQ persons are adherents of different Yoruba orisa, including Osun, Yemanja, Obatala, and Ifa. They play roles as followers and leaders, irrespective of gender. However, as we saw earlier, in the diaspora the sexual orientation of adherents is seriously taken into account when a person is being considered for initiation to priesthood, which may include capacity for spirit possession in Santería and Candomblé. This is not an overt issue with adherents of Yoruba religion in Yorubaland. Thus, the boundaries of Yoruba gender ideology are being expanded in the practice of the religion in the diaspora, but the negotiations are ongoing.

The significance of motherhood for the practice of Yoruba religion in Africa and the diaspora remains. Motherhood is a position of authority and power among the Yoruba, both biologically and symbolically, with connotations of mystic capacities derived from the blood, fluid, and breast milk (biologically) or mentorship and prayers (symbolically) expended as investments in the child's life. The position of the mother is extolled in Yoruba religious practices in the diaspora, especially as being spiritual leaders with profound authority and power. For instance, the ilê in Candomblé in Brazil is usually headed by a spiritual mother, just as women leaders hold sway in Santería and Haitian Vodou. It is worth mentioning, though, that the *Ìyà Mi* group (powerful mothers) is yet to be confirmed as a functioning institution in the practice of Yoruba religion in the diaspora.

Women's Roles in the Practice of Immigrant and Convert Yoruba Religion in the Diaspora

Historically, as we have seen, women have played prominent roles at all levels of Yoruba religion. Throughout the past four hundred years, with the experiences of the transatlantic slave trade up to contemporary times, women have remained in the vanguard of the sustenance and creativity of Yoruba religion in the diaspora.

As is true of many religions, women constitute the majority of adherents and worshippers in Yoruba religion in the diaspora. Consequently, as noted of women in Yorubaland, women in in the diaspora are the sustainers of the Yoruba religion through their daily activities.[55] Such activities include cleaning of the sacred space (altar, shrine, or temple), cooking and preparing food items to be offered to the deity, recitations (*oríkì*, praise poetry of the deity; *ìjúbà*, homage to the deity), and music and dance where applicable. Thus, women play the roles of active regular worshippers of deities for the general well-being of every member of the family and, by extension, of the community of believers.

In addition, women teach the tenets of orisa traditions to children as well as to new members coming into the religion, both at the informal and the formal levels. On the informal level, this is done through the process of socialization of children in Yoruba ethos, language, and cultural practices. Mothers who are adherents of an orisa tradition conduct worship with the children present. Women often establish schools and centers where Yoruba language, drumming, dance, and other components of Yoruba religion and culture are taught. In addition, cultic functionaries—female and male—are often invited by such centers and schools to teach and impart knowledge on Yoruba religion and culture. Women transmit knowledge of the religion through home decorations themed on an orisa, fashion using *àdìre eléko* (indigo resist-dyed cotton cloth) in beautiful designs, and music, paintings, sculpture, and dance. Thus, women in orisa traditions in the diaspora display Yoruba religion in everyday activities, thereby confirming the all-inclusive influence of the orisa.

Priestesses of different Yoruba orisa play the roles of leaders and custodians of tradition in the diaspora. To lead in Yoruba religion, initiation into the deity's worship is crucial. This involves acquiring knowledge of the practices and taboos of each orisa. There are controversies associated with the location of initiation into a Yoruba orisa worship community, which may not necessarily be true for Santería or Candomblé. Some people opine that it is best to hold initiations, especially into Ifa priesthood, in Yoruba towns in Africa rather than a location in the diaspora, principally because of the availability of ritual items needed and the fulfillment of the requirement by Ifa that at least ten babalawo must be in attendance for the three-day program in the *ìwo-gbódù* (forest of odù Ifá) to initiate a new babalawo or iyanifa.[56] Presently the initiation of women leaders in Yoruba religion in the diaspora take place in both types of locations, Yoruba towns and the diaspora.

Orisa priestesses are at the forefront of the propagation of Yoruba religion on the internet, as shown by the many websites that promote the knowledge of different orisa traditions.[57] Further, some of these websites sell ritual items of different orisa as well as offering tours to Yoruba towns in Nigeria, which usually target specific festivals such as Osun Osogbo and Sango festivals in Osogbo and Oyo towns, respectively.[58] The activities of orisa priestesses on the internet simultaneously serve as advertisement, documentation, and sustenance of Yoruba religion worldwide. In addition, orisa priestesses play salient roles in the administrative structures of Yoruba religion, as iyanifa, *apètèbí* (wife of a babalawo), writers, and life coaches.[59]

Women play roles in Yoruba religion in the diaspora that include priestesses, teachers, custodians of tradition, diviners, drummers, singers, painters, sculptors, cooks, and cleaners of worship places. Women's involvement with Yoruba religion has been enabled in significant ways by the internet and social platforms such as Facebook, Twitter, and chat groups. It is clear that the practice of Yoruba religion in the diaspora is marked largely by dynamism, with boundaries that are ever widening with regard to membership demography and innovative practices, and women feature prominently in these initiatives.

Yoruba Christians and Muslims in the Diaspora

In addition to the growing practice of the Yoruba religion in the diaspora, there is the ever-increasing presence of Yoruba Pentecostal denominations, including the Mountain of Fire and Miracles Ministries, the Redeemed Christian Church of God, and the Winners Chapel International, as well as branches of African independent churches like the Cherubim and Seraphim movement. In Pentecostal churches in the diaspora, which emphasize the manifestations of the Holy Spirit in divine healing and speaking in tongues, women's roles are the same as their roles in the churches in Yorubaland, described earlier, including as choir members, pastors, Sunday-school teachers, and members of church councils.[60] Women's roles in the African independent churches in the diaspora also play similar roles as women in these churches in Yorubaland.

Women in African independent church denominations and movements serve as church founders. For example, the Reverend Mother Esther Abimbola Ajayi, known as Iya Adura, founded and pastors the Love of Christ Generation Church C&S (Cherubim and Seraphim; London Branch) at 412–412a, Clapham Road, London SW9 9DA.[61] Women in the African independent churches also serve as prophetesses, Bible-study teachers, ushers, and choir members. Prophetess Dorcas Obagbemiro of the Cherubim and Seraphim Movement No. 6, Sabo-Oke area, Ilorin, reports that she preaches the gospel of Jesus Christ in Nigeria and in the United States, and she observes that women in C&S churches play the same roles in Nigeria and the diaspora. She asserts that women in the church determine the fervency of the spiritual growth of the church as committed members and as mothers and wives in their homes. She avers that although women in the church face various existential challenges, God can solve these challenges if women depend on God totally, and this in turn will build the church.[62]

Similarly, in the diaspora, Yoruba women's roles in Islamic organizations such as the Ansar-ud-Deen Society of Nigeria (committed to education) and the Nasrul-lahi-li Fathi Society of Nigeria (NASFA; committed to the formation of prayer groups) and in mosques such as the Bow Central Mosque in London are the same as women's roles in Islam in Yorubaland. These Yoruba Muslim women engage in prayers to Allah, submit themselves to doing the will of Allah in their daily lives, and carry out works of charity.[63]

Conclusion

The diaspora of Yoruba people during the transatlantic slave trade and, beginning in the twentieth century, through immigration of Yoruba to countries outside Yorubaland has resulted in the indigenous Yoruba religion becoming one of the notable religious traditions of the world.[64] The Yoruba religious tradition is characterized by internal diversity, widespread continuities, and syncretic offshoots. Women constitute important agents in the practice of Yoruba-derived religions in the diaspora. This is especially true of women's roles in ritual spaces. Priestesses are active participants and leaders in Santería, Candomblé, and Haitian Vodou. In addition, women are diviners, custodians of tradition, sculptors, and painters, and they participate in the recitation of diverse oral genres. Also, women feature prominently during religious festivals of Yoruba religion in the diaspora. Women's leadership is exemplified in women's headship of some ilê in Candomblé, as santeras in Santería, and as mambo asogwe in Haitian Vodou. The act of cooking is ritualized in Candomblé to emphasize the importance of women's cooking activities. The significant roles of women in the founding of temples and orisa worship in New York City is also worthy of note. In addition, women ensure the continuity of Yoruba religion in the diaspora through the socialization of their children according to Yoruba ethos and worldview.

The influence of Yoruba religion on Santería, Candomblé, and Haitian Vodou, in addition to the Vodun worship of Fon and Ewe peoples, demonstrates that Yoruba religion is a major religious tradition of the world. This is seen also in the increasing number of converts, many of whom are women, to various forms of Yoruba religion by people not born into Yoruba culture, including African Americans and people of European descent. The different adherents of Yoruba religion interact at various levels, including festivals and the public worship sessions of different orisa.

Every significant religious tradition interacts with the processes of globalization at many levels. Yoruba religion is no exception, and this proffers opportunities for women's roles in Yoruba religion worldwide. Chapter 6 explores the place of women in the practice of Yoruba religion in a globalized world.

6

Women in the Yorùbá Religion and Globalization

Yeye Chief (Mrs.) Doyin Olosun-Faniyi (b. 1962) is a Yoruba priestess who participates in the globalization of the Yoruba religion, traveling to other countries, teaching about Yoruba religion, and initiating new devotees of the òrìṣà.[1] She is the adopted daughter of the Austrian artist and adherent of Yorùbá religion Iya Susanne Wenger (1915–2009), known in the Yoruba religion as Adunni Olorisa (adored one of the orisa) of the Osun-Osogbo Sacred Grove in Osogbo, Osun State. Susanne Wenger arrived in Nigeria in 1950. Prior to coming to Nigeria, she was an artist who exhibited her works in Paris, Zurich, and other parts of Europe. Wenger's primary effort in Nigeria for many years was to collaborate with local artists and workers on the construction, renovation, and preservation of shrines and sculptures in the Osun-Osogbo grove along the Osun River.[2] Her efforts led to the recognition of the Osun-Osogbo Sacred Grove as a World Heritage Site by UNESCO (United Nations Educational, Scientific, and Cultural Organization) in 2005. She died at the age of ninety-three in Osogbo. Yeye Chief Doyin Olosun-Faniyi lived with and worked closely with Adunni Olorisa from the time she was five years old, and she consequently grew up enmeshed in Yoruba religious sensitivities.

Yeye Chief Doyin Olosun-Faniyi is a priestess of Osun and an ìyánífá with many years of experience in Yoruba religion in Nigeria and the diaspora. She consults, mentors, and performs different rituals as occasion demands in many countries worldwide. Olosun-Faniyi's first awareness that Osun was worshipped beyond Nigeria occurred when she was nine years old, with the visit of a Puerto Rican Osun priestess, popularly called Iya Sonta, who lived in New York City. Iya Sonta was a friend of Iya Adunni Olorisa and annually visited her residence on Ibokun Road in Osogbo to initiate adherents (omo-òòsà) to Osun worship.[3]

In 1993, Olosun-Faniyi made her first trip outside Nigeria as an Osun priestess on official duty to Portugal. She went to perform rituals for

Yeye Chief Doyin Olosun-Faniyi, wearing òrìṣà parapọ̀ beads, in front of her house, also a museum for her mother, Susanne Wenger, on Ibokun Road in Osogbo next to the fence by the artist Adebisi Akanji, 2015. (Courtesy of Yeye Chief Doyin Olosun-Faniyi and Moussa Kone)

a Portuguese Osun adherent who remained infertile after many years. According to Olosun-Faniyi, she had to travel with the ritual items needed because such items were unavailable in Portugal. She identified a flowing river in Portugal to which necessary ritual prayers were made to symbolize Osun River, in line with the Yoruba stance we saw earlier that *omi gbogbolò'sun*, "all waters are Osun water." The trip was a success. The woman became pregnant shortly thereafter, and the child was named Osuntoyin, meaning "Osun is worthy of praise." Since then, Olosun-Faniyi has traveled to many countries in the Yoruba diaspora, including Germany, Austria, Brazil, the United Kingdom, the United States, Ghana, and Togo, to perform religious duties. These trips include divination for clients on diverse existential issues, mentoring of omo-oosa, holding workshops and seminars on aspects of the Yoruba belief system, and offering sacrifices if they are prescribed by Ifá divination.[4]

The need to make ritual items, religious objects, and services available to every adherent of Yoruba religion who needs them in Yorubaland and the diaspora opens wide the doors of commercialization. Olosun-Faniyi sends fashion items with Yoruba religious themes and religious items out into the diaspora for sale. She is the originator of *òrìṣà parapọ̀* beads, which signify the unity of all orisa that should be emulated among adherents of different deities in Yoruba religion. She has students in Germany, Austria, and the United States with whom she is in constant communication and with whom she exchanges visits regularly. Yeye Chief Olosun-Faniyi's life experiences illuminate the effects of globalization on Yoruba religion, its adherents, and its practices. They also demonstrate women's agency, activities, and leadership in religious, economic, and leadership roles among the Yoruba.

"Globalization" is a term that refers to "increasing global connectivity, integration, and interdependence in the economic, social, technological, cultural, political, and ecological spheres."[5] Globalization has proven to be a decisive factor in prevailing trends in all ramifications of human experience in recent times. The advent and process of globalization across different sectors have been marked by controversies, with arguments made for and against the phenomenon. Some people highlight the positive influences of globalization on different spheres of human endeavors. According to the economist Jagdish Bhagwati, statistics show the stupendous increase in world trade and GDP (gross domestic product) after opening of markets to global trade. Bhagwati argues that globalization has benefited the poor because trade enhances economic growth and growth reduces poverty. Participation of women in the workforce and in other aspects of life has also improved.[6]

However, globalization also creates challenges for countries and their citizens. As reported by Ahmadu Ibrahim, the economist T. A. Oyejide notes the negative impact of globalization as including "the erosion of sovereignty, especially on economic and financial matters, as a result of the imposition of models, strategies and policies of development on African countries by the International Monetary Fund, the World Bank and the World Trade Organization." Ibrahim concludes that "globalization for [the] most part does not facilitate the establishment of the economic conditions necessary for genuine democracy and good governance to take solid roots and thrive."[7] In addition, Ibrahim states that as a result of the "cultural domination from outside that goes with globalization, African countries are rapidly losing their cultural identities and therefore their ability to interact with other cultures on an equal and autonomous basis."[8] Thus, the concept and manifestations of globalization remain complex and contentious, including their influence on religions worldwide.

Globalization significantly affects Yoruba women in religions on the African continent and in the diaspora. The impact of globalization on Yoruba women can be discerned in cultural erosion and heightened immersion in globalized popular culture disseminated by media. Moreover, in Nigeria there is dwindling appreciation of African cultural values such as respect and hospitality in interpersonal relations. The outcome of these developments is a lack of transmission of Yoruba values in the socialization of children. On the other hand, Yoruba women who are adherents of Yoruba religion experience globalization through opportunities to interact with adherents of Yoruba religion in the diaspora for the purposes of social networking and religious mentorship. Oftentimes, this has resulted in international travels for Yoruba women. Moreover, as a consequence of globalization, women who are active in Yoruba religion have had opportunities to conduct commercial ventures such as the sale of beaded handicrafts, traditional batik, and items such as kola nut and bitter kola to orisa worshippers in the diaspora.

Globalization and Religion

Religion is an agent of globalization in structure and practice. The relationship between religion and globalization is marked by tension, though these forces operate as partners in some settings. Religion and religious organizations are influential throughout the world, while "religions previously isolated from one another . . . now have regular and unavoidable contact."⁹ Globalization serves religion through its many tools of communication and travel, such as information technology, migration, and the media. "For example, websites provide information and explanations about different religions," while videos and television supply "visual religious teachings and practices."¹⁰

According to the sociologist David Lehmann, the interaction between religion and globalization manifests itself in two ways: one, it "brings old practices to new groups in new settings" ("disembedding" the practices and beliefs from their indigenous setting); and two, it "intensifies transnational links among groups similar in their practices, and creates networks and sometimes even tightly-knit communities of people" across vast distances and across "boundaries of language, ethnicity and race."¹¹ Both manifestations of globalization noted by Lehmann are true for Yoruba religion in Nigeria and the diaspora, especially in the existence and relevance of African-derived religions such as Santería, Candomblé, and Haitian Vodou in the diaspora and increasing connections of Yoruba priestesses and priests with orisa worshippers throughout the world. The spread of religions is predicated on human agency, which is also crucial to the process of globalization. However, the process of globalization often threatens the distinctive features of a religion, and this results in tensions that may be resolved through syncretism (blending elements of different religions) or adaptations. Thus, any religion that is affected by the process of globalization cannot remain static. As noted by the religious studies scholar Asonzeh Ukah, "In the last four centuries—or in the course of all the phases of interpenetration of Africa...—African religions and other religious systems derived from them have crossed boundaries, deserts and oceans drawing diverse populations and cultures in Europe, the Americas, parts of Asia—and of course Africa itself—into a unique globalized religioscape. Thus, African religions are an important structure and vehicle of contemporary globalization."¹²

Globalization and Yoruba Religion

The globalization of Yoruba religion may be attributed to many interrelated factors. The Yoruba diaspora scholar Olabiyi Babalola Yai identifies three phases in the globalization of Yoruba religious traditions: West African, Atlantic, and Post-Atlantic.¹³

The West African period involved social interactions, including commercial activities and the spread of Yoruba religion, among different neighboring societies, such as those of the Edo, Yagba, Itsekiri, Nupe, Ibariba, Igbo, Igala, Fon, Ewe, Gun, Akan, and others.[14] Influences of Yoruba culture and religious traditions survive among these West African peoples. This is especially true of Ifa divination practices, which could be described as "the most 'globalized' indigenous religious tradition in West Africa."[15] Additionally in West Africa, Yoruba religion encountered Islam through the trans-Saharan trade, as reflected in the content of Ifa, in which there is a chapter titled "Odù Ìmàle," the Muslim chapter, also called "Odù Òtúá."[16]

The Atlantic period refers to the experiences of Yoruba people during the years of the transatlantic slave trade and enslavement in the New World. It was a horrific collective experience, and Yoruba utilized survival tactics to preserve themselves and their Yoruba religion. As we have seen, Santería, Candomblé, Haitian Vodou, Orisha (Shango) in Trinidad and Tobago, and other African-derived religions were developed during the Atlantic period through the interaction and blending of Yoruba religion with the religions of enslaved Central Africans, other West Africans, and religions of indigenous Americans within a context of Catholic European colonialism.[17] These religions have many aspects that are derivatives of Yoruba worldview and religious practices, including deities, language of worship, music, songs and incantations, and dance.[18]

The Post-Atlantic period began in the late twentieth century, approximately in the 1980s, with the more recent diaspora of Yoruba throughout the world as well as converts to Yoruba religion coming to visit or live in Yorubaland in order to learn and be initiated in the religion. Yoruba religion as it is practiced in Yorubaland exists in the diaspora, with investments of time, intelligence, and money by cultic functionaries of Yoruba religion from Nigeria. The Post-Atlantic period involves converts to Yoruba religion from among Yoruba people, other Africans on the continent, and in the diaspora, people with African and non-African ethnic backgrounds.[19]

These three periods delineated by Olabiyi Babalola Yai are connected by migration, education, media, and transborder economics that have variously influenced the globalization of Yoruba religion. In addition, tourism and the use of new media technologies have facilitated the introduction of Yoruba belief systems and practices to the countries of the diaspora. Worthy of mention is the recognition and declaration of the Osun-Osogbo Sacred Grove as a World Heritage site and Ifa oracular practice as an Intangible Cultural Heritage of Humanity by UNESCO.[20]

Globalization as Experienced by Women in Yoruba Religion

Women encounter and facilitate globalization through Yoruba religion in diverse ways. Female adherents, who may be priestesses of an orisa or who may be worshippers, are involved in the sale of religious items such as kola nuts, alligator pepper, and fashion items on the internet. Moreover, some women specialize in the prescription and sale through the internet of different types of herbs to heal ailments. Women's prominence in business enterprises is often an effective means of globally propagating, sustaining, and publicizing Yoruba religion. Examples of such enterprises include the Aṣẹ Ire website of Dr. Funlayo Easter Wood-Menzies (Iya Funlayo), an African American iyanifa and priestess of Ọbàtálá whom we met in chapter 5.[21] Through the site, she offers divination services (including orisa-inspired Tarot card readings) and spiritual counseling. Other examples of websites related to Yoruba commercial ventures include Yoruba Imports, which provides Yoruba artworks, religious items, and foods, soaps, and oils; Owa Afrikan Market, which provides items related to Ifa and orisa and African herbs used in Yoruba and Yoruba-derived religious rituals; and Orisha Marketplace, which offers herbs, consecrated orisa shrines, religious objects, medicines, charms, baths, prayer flags, sacred stones, and many other items.[22] Women play important roles in the administration and operation of these websites. Similarly, women leaders in Yoruba religion in the diaspora offer spiritual consultations and training in Europe, South America, and North America. Women operate websites where consultation services and sale of fashion items and religious paraphernalia in Yoruba religion are available.

Media may thus be described as contributing to the globalization of African religion. In addition to websites, these include print and electronic media and social media platforms such as Facebook, Instagram,

YouTube, and WhatsApp. Different apps have been developed to facilitate the globalization of Yoruba religion. It is now possible to have divination for clients on the telephone and/or through email, at a fee, which sometimes can be exorbitant.

Globalization affords women leaders in Yoruba religion from Yorubaland opportunities to mentor and guide adherents on the African continent and in the diaspora. Sometimes this may entail residency of the mentor (*ìyálóòsà*, mother of orisa) and instruction of her student (omo-oosa, child of orisa) during short visits or on a long-term basis. The relationship of these two persons is similar to that of mother and child. When residency is possible for a long period, the student gets to learn a great deal about Yoruba religion and culture by memorization and participation in ritual activities at different stages. Oftentimes for students who are in the diaspora, whether the mentor travels to a location in the diaspora or the student travels to Yorubaland, the time spent together physically is short. Attempts are made to impart as much knowledge as possible during such brief stays. Also, some women leaders of Yoruba religion from North America organize annual workshops, seminars, and competitions for young adherents of Yoruba religion in Osogbo to validate their self-esteem and knowledge in the face of intimidation from Christians and Muslims. This is especially desirable as youths who practice Yoruba religion in Nigeria are in the minority and may feel threatened by their counterparts in these other religions. Thus, women are at the forefront of the management of the effects of globalization on young adherents of Yoruba religion worldwide. However, these efforts, if not properly managed, may become avenues for the crass commercialization of Yoruba religion.

Commercialization is a process involving exchange of money in any currency for services rendered, and it may be abused. The commercialization of religion may manifest itself on two main fronts: charges for spiritual services that may include consultations, prayers, and offerings; and commercial businesses of different types that are conducted by religious bodies. These businesses may include ventures such as schools, water-packaging industries, and computer centers, plus sales of soap, anointing oils, and mantles to convey blessings. Individual members of any religion can engage in such commercial activities, and it will be construed as efforts to earn a living. However, when religious organizations embark on business ventures solely to make money, it distracts from spiritual goals that should be the major concern of religious bodies. The ultimate aim of the commercialization of religion is profit. The commercialization of religion is a reality in Nigeria and many African countries, and it cuts across religions. For example, Christian churches and Muslim organizations own universities in contemporary Nigeria, and the school fees are well beyond the reach of an average Nigerian because the aim is for the organization to make a profit.[23] Religion has become a lucrative business in Nigeria in which people pay for religious services rendered.

Moderate and oftentimes voluntary gifts are expected from the client to the priestess or priest in any religious setting of Yoruba religion, but exploitation is abhorred and discouraged. However, this has not totally eradicated instances of exorbitant charges for spiritual services in Yoruba religion, especially between priestesses and priests on the African continent and clients in the diaspora. But such actions are generally frowned upon and condemned. When evidence is convincing, sometimes disclaimers stating why other adherents of Yoruba religion should not have any dealings with such a person are posted on social media platforms.[24]

Conclusion

This chapter has highlighted women's agency and leadership roles in Yoruba religion in a globalized world. Globalization and religion are closely knitted and serviced through migration, communication, and the media. Globalization has facilitated the relevance and influence of Yoruba religion in the host societies in the diaspora, and women are at the forefront of this inventiveness.

Globalization is experienced by women in Yoruba religion through economic activities, women's leadership across nations as spiritual counselors, women's utilization of social media platforms, and women's religious mentorship of women and men between Yorubaland and the diaspora. Some challenges emerge for women from the globalization of Yoruba religion, including commercialization of religion and related abuses of trust concerning fees charged for divination consultation, initiation, and the sale of fake products. There are reports of sexual harassment in some instances, in which women are compelled to engage in sexual relations as an alleged prescribed requirement for initiation into orisa worship. Also, the lack of knowledge of Yoruba language and culture remains a formidable challenge to practitioners of Yoruba religion in the diaspora.[25] However, there are efforts being made to mitigate these challenges.

Yet the ease of communication and travel that are part of globalization have aided the spread of the knowledge of Yoruba language and culture worldwide. The economic potential of the export of religious items that are abundant on the African continent but are scarce on other continents has been facilitated by the technologies that promote globalization. Globalization is fostering lasting religious and social networks of women adherents of Yoruba religion across continents.

Conclusion

As this book has shown, gender is an important category in Yorùbá society, interpersonal relations, and religion, although it is complex and fluid in the people's daily life experiences. This position is contrary to the assertion by the sociologist Oyeronke Oyewumi that gender was introduced to the Yoruba when they encountered Western colonial powers.[1] Yoruba have always had gender constructions. This book has placed Yoruba gender relations in historical and social contexts to elucidate the complex dynamics of the influence of women in the Yoruba religious traditions—Yoruba religion, Christianity, and Islam.

As we have seen, Yoruba operate within a system of gender complementarity, which is based on notions of balance, so that neither of the sexes can be subsumed in the other. Yoruba gender constructions are informed by a socially diffused form of male dominance that is mitigated by the fact that Yoruba women have always been economically productive and active in society. Yoruba women's economic contributions and women's corresponding significance in Yoruba cosmological narratives provide women with a basis on which to assert their position as stakeholders in Yoruba society and religions. In the Yoruba culture and indigenous thought system, there is acknowledgment and appreciation of female leadership in religion as well as in other areas of society, including the marketplace and politics. The profound influence of the Yoruba culture's active gender roles for women is reflected in the roles of women in the three religious traditions under consideration in this book: Christianity, Islam, and the worship societies devoted to specific òrìṣà. While the coming of Christianity and Islam to Yorubaland has posed some significant challenges to this gender balance through the propagation of patriarchal gender roles, the resources within Yoruba culture have enabled women to contest the full acceptance of those new norms.

Women in Yoruba religion, Christianity, and Islam in Yorubaland utilize women's groups or associations (*egbẹ́*) for mobilization, social networking and support, and political influence. Such women's groups afford Yoruba women in these three religious traditions the opportunity to influence decisions within male-dominated religious and cultural structures that tend to ignore women's views and concerns. Additionally, Yoruba women utilize their group organizations to facilitate social networking for celebration during good times and solidarity and comfort during challenging times. Such groups are formed in Christian denominations, where women's associations serve as forums of interaction, and in Islamic organizations, where women gather in prayer societies (ẹgbẹ́ alasalatu). Diverse orisa worship sessions are enhanced by the singing and dancing of women's groups both on the African continent and in the diaspora. Unfortunately, the potential of women's groups to sponsor and sustain females in positions of leadership within male-dominated religious structures remains elusive at present, especially within Christian and Muslim religious institutions, though the establishment of independent prayer groups by women and their visibility in Yoruba society is a welcome development.

Motherhood, both biological and symbolic, continues to be exalted in the three religious traditions in Yorubaland and in the diaspora. Motherhood is a state of empowerment among the Yoruba, irrespective of religious affiliation, and thus represents a point of agreement among the three religions. This stance is recorded in the Yoruba people's oral genres, as exemplified in the following song (oríkì):

Ìyá ni wúrà íyebíye	Mother is gold and so precious
Tí à ko le f'ówo rà	that we cannot purchase with money.
O loyún mi f'ósu mèsán	She carried my pregnancy for nine months.
O pon mí f'ódun metà	She put me on her back for three years.

The expressed appreciation in this song is applicable to every Yoruba mother. Symbolic motherhood is a means to ameliorate the lack of children in a woman's life, usually through adoption. For the Yoruba, all women are mothers. In Yoruba religion, the Ìyà Mi group of powerful women (àjẹ́) symbolizes the zenith of motherhood and women's empowerment, which exerts profound influence on the people's outlook.

Women's economic productivity and independence in Yorubaland and in the diaspora undergirds women's religious leadership in Yoruba religions. The present reality of women as leaders in the Yoruba religious traditions confirms the overarching argument of this book that women in Yoruba religions have agency through religious roles and influence on issues of authority and gender relations because Yoruba women are income earners, traditionally in the markets but now in occupations afforded by urbanization, education, and globalization. Women's leadership roles bestow both religious and social responsibilities, and this cuts across the three religious traditions. Thus, women's independent economic ability serves as a potent basis on which to challenge patriarchy in religion and negotiate power in the structures of religion. This has implications for the education of females, which should be prioritized, because a well-educated woman is likely to attain economic power and social status in society. Consequently, education equips women to negotiate gender relations and gain appreciation as stakeholders, especially in religion.

However, women leaders in these three religious traditions encounter challenges of diverse types, which they negotiate by means of the Yoruba cultural paradigm of female assertiveness. For women leaders of Yoruba religion in Yorubaland, the challenge of established male-dominated authority structures is a reality. For example, no association of priestesses or women custodians of the Yoruba religious tradition exists currently. Moreover, the reluctance of the Nigerian government to recognize and give Yoruba religion the same respect accorded to Christianity and Islam, as manifested in public holidays on days of celebration, undermines the status of women leaders in Yoruba religion.

Women's involvement in scriptural interpretation and propagation in any religion constitutes an avenue for the empowerment of women. Yoruba religion is largely oral, and women are actively involved in the recitation of these oral genres. This bestows tremendous authority on women as they serve as custodians and make decisions on which genre to prioritize for each setting. Thus, women exert influence on the content and performance of Yoruba oral genres in ritual settings. However, there is controversy over the initiation and practice of women as priestesses of Ifa divination (*iyánífá*) in some traditions in the diaspora, particularly Santería.

Yoruba women leaders in Christianity and Islam face limitations and restrictions that can be traced to patriarchal scriptural interpretations and implementation, especially concerning women teaching theology to men and menstruation and women's access to sacred spaces in places of worship. Some feminist interpretations of scriptures in Christianity that appreciate women's roles can now be cited by Yoruba women, but more needs be done. Scriptural interpretation remains under male control in Islam as practiced in Yorubaland, although practices are modified by Muslim women through implementing Yoruba reliance on associations to facilitate women's leadership in women's prayer groups.

As initiated priestesses in Yoruba religion, women have access to the orisa and to *àṣẹ*—the power to make things happen—through prayers, recitations, offerings, and/or divination. In the diaspora, women serve as leaders in the practice of African-derived religions formed as a result of the movement of persons by the transatlantic slave trade. This is especially true of women's roles in the ritual spaces; for instance, priestesses are active participants and leaders in Santería, Candomblé, and Haitian Vodou. Women are diviners, custodians of tradition, sculptors, and painters, and they participate in the recitation of oral genres. Women feature prominently during religious festivals of Yoruba religion in the contemporary diaspora due to immigration. Women are religious leaders, as exemplified in women's headship of some *ilê* (houses of worship) in Candomblé.

The ordination of women is another possible means of empowering women in the ritual spaces in Christian denominations. Some churches in Yorubaland do ordain women, while others have yet to do so. However, an increasing number of women in all churches in Yorubaland feature in leadership capacities, though largely informally. Being called by the Holy Spirit to preach and/or prophesy, including receiving prophetic visions or dreams, remains the primary way some women become religious leaders in Christian churches in Yorubaland and in the diaspora. Therefore, women have more opportunities to exercise religious leadership in Pentecostal churches and African independent churches than as ordained women in denominations stemming from mission Christianity. Women who are the wives of male leaders in Pentecostal churches play honored roles as ordained ministers in those churches and denominations. Some women may become church pastors in Pentecostal denominations or leave denominations to found separate women's prayer groups. Women who are prophetesses in African independent churches have respected roles in those churches, and they may found and pastor their own churches. Islam does not have ordained clergy, although respected educated persons are asked to preach and lead the community in prayer. Muslim women take on these roles in women's worship groups.

Women leaders in Yoruba religion and African-derived religions have displayed economic entrepreneurship during the present era of globalization. Of note are commercial activities by some women leaders of Yoruba/Orisa religion on websites for the sale of ritual items, Yoruba-themed fashion, and spiritual readings and consultation for assistance. Some women leaders in Yoruba/Orisa religion in the diaspora engage in religious tourism and conduct tours of spiritual sites in Yoruba cities in Nigeria, thereby building bridges between adherents and admirers of Yoruba religion in Africa and the diaspora.

In sum, women have agency as they play different roles in their religions, and this has a profound influence on issues of power and gender relations in Yoruba religions. The Yoruba cultural template for women's gender roles has served as a tool for the effectiveness of women's active roles in religions in Africa and the diaspora. The influences of Yoruba women's roles in religions extend to other sectors of Yoruba society, including economics and fashion, even as it is their active participation in society and particularly the economic sphere that undergirds their power within religious traditions. This ongoing enterprise will probably continue to evolve as Yoruba women negotiate ascribed roles in these three religious traditions.

ACKNOWLEDGMENTS

I thank God for the opportunity to write another book and contribute to scholarly discourse on women in religion. The ultimate aim is to see women live as the creator purposed, in a joyful and free spirit, especially during worship to their creator.

I am grateful for the cooperation of my resource persons who were interviewed on women in Christianity, Islam, and Yoruba religion. I will mention with gratitude facilitators of such interviews to include Mr. Oluwaseun Grillo and Chief (Mrs.) Doyin Olosun-Faniyi (Yoruba religion), Professor Mrs. Sidikat Ijaiya and Mrs. Wulemot Motunrayo Olanrewaju (Islam), Prophetess Dorcas Obagbemiro and the Reverend Father Uchenna Nwosu (Christianity), and Dr. Funlayo E. Wood-Menzies (Yoruba religion in diaspora).

I register my profound appreciation to the editor of the Women in Religion series, Catherine Wessinger, for her significant editorial input throughout the process of writing this book. I value her utilization of the manuscript in her classes, which resulted in good feedback. The acquisition editor at New York University Press, Jennifer Hammer, has been very helpful, and I am grateful to her.

My appreciation goes also to Professor Jacob Kehinde Olupona, for his mentorship, insights, and support. I want to thank the anonymous readers of the manuscript for the useful feedbacks that added substance to the arguments of the manuscript.

Finally, my great appreciation goes to my children, Oluwatobiloba (God is great), Ifeoluwa (the will of God), and Ebunoluwa (the gift of God) for patiently bearing with my absence and encouragement on occasions when I was overwhelmed by this project. Their love and support made this project a success.

QUESTIONS FOR DISCUSSION

INTRODUCTION: WHY STUDY WOMEN IN YORÙBÁ RELIGIONS?

How did the transatlantic slave trade cause the spread of Yoruba religion across other parts of the world?

How do women serve as key sustainers of Yoruba religious traditions?

What profound changes did the introduction of Christianity and Islam bring to Yoruba religiosity?

What are some of the features of Yoruba religion?

CHAPTER 1: WOMEN'S FAMILY, ECONOMIC, SOCIAL, AND POLITICAL ROLES IN YORÙBÁLAND

How did the colonization and subjugation of Yorubaland by the British in the late nineteenth century affect the status of Yoruba women?

Give examples to buttress the assertion that women were active participants in the traditional Yoruba society.

Why are mothers idolized among the Yoruba? What is the implication of this for infertile women?

How do women's access to and dissemination of Yoruba oral genres constitute an avenue for empowerment?

What is *àṣẹ*? Is it different from *agbára*?

How does the Yoruba cyclical worldview encourage high ethical standards?

What does "respect" connote among the Yoruba?

CHAPTER 2: WOMEN'S LEADERSHIP IN RITUALS OF THE YORÙBÁ RELIGION

How is spirit possession manifested and understood in the rituals of Yoruba religion?

What does the yearly Itapa festival in Ilé-Ifẹ̀ signify?

How would you describe the role and status of priestesses in Yoruba worship sessions?

Who is the *arugbá* in Yoruba religion? What does her role indicate for gender classification among the Yoruba?

Discuss the dynamic position of the *awo* and knowledge acquisition and use in Yoruba religion.

Who are the àjẹ́ (the powerful mothers)? Would you agree that the àjẹ́ occupy a central position in Yoruba religion?

How does the Gẹ̀lẹ̀dẹ́ festival celebrate the powers of the "mothers"?

CHAPTER 3: YORÙBÁ WOMEN IN CHRISTIANITY

How has Yoruba religion and culture impacted the practice of Christianity and Islam among the Yoruba?

How do women create and utilize alternative spaces of power to function effectively within the churches among the Yoruba?

What roles do prophetesses play in the Celestial Church of Christ and the Eternal Sacred Order of Cherubim and Seraphim?

What are the social implications of women's leadership roles in religions among the Yoruba?

Discuss examples of women's groups (ẹgbẹ́) in religions and their influence on Yoruba societies.

What are the implications of the creation and relevance of independent women's prayer groups in Christianity for mainstream structures of Christian denominations among the Yoruba?

CHAPTER 4: YORÙBÁ WOMEN IN ISLAM

How has Yoruba religion and culture impacted the practice of Islam among the Yoruba?

How do women exercise agency and leadership in Islam among the Yoruba people?

How do Yoruba women create alternative spaces of power in Islam?

State and discuss the roles of the Muallimaat and the Amirah in Islam among the Yoruba.

What changes did Western education bring to Yoruba women's awareness in the practice of Islam in Yorubaland?

What do you think is the prospect of feminist interpretation of the Qur'an among Yoruba Muslim women?

Describe Yoruba Muslim women's activities in Yorubaland.

How has globalization influenced women's roles in Islam among the Yoruba people?

Discuss an example of a Muslim women's group among the Yoruba people.

CHAPTER 5: WOMEN AND THE YORÙBÁ RELIGIONS IN THE DIASPORA

How has the practice of Yoruba religion in the diaspora challenged the concept of what constitutes religion in these societies?

How has the practice and sustenance of Yoruba religion in diaspora aided migration of goods, services, and people?

State and discuss the two main strands of Yoruba religion as practiced in the diaspora.

What is the relation between Yoruba religion and African diaspora religions?

What are the social implications of private and public worship sessions in the diaspora?

How does the practice of Yoruba religion in the diaspora sustain the teaching and learning of Yoruba language?

What reasons can you adduce for the conversion of some African Americans and people of European descent to Yoruba religion in the diaspora?

Discuss how women leaders in Yoruba religion facilitated the surge in membership for orisa worship in the diaspora.

How is Yoruba religion propagated on the internet?

CHAPTER 6: WOMEN IN THE YORÙBÁ RELIGION AND GLOBALIZATION

What is your assessment of the interactions between Yoruba religion and globalization?

How have migration, education, media, and transborder economics influenced Yoruba religion?

How do women experience and participate in the globalization of Yoruba religion?

CONCLUSION

How can the viability of Yoruba culture as a platform to negotiate and promote gender equality in religions be sustained?

What changes do you envisage with the increase in women leaders in religions, with regard to policy formation and priorities?

What can women in other religions and cultures learn from women's status and activities in Yoruba religions and culture?

FOR FURTHER READING

Ashcraft-Eason, Lillian, Darnise C. Martin, Oyeronke Olademo, eds. *Women and New and Africana Religions*. Santa Barbara, CA: Praeger, 2010.

Clark, Mary Ann. *Where Men Are Wives and Mothers Rule: Santería Ritual Practices and Their Gender Implications*. Gainesville: University Press of Florida, 2005.

Drewal, John Henry, and Margaret Thompson Drewal. *Gẹlẹdẹ: Art and Female Power among the Yoruba*. Bloomington: Indiana University Press, 1983.

Gbadamosi, T. G. O. *The Growth of Islam among the Yoruba, 1841–1908*. London: Longman, 1978.

Harding, Rachel E. *A Refuge in Thunder: Candomblé and Alternative Spaces of Blackness*. Bloomington: Indiana University Press, 2000.

Johnson, Samuel. *The History of the Yorubas: From the Earliest Times to the Beginning of the British Protectorate*. 1921. Edited by Obadiah Johnson. Cambridge: Cambridge University Press, 2010.

Lawal, Babatunde. *The Gẹ̀lẹ̀dẹ́ Spectacle: Art, Gender, and Social Harmony in an African Culture*. Seattle: University of Washington Press, 1997.

Ogungbile, David O., ed. *African Indigenous Religious Traditions in Local and Global Contexts: Perspectives on Nigeria*. Lagos: Malthouse, 2015.

Olajubu, Oyeronke. *Women in the Yoruba Religious Sphere*. Albany: State University of New York Press, 2003.

Olupona, Jacob K., and Rowland O. Abiodun, eds. *Ifá Divination, Knowledge, Power, and Performance*. Bloomington: Indiana University Press, 2016.

Olupona, Jacob K., and Terry Rey, eds. *Òrìṣà Devotion as World Religion: The Globalization of Yoruba Religious Culture*. Madison: University of Wisconsin Press, 2008.

Peel, J. D. Y. *Christianity, Islam, and Oriṣa Religion: Three Traditions in Comparison and Interaction*. Oakland: University of California Press, 2016.

———. *Religious Encounter and the Making of the Yoruba*. Bloomington: Indiana University Press, 2000.

NOTES

NOTE ON THE SPELLING OF YORÙBÁ WORDS
1. Adetugbo, "Yoruba Language in Yoruba History," 176.
2. Simon Ager of Omniglot, email to the author, May 20, 2021.

INTRODUCTION
1. Akinyemi, "Deities."
2. Olupona, introduction to *African Spirituality*, xvii.
3. Wessinger, *Theory of Women in Religions*, 2, 15, 70–73.
4. For example, see Orisha Marketplace, http://orishamarketplace.com.
5. Olupona and Rey, introduction to *Òrìṣà Devotion as World Religion*, 4.
6. Ruether, "Christianity."
7. Wessinger, *Theory of Women in Religions*.
8. Olajubu, *Women in the Yoruba Religious Sphere*, 122.
9. Olademo, "Paradox of Love," 18.
10. Gbadamosi, *Growth of Islam among the Yoruba*; Kalu, *Christianity in West Africa*.
11. "Funmilayo Ransome-Kuti." Funmilayo Ransome-Kuti is the mother of the famous Nigerian musician Fela Anikulapo-Kuti, or Fela Kuti (1938–97).
12. Badejo, *Ọṣun Ṣẹ̀ẹ̀gẹ̀sí*.
13. Matory, *Sex and the Empire That Is No More*.
14. M. Clark, *Where Men Are Wives and Mothers Rule*, 30.
15. Oyewumi, *Invention of Women*; Olajubu, "Seeing from a Woman's Eye."
16. See the chapters in Lopes and Alvaré, *Not Just Good, but Beautiful*.
17. Apter, "Embodiment of Paradox," 221.
18. Wessinger, *Theory of Women in Religions*, 77–82.
19. Hallen and Sodipo, "Comparison of the Western 'Witch' with the Yoruba 'Aje,'" 5.
20. Pearce, "She Will Not Be Listened To in Public."
21. Oyewumi, *What Gender Is Motherhood?* 58.
22. Olajubu, *Women in the Yoruba Religious Sphere*, 64.
23. Ogungbile, "Religious Experience and Women Leadership in Nigerian Islam."
24. Friedl, *Women and Men*, 73.

CHAPTER 1. WOMEN'S FAMILY, ECONOMIC, SOCIAL, AND POLITICAL ROLES IN YORÙBÁLAND
1. The Egba are one of the Yoruba subgroups.
2. O. Ilesanmi, "Efunsetan Aniwura."

3. Africa Launch Pad, "Richest Women in Nigeria."
4. Olademo, *Gender in Yoruba Oral Traditions*, 5.
5. Sudarkasa, *Where Women Work*, 25.
6. "Yoruba."
7. Countries of the World, "Nigeria People 2020."
8. Parfitt, "Construction of Jewish Identities in Africa," 126; Johnson, *History of the Yorubas*, 21; Adetugbo, "Yoruba Language in Yoruba History."
9. "Yoruba Are 99.9% Identical to Igbos, Akan and Gaa-Adangbe."
10. Eltis, "Diaspora of Yoruba Speakers," 17.
11. Ojo, "Yorùbá Omo Odùduwà," 17.
12. Fabunmi, *Ife*, 11–23; Bascom, *Yoruba of Southwestern Nigeria*, 22–24; Falola and Heaton, *History of Nigeria*, 57; Rodney, *How Europe Underdeveloped Africa*, 145.
13. O'Hear, "Enslavement of Yoruba."
14. Johnson, *History of the Yorubas*, 567–70.
15. Olajubu, *Women in the Yoruba Religious Sphere*, 48.
16. Fadipe, *Sociology of the Yoruba*, 29.
17. Caldwell, Orubuloye, and Caldwell, "Destabilization of the Traditional Yoruba Sexual System," 234.
18. Author interviews with three Yoruba women in Abeokuta who are wives in three polygynous marriages about their experiences: Mrs. Fadeke Abiodun, Mrs. Shade Oluwasanmi, and Mrs. Wuraola Akanbi.
19. Ogunyemi, *Africa Wo/man Palava*; see also Ologundudu, *Cradle of Yoruba Culture*, 126.
20. Pearce, "She Will Not Be Listened To in Public."
21. Author interview with Mrs. Bose Folorunsho and Mrs. Tomilola Ayano of Ilorin, Kwara State, March 20, 2019; both women are childless in monogamous marriages.
22. M. Abimbola, "Role of Women in the Ifá Priesthood," 250.
23. Oyewumi, *What Gender Is Motherhood?*, 58.
24. Olajubu, *Women in the Yoruba Religious Sphere*, 8.
25. M. Clark, *Where Men Are Wives and Mothers Rule*, 39.
26. Oni-Orisan, "To Be Delivered," 27.
27. Oni, "Discriminatory Property Inheritance Rights," 33; Ajiboye and Yusuff, "Inheritance Rights, Customary Law and Feminization of Poverty," 127.
28. Oni, "Discriminatory Property Inheritance Rights," 32.
29. Oni, 33.
30. Ajiboye and Yusuff, "Inheritance Rights, Customary Law and Feminization of Poverty," 127.
31. Oni, "Discriminatory Property Inheritance Rights," 37, 41, 42.
32. Ajiboye and Yusuff, "Inheritance Rights, Customary Law and Feminization of Poverty," 122, 129; Oni, "Discriminatory Property Inheritance Rights."
33. Oni, "Discriminatory Property Inheritance Rights," 32, 33.
34. Olupona, "Yorùbá Goddesses and Sovereignty in Southwestern Nigeria."

35. Abiodun, "Hidden Power," 16.
36. Ogungbile, "Ẹẹ̀rìndínlógún," 190.
37. Abiodun, "Hidden Power," 29.
38. Olademo, *Gender in Yoruba Oral Traditions*.
39. Olupona with Ajíbádé, "Ẹkuǹ Ìyàwó."
40. Barber, *I Could Speak until Tomorrow*.
41. Olarinmoye, "Images of Women in Yoruba Folktales."
42. Akinsipe and Babarinde-Hall, "Dance in the Yoruba Family Rites of Birth, Marriage and Death."
43. Author interview with Yeye Chief (Mrs.) Doyin Olosun-Faniyi at the Susanne Wenger House, Ibokun Road, Osogbo, Nigeria, June 12, 2015, and January 4, 2017.
44. Topping, "Nigeria's Female Genital Mutilation Ban Is Important Precedent." See also Richards, "History Has Been Made."
45. Kandala et al., "Female Genital Mutilation/Cutting in Nigeria."
46. Kandala et al., 16. Statistics are not cited here for other zones in Nigeria.
47. Kandala et al., ix.
48. Onyeocha, "Formation of Character in Traditional Nigerian Moral Education," 79–80; Omoyajowo, "Role of Women in African Traditional Religion and among the Yoruba," 75–76.
49. Omoyajowo, "Role of Women in African Traditional Religion and among the Yoruba," 77.
50. Matory, *Sex and the Empire That Is No More*, 74, 139, 184, 185, 188, 189, 191–93, 198, 207, 215, 216.
51. Matory, 74, 139, 198, 207, 215, 216.
52. Olajubu, *Women in the Yoruba Religious Sphere*, 115.
53. Lawal, *Gẹ̀lẹ̀dẹ́ Spectacle*, 37.
54. M. Abimbola, "Role of Women in the Ifá Priesthood," 249–50.
55. M. Abimbola, 255.
56. M. Abimbola, 255.
57. M. Abimbola, 255.
58. Olupona and Abiodun with Afolabi, introduction to *Ifá Divination, Knowledge, Power, and Performance*, 1.
59. Abiodun, "Who Was the First to Speak?," 56.
60. Olupona and Abiodun with Afolabi, introduction to *Ifá Divination, Knowledge, Power, and Performance*, 1–3.
61. Abiodun, "Who Was the First to Speak?," 56.
62. W. Abimbola, *Ifá*, 12.
63. Ogungbile, "Ẹẹ̀rìndínlógún," 189–91; W. Abimbola, "Bag of Wisdom."
64. Ogungbile, "Ẹẹ̀rìndínlógún," 191, 196.
65. Ogungbile, 196.
66. Obanifa, "Obi Divination." See also Ologundudu, *Cradle of Yoruba Culture*, 176–80.
67. Idowu, *Olódùmarè*, 53.

68. Awoniyi, "*Omoluwabi*"; see also Afọláyan, "Ọmọlúwàbí (Ọmọlúàbí)."
69. Olupona, *City of 201 Gods*, 111.
70. Aluko, *Osomalo*, 6–7. See also Awe, "Yoruba Women in History"; and T. Ilesanmi, *Ipa ti awon Obinrin nko Lawujo Yoruba laye Atijo boti han ninu Litereso Atenudenu*, 24.
71. Arewa and Stroup, "Ogboni Cult Group (Nigeria)."
72. Cole, *Modern and Traditional Elites in the Politics of Lagos*, 16.

CHAPTER 2. WOMEN'S LEADERSHIP IN RITUALS OF THE YORÙBÁ RELIGION

1. Washington, *Our Mothers, Our Powers, Our Texts*, 33–34.
2. Abiodun, "Hidden Power," 19.
3. Author interview with Madam Ajiun Funke Adisa at the Erinle orisa shrine (ojuba) in Agbole Bameke Ijaiye, Abeokuta, July 23, 2019.
4. Weber, *Theory of Economic and Social Organizations*, 358.
5. Van Gennep, *Rites of Passage*, 34.
6. Matory, *Sex and the Empire That Is No More*, 184.
7. Abiodun, "Hidden Power," 10–15. Heterosexuality prevails among the Yoruba and has continued to do so. Though the existence of homosexuality may be a possibility, it is considered obscene, shameful, and offensive. In January 2014, a law was instituted in Nigeria that made homosexuality a crime. A person convicted in a secular court could be sentenced to up to fourteen years in prison. A person convicted of homosexuality in an Islamic court could be sentenced to twenty lashes with a cane. See Ajibade, "Same-Sex Relationship in Yoruba Culture and Orature"; Murdock, "Nigerians Applaud Anti-gay Law."
8. Olajubu, *Women in the Yoruba Religious Sphere*, 113.
9. Idowu, *Olódùmarè*, 18–21. Another version of the stories says that before Orisa Nla followed Olodumare's instructions to create the Earth, he got drunk and fell asleep. Then another orisa, named Odùduwà, completed the task of creating the Earth. Idowu, 22.
10. Lawuyi, "Obatala Factor in Yoruba History."
11. Author interview with Osunfunke Obitosin (age seventy) in Abeokuta, June 12, 2016. She is the chief priestess at Ojuba Obatala, Ijemo Alape, Abeokuta.
12. Author interview with Ibitooke Amoke Badru (age sixty-five) in Abeokuta, June 12, 2016. She is Iyalode Onisegun of Erunwon, Abeokuta.
13. For example, see Udobang, "How Nigeria's Millennial Priestess Is Revitalizing Spirituality"; Adjovi, "My Life as a Millennial Yoruba Priestess."
14. Oladẹmọ, "Women in Yoruba and Igbo Spirituality."
15. M. Abimbola, "Role of Women in the Ifá Priesthood," 256.
16. Witte, "Fishes of the Earth," 161–62.
17. Hoad, *African Intimacies*, 35.
18. Author interview with Agbaakin Sunday Oyelade (age sixty-eight) in Abeokuta, June 15, 2016. He is a custodian of tradition at Itokun, Abeokuta.

19. "Erinle."
20. Author interview with Mr. Saidi Osunibi, an asogun at the ojuba Erinle Ijaiye, Abeokuta, August 12, 2016.
21. Probst, *Osogbo and the Art of Heritage*.
22. Olademo, *Gender in Yoruba Oral Traditions*, 41.
23. Author interview with Osunfunke Obitosin.
24. See, for example, discussions in Abiodun, "Women in Yoruba Religious Images," 4; Awolalu and Dopamu, *West African Traditional Religion*, 54; Crumbley, "Impurity and Power."
25. Olajubu, *Women in the Yoruba Religious Sphere*, 22–23.
26. Olajubu, "Seeing from a Woman's Eye."
27. Author interview with Iya Agan, Iya Oloya, Idayat Irele (age forty-eight) of Okeipa Area, Lagos, December 5, 2015.
28. There have been consistent efforts urging President Muhammadu Buhari of Nigeria to send an executive bill to the National Assembly to declare August 20 every year as Isese Day and a public holiday to celebrate traditional religions across the country. Buhari has been president of Nigeria from 2015 to the present (2021).
29. Author interview with Aina Ogunsanya (age forty-nine), an Ifa priest-babalawo, in Abeokuta, June 16, 2016.
30. Lawal, *Gẹ̀lẹ̀dẹ́ Spectacle*, 291.
31. Abiodun, "Hidden Power," 19.
32. Drewal, "Art and the Perception of Women in Yorùbá Cultures," 549.
33. Lawal, *Gẹ̀lẹ̀dẹ́ Spectacle*, 267.
34. Abiodun, "Hidden Power," 19.
35. Lawal, *Gẹ̀lẹ̀dẹ́ Spectacle*, 31.
36. Morton-Williams, "Àtíngà Cult among the Southwestern Yoruba."
37. Olademo, "Paradox of Love."
38. Eboiyebi, "Convicted without Evidence," 251.
39. Eboiyebi, 255.
40. Eboiyebi, 255.
41. Eboiyebi, 257–58.
42. Lawal, *Gẹ̀lẹ̀dẹ́ Spectacle*, 46–48; Drewal and Drewal, *Gẹlẹdẹ*, 227; Willis, *Masquerading Politics*, 40–41.
43. Lawal, *Gẹ̀lẹ̀dẹ́ Spectacle*, 48–49.
44. Lawal, 49–50.
45. Lawal, 39.
46. Lawal, 39–40.
47. See Drewal, "Yoruba Gelede Masquerade"; Drewal, "Art and the Perception of Women in Yorùbá Cultures"; Drewal and Drewal, *Gẹlẹdẹ*; Lawal, *Gẹ̀lẹ̀dẹ́ Spectacle*, 71.
48. Lawal, *Gẹ̀lẹ̀dẹ́ Spectacle*, 71.
49. Lawal, 71, 73.
50. Lawal, 74–75.

51. Lawal, 75.
52. Author interview with Mohammed Adegboyega (age fifty-five), in Abeokuta, June 15 and September 30, 2016. He is a priest of Gelede termed *Ogalagbo Onigelede* (Ogalabo the carrier of Gelede) and an artisan by profession.
53. Author interview with Waheed Balogun (age sixty-three), in Abeokuta, June 16 and September 28, 2016. He is the Jagunnailu ago-egun (Jagunna of egun [ancestral cult] cult) of Gelede and a retired footballer of the Abiola Super Babes. I wish to acknowledge the significant assistance received on the fieldwork from Mr. Seun Grillo.
54. Author interview with Mohammed Adegboyega.
55. Author interview with Waheed Balogun.
56. Lawal, *Gẹ̀lẹ̀dẹ́ Spectacle*, 79.
57. Drewal, "Art and the Perception of Women in Yoruba Culture," 557.
58. Drewal, 553–54.
59. M. Abimbola, "Role of Women in the Ifá Priesthood," 248.

CHAPTER 3. YORÙBÁ WOMEN IN CHRISTIANITY

1. Canaan Ministries, "Focus"; Rhema Chapel International Churches Agege, "About Us."
2. Redeemed Christian Church of God, www.rccg.org.
3. Daughters of Deborah International Ministry, www.facebook.com/Daughters-of-Deborah-Intl-Ministry-657452060932577/.
4. Olademo, "New Dimensions in Nigerian Women's Pentecostal Experience," 65.
5. Omotoye, *Christianity as a Catalyst*, 4.
6. Igenoza, *Polygamy and the African Churches*, 32.
7. Peel, *Christianity, Islam, and Orișa Religion*, 6.
8. Olajubu, *Women in the Yoruba Religious Sphere*, 1.
9. Olajubu, "Seeing from a Woman's Eye"; Logan, *From Women's Experience to Feminist Theology*; Adewale et al., *Biblical Studies and Feminism in the African Context*; Mercy Oduyoye, *Daughters of Anowa*.
10. Olajubu, *Women in the Yoruba Religious Sphere*, 58–59.
11. Olajubu, 56; Adogame, "Engaging the Rhetoric of Spiritual Warfare," 498.
12. Ukpong, *Nigerian Pentecostalism*, 75.
13. Okure, "Unwise Words in a Wise Word," 18–19; Oduyoye and Kanyoro, *Will to Arise*; Akintunde, *Lukan Narratives about Women*.
14. Modupe Oduyoye, *Planting of Christianity in Yorubaland*, 61.
15. A Nun's Life Ministry, "What Is the Difference between a Sister and a Nun?"
16. Wallace, "Catholic Women and the Creation of a New Social Reality," 27.
17. Wallace, "Social Construction of a New Leadership Role," 33.
18. "Call of Their Own."
19. Wessinger, *Theory of Women in Religions*, 137–40.
20. O'Connell and Dulle, "Pope Francis Has Set Up a New Commission."
21. McElwee, "Francis Creates New Women Deacons Commission."

22. Glatz, "Pope Francis: More Must Be Done to Include Women."
23. McElwee, "Francis Officially Creates Catholic Ministry of Catechist."
24. Author interview with the Reverend Father Lawrence Adekunle Abiona, principal of St. Joseph Centenary Catholic College, Ilorin, Kwara State, Nigeria, May 19, 2016, and May 17, 2021; author interview with catechist Mrs. Dupe Folashade Omole, May 17, 2021.
25. Author interview with the Reverend Father Uchenna Nwosu, St. Thomas Aquinas Catholic chaplaincy, University of Ilorin.
26. "Mothering Sunday" is a British term for Mother's Day.
27. Author interview with Reverend Sister Irene Mildred Anaeke, Department of Religion and Human Values, University of Cape Coast, Ghana, May 6, 2016; also author interviews with the Reverend Father Uchenna Nwosu and Sisters Josefa Umeugo and Cynthia Mbamalu of the St. Thomas Aquinas Catholic chaplaincy, University of Ilorin, minicampus, May 17, 2021, and June 27, 2020.
28. Author interview with the Reverend Father Lawrence Adekunle Abiona. See also Olateju and Olusegun, "Chieftancy Titles in Yorubaland," 86.
29. Ajayi, "Place of Ogbomoso," 17.
30. Nigerian Baptist Convention, www.nigerianbaptist.org.
31. Nigerian Baptist Convention, "Highlights on History."
32. Ayegboyin, "Women in the Nigerian Baptist Convention," 145.
33. Ayegboyin, 152.
34. Author interview with Pastor (Mrs.) Abigail Adedayo, Minister of Counseling and Administration, Associate Pastor, First Baptist Church, Abuja, Nigeria, May 25, 2016.
35. Author interview with Reverend (Mrs.) Olayemi Titilope Aderibigbe, Church Pastor, Ijero Baptist Church, Apapa Road, Ebute-Meta, Lagos, Nigeria, May 19, 2016.
36. Author interview with Reverend (Mrs.) Olayemi Titilope Aderibigbe.
37. Author interview with Mr. John Fashiku, Elder, Emmanuel Baptist Church, Ilorin, Nigeria, May 23, 2016.
38. Osun, "Christ Apostolic Church of Nigeria"; Adamolekun, "Historical Account of the Advent and Growth of Christ Apostolic Church"; Omoyajowo, *Cherubim and Seraphim*; Adogame, *Celestial Church of Christ*.
39. Olajubu, *Women in the Yoruba Religious Sphere*, 55.
40. Author interview with Dr. Oyewole Ogunbiyi, Department of Religions, University of Ilorin, and member of Cherubim and Seraphim Church, June 27, 2020.
41. Omotoye, "Pentecostalism and the Yoruba Worldview."
42. Ayegboyin, "But Deliver Us from Evil," 37.
43. MFM Women Foundation, www.mfmprovidence.org.
44. Pastor (Mrs) Foluke Adenike Adeboye, https://faadeboye.com.
45. Ukah, "Roots and Goals."
46. For example, see the video RCCG, "Thanksgiving Service."
47. Feast of Esther, "About Feast of Esther"; see also the video Orogun, "Feast of Esther."

48. RCCG Solution Centre, "School of Disciples (SOD)"; Redeemed Christian Bible College, www.rcbc.edu.ng.
49. Redeemed Christian Church of God Victory Centre, "Good Women Fellowship."
50. Author interview with Associate Pastor (Mrs.) Julie Ileuma of the Redeemed Church of God, Abuja, June 4, 2016.
51. Peel, *Christianity, Islam, and Orișa Religion*, 138.
52. See Busola Olotu's Blog, https://busolaolotu.wordpress.com; Olademo, "New Dimensions in Nigerian Women's Pentecostal Experience."

CHAPTER 4. YORÙBÁ WOMEN IN ISLAM

1. Author interview with Dr. (Mrs.) Hassanat Funmilayo Abubakar-Hamid, Lecturer, Department of Arabic, University of Ilorin, Ilorin, Nigeria, August 31, 2019.
2. Gbadamodsi, *Growth of Islam among the Yoruba*, 14.
3. Hiskett, *Development of Islam in West Africa*, 113.
4. Adelowo, "Imperial Crises and Their Effect on the Status of Islam."
5. Peel, *Religious Encounter and the Making of the Yoruba*, 187.
6. P. Clark, *West Africa and Islam*, 225; Oyewole, "Humuani's Life Is a Pride to Muslims."
7. Wadud, *Qur'an and Woman*.
8. The Noble Qur'an, Surah 49:13, Sahih International, https://quran.com/49.
9. The Noble Qur'an, Surah 33:35, Sahih International, https://quran.com/33.
10. Hadith 1912 in Tirmithi, *Sunanu Tirmithi*, 318. English translation kindly provided by Dr. Sulayman Adeniran Shittu, University of Ilorin.
11. Author interview with Mrs. Wulemat Motunrayo Olanrewaju, the Atesinse Adinni, Asalatu Laola and Iya Adinni at Oke Aluko Street, Ilorin, August 22, 2019.
12. The Noble Qur'an, Surah 4:34, Sahih International, https://quran.com/4/34.
13. Sabbah, *Woman in the Muslim Unconscious*, 45.
14. Mernissi, *Women's Rebellion and Islamic Memory*, 111.
15. Olanipekun, "Women and Mosque Attendance in Islam."
16. Mernissi, *Women's Rebellion and Islamic Memory*, 15, 38; Mernissi, *Beyond the Veil*; Sabbah, *Woman in the Muslim Unconscious*; Shaarawi, *Harem Years*; Wadud, *Qur'an and Woman*.
17. Wadud, *Qur'an and Woman*, 29.
18. Rufai, "Rethinking the Proliferation of Muslim Chieftancy Titles."
19. Fateh al-Bari, vol. 1: 177; also author interview with Dr. Mrs. Hassanat Funmilayo Abubakar-Hamid.
20. L. Clarke, "Women in Islam," 231–32.
21. Author interview with Alhaja Sikiratu Saliu, clerk at the Faculty of Law, University of Ilorin, May 17, 2021.
22. Author interview with Olori (Queen) Roheemat Olabimpe Adeyemi, the Iya Adinni, Anwarul Islam Society of Nigeria, Igboho branch, Oyo State, Department of Linguistics, University of Ilorin, Nigeria, August 25, 2019; author interview with Mrs. Wulemat Motunrayo Olanrewaju.

23. Author interview with Professor (Mrs.) Sidikat Ijaiya, telephone conversation in Ilorin, Kwara State, Nigeria, August 11, 2019; author interview with Dr. (Mrs.) Modinat Abdulraheem, University of Ilorin, Ilorin, Kwara State, Nigeria, August 31, 2019; author interview with Dr. (Mrs.) Barakat Raji, Faculty of Law, University of Ilorin, the current coordinator of University of Ilorin Muslim Ladies Circle, September 11, 2019; and author interview with Olori (Queen) Roheemat Olabimpe Adeyemi.
24. Author interview with Mrs. Wulemat Motunrayo Olanrewaju.
25. Kerr, "Islamic *Da'wa* amd Christian Mission."
26. Mohammed, introduction to *Education for All (Islamic Perspectives)*, 4.
27. Fahm, "Muslim Women and Social Responsibility in Nigeria," 180.
28. Fahm, 177.
29. Author interview with Professor (Mrs.) Sidikat Ijaiya.
30. Author interview with Mrs. Wulemat Motunrayo Olanrewaju.
31. Peel, *Christianity, Islam, and Orișa Religion*, 138.
32. Ogungbile, "Religious Experience and Women Leadership in Nigerian Islam."
33. Author interview with Professor David O. Ogungbile, Department of Religious Studies, Obafemi Awolowo University, Ile-Ife, Nigeria, by telephone, June 30, 2020.

CHAPTER 5. WOMEN AND THE YORÙBÁ RELIGIONS IN THE DIASPORA

1. Author interview with Dr. Funlayo E. Wood-Menzies, a postdoctoral scholar at the University of California, Santa Barbara, and scholar-priestess of Ase Ire, January 6, 2020; Ase Ire, "About Iya Funlayo."
2. Schmidt, "Discourse about 'Africa' in Religious Communities in Brazil."
3. Hucks, *Yoruba Traditions and African American Religious Nationalism*, 292.
4. Yai, "Yorùbá Religion and Globalization," 236.
5. Oroge, "Iwofa."
6. Olajubu, "Socio-cultural Analysis of Celibacy among the Yoruba," 275.
7. Gates, "How Many Slaves Landed in the U.S.?"
8. Oladimeji, "Barubas." Baruba, also known as Bariba people, are currently found in the Baruten local government area of Kwara State, Nigeria, and in neighboring Benin Republic.
9. Lovejoy, "Yoruba Factor in the Trans-Atlantic Slave Trade," 40, 43.
10. O'Hear, "Enslavement of Yoruba," 57. See also Ajayi and Smith, *Yoruba Warfare in the Nineteenth Century*, 108.
11. O'Hear, "Enslavement of Yoruba," 57.
12. Diakite, "Orisha Traditions in the West," 340.
13. K. Clarke, "Ritual Change and the Changing Canon," 288; Kamari Maxine Clarke, email message, January 12, 2019. Dr. Clarke's elaboration of the fourth category is greatly appreciated.
14. Epprecht, "Religion and Same Sex Relations in Africa," 515. See also Ajibade, "Same-Sex Relationships in Yorùbá Culture and Orature."

15. Ajibade, "Same-Sex Relationship in Yorùbá Culture and Orature."
16. See Connor and Sparks, *Queering Creole Spiritual Traditions*.
17. Vega, "Dynamic Influence of Cubans, Puerto Ricans, and African Americans," 321.
18. Vega, 322–23.
19. Hucks, "From Cuban Santería to African Yorùbá," 338.
20. Hucks, *Yoruba Traditions and African American Religious Nationalism*, 98–99, 106–7; Hucks, "From Cuban Santería to African Yorùbá," 340.
21. Hucks, *Yoruba Traditions and African American Religious Nationalism*, 106.
22. Hucks, 92–93, 106, 108–9; Hucks, "From Cuban Santería to African Yorùbá," 344–45.
23. Sandoval, *Worldview, the Orichas, and Santería*, 257.
24. Moussa Kone explains that *Lucumí* is the Spanish version of the word and that in Yoruba orthography, no *c* is used. Therefore, he prefers to spell the word as *Lukumí*. See "About the Term Lukumí."
25. M. Clark, *Where Men are Wives and Mothers Rule*, 26.
26. Clark, 77.
27. Matory, *Black Atlantic Religion*, 210.
28. Matory, 212.
29. Beliso-De Jesús, "Contentious Disporas."
30. Beliso-De Jesús, 831, 835.
31. Pessoa de Barros, "Myth, Memory, and History," 400.
32. Pessoa de Barros, 400.
33. Matory, *Black Atlantic Religion*, 1.
34. Hayes, "Serving the Spirits, Healing the Person," 103–4, 109–10.
35. Parés, "Birth of the Yoruba Hegemony in Post-Abolition Candomblé."
36. Hayes, "Serving the Spirits, Healing the Person," 108–9.
37. Hayes, 109.
38. Olosun, "Candomblé Priesthood."
39. Brown, *Mama Lola*, 4.
40. Brown, 220.
41. Bibbs, "Vodou," 78–80.
42. Bibbs, 80.
43. See the video Balogum, "Orisha Oshun."
44. Author interview with Chief Adigun Olosun, Baba Osun of Osogbo and a babalawo in Yoruba religion, October 8, 2016. He has been living in Germany since 2004.
45. African Studies Institute, Franklin College of Arts and Sciences, University of Georgia, http://afrstu.uga.edu.
46. Murphy and Sanford, introduction *Ọṣun across the Waters*, 4.
47. See the video Matthew 280811, "Oshun Festival in Matura."
48. Hunt, *Oyotunji Village*, 52.
49. See the festival schedule at Oyotunji African Village, www.oyotunji.org.
50. Odun Ifa and Oya Festival at Lite House, 50 Mother Gaston, Brooklyn, New York.

51. Author interview with Chief Adigun Olosun. See the video Vasquez, "First Yoruba Egungun Festival in Mexico of Baba Olosun."
52. "It's Tough Carrying Out Rituals in US, Europe."
53. "It's Tough Carrying Out Rituals in US, Europe."
54. Hucks, "I Smoothed the Way, I Opened the Doors," 22.
55. Olajubu, *Women in the Yoruba Religious Sphere*, 8.
56. Author interview with Chief Adigun Olosun. Ifa says, *Enu won là n boní ifè, enu won. Mo fúngbá mo fawo, enu won kòle rìí mi bájà, enu won*, meaning "It is their mouths we feed at Ife, I will give each one so their mouths would not abuse me." The initiation of a new babalawo must entertain many people, and there is feasting and happiness. A lot of prayers will be said for the initiate on that occasion.
57. Sandoval, *Worldview, the Orichas, and Santería*, 323.
58. For example, see Aṣẹ Ire, "About Iya Funlayo."
59. The apetebi cooks, attends to the children, may engage in economic activities, and participates in rituals.
60. For example, Mountain of Fire and Miracles Ministries, 10000 Kleckley Drive, Houston, TX 77075, USA; Winners Chapel International, 310 Fulton Avenue, Hempstead, NY 11550, USA; Redeemed Christian Church of God, 44–45 Geddes House, Kirkton North, Livingston EH54 6GU, United Kingdom.
61. Instagram: love_of_christ_generation, Rev. Esther Ajayi; Facebook: Esther Ajayi (Iya Adura), www.facebook.com/A.E.Ajayi.
62. Author interview with Dorcas Obagbemiro, Prophetess in Cherubim and Seraphim Movement Church, Branch 6, Ilorin, Kwara State, Nigeria, February 16, 2021.
63. Ansar ud Din Society of Nigeria, Washington, DC, Chapter, https://ansaruddeen-northamerica.com; Bow Central Mosque, www.bowcentralmosque.co.uk.
64. Olupona and Rey, *Òrìṣà Devotion as World Religion*.

CHAPTER 6. WOMEN IN THE YORÙBÁ RELIGION AND GLOBALIZATION

1. *Yèyé* means "mother" and is used to show respect for the person so addressed.
2. Olajubu, "Place of Susan Wenger's Art in Yoruba Religion." The blog of Moussa Kone, titled *Orisha Image*, contains photographs of the Osun-Osogbo Sacred Grove as well as of other aspects of Yoruba religion. See www.orishaimage.com.
3. I do not have convincing data on whether this Sonta is the same person as Sunta Serrano (Asunción Rodriguez Serrano) discussed in chapter 5.
4. Author interview with Yeye Chief (Mrs.) Doyin Olosun-Faniyi at the Susanne Wenger House, Ibokun Road, Osogbo, Nigeria, June 12, 2015, and January 4, 2017.
5. Raju and Bhaskar, "Impact of Globalization," 109.
6. Bhagwati, *In Defense of Globalization*, 47.
7. Ibrahim, "Impact of Globalization on Africa," 87.
8. Ibrahim, 88.
9. Golebiewski, "Religion and Globalization," 2.

10. Golebiewski, 2.
11. Lehmann, "Religion and Globalization," 415.
12. Ukah, "Religion and Globalization," 511.
13. Yai, "Yorùbá Religion and Globalization," 235–42.
14. Yai, 235.
15. Yai, 235.
16. Yai, 236; Apter, "Recasting Ifá," 44; Akinyemi, "Art, Culture, and Creativity," 352–53.
17. Yai, "Yorùbá Religion and Globalization," 237.
18. Sandoval, *Worldview, the Orichas, and Santería*, 357.
19. Yai, "Yorùbá Religion and Globalization," 238–39.
20. In 2005, UNESCO declared the Osun-Osogbo Sacred Grove as a World Heritage site and the Ifa divination system as an Intangible Cultural Heritage of Humanity. See UNESCO, "Osun-Osogbo Sacred Grove"; and UNESCO, "Ifa Divination System."
21. Aṣẹ Ire, https://aseire.com.
22. Yoruba Imports, https://yorubaimports.ecwid.com; Owa African Market, www.owamarket.com; Orisha Marketplace, http://orishamarketplace.com.
23. For instance, Covenant University in Ota, Ogun State, and Landmark University in Omu-Aran, Kwara State, established by the Living Faith Church; Bowen University in Iwo, Osun State, established by the Baptist Church; and Fountain University, established by the Islamic group NASFAT (Nasirillahi 'al Fatir Society of Nigeria).
24. Daniel, "Alaafin of Oyo Declares Ifa Priests Wanted"; see also "3 Ifa Priests Turned Yahoo Boys Arrested."
25. There is great commitment in the United States to the teaching and learning of Yoruba language; hence, the number of Yoruba language programs in the United States is now in the double digits compared to two decades ago, according to an unpublished paper by Ojo, "Yoruba Language Pedagogy in the United States of America."

CONCLUSION

1. Olajubu, "Seeing from a Woman's Eye"; Oyewumi, *What Gender Is Motherhood?*

BIBLIOGRAPHY

Abimbola, M. Ajisebo McElwaine. "The Role of Women in the Ifá Priesthood: Inclusion versus Exclusion." In *Ifá Divination, Knowledge, Power, and Performance*, edited by Jacob K. Olupona and Rowland O. Abiodun, 246–59. Bloomington: Indiana University Press, 2016.

Abimbola, Wande. "The Bag of Wisdom: Ọ̀ṣun and the Origins of Ifá Divination." In *Ọ̀ṣun across the Waters: A Yoruba Goddess in Africa and the Americas*, edited by Joseph M. Murphy and Mei-Mei Sanford, 141–54. Bloomington: Indiana University Press, 2001.

———. *Ifá: An Exposition of Ifa Literary Corpus*. Ibadan: Oxford University Press, 1976.

Abiodun, Rowland. "Hidden Power: Ọ̀ṣun, the Seventeenth Odù." In *Ọ̀ṣun across the Waters: A Yoruba Goddess in African and the Americas*, edited by Joseph M. Murphy and Mei-Mei Sanford, 10–33. Bloomington: Indiana University Press, 2001.

———. "Who Was the First to Speak? Insights from Ifá Orature and Sculptural Repertoire." In *Òrìṣà Devotion as World Religion: The Globalization of Yorùbá Religious Culture*, edited by Jacob K. Olupona and Terry Rey, 51–69. Madison: University of Wisconsin Press, 2008.

———. "Women in Yoruba Religious Images." *African Languages and Cultures* 2, no. 1 (1989): 1–18.

"About the Term Lukumí." *Orisha Image* (blog), December 13, 2018. www.orishaimage.com.

Adamolekun, Taiye. "A Historical Account of the Advent and Growth of Christ Apostolic Church in Akoko, Nigeria." *British Journal of Arts and Humanities* 8, no. 1 (August 2012): 73–86. http://docplayer.net.

Adelowo, E. Dada. "Imperial Crises and Their Effect on the Status of Islam in Yorubaland in the Nineteenth Century." *Journal of the Historical Society of Nigeria* 11, nos. 1–2 (December 1981–June 1982): 128–37.

Adetugbo, Abiodun. "The Yoruba Language in Yoruba History." In *Sources of Yoruba History*, edited by S. O. Biobaku, 176–204. Ibadan: Ibadan University Press, 1987.

Adewale, Olabiyi Adeniyi, D. D. Adegbite, Olatunde Abosede Oderinde, E. O. Adeogun, and A. O. Ojewole, eds. *Biblical Studies and Feminism in the African Context: In Honour of the Late Dorcas Olubanke Akintunde*. Ibadan: Nigerian Association for Biblical Studies–NABIS (Western Zone), 2012.

Adjovi, Laeila. "My Life as a Millennial Yoruba Priestess." *BBC News Outlook* (podcast), January 20, 2019. 23 mins. www.bbc.co.uk.

Adogame, Afe. "Engaging the Rhetoric of Spiritual Warfare: The Public Face of Aladura in Diaspora." *Journal of Religion in Africa* 34, no. 4 (November 2004): 493–522.

Adogame, Afeosemime U. *Celestial Church of Christ: The Politics of Cultural Identity in a West African Prophetic-Charismatic Movement*. Bern: Peter Lang, 1999.

Afọláyan, Michael Ọládẹ̀jọ. "Ọmọlúwàbí (Ọmọlúàbí)." In *Encyclopedia of the Yoruba*, edited by Toyin Falola and Akintunde Akinyemi, 223. Bloomington: Indiana University Press, 2016.

Africa Launch Pad. "Richest Women in Nigeria: Top 10 in 2020." Accessed May 12, 2020. https://africalaunchpad.com.

Ajayi, J. F. Ade, and Robert Smith, *Yoruba Warfare in the Nineteenth Century*. 2nd ed. Ibadan: Ibadan University Press, 1971.

Ajayi, S. Ademola. "The Place of Ogbomoso in Baptist Missionary Enterprise in Nigeria." *Ogirisi: A New Journal of African Studies* 8 (2011): 16–38.

Ajibade, George Olusola. "Same-Sex Relationships in Yorùbá Culture and Orature." *Journal of Homosexuality* 60, no. 7 (2013): 965–83.

Ajiboye, Olanrewaju Emmanuel, and Olabisi Sherifat Yusuff. "Inheritance Rights, Customary Law and Feminization of Poverty among Rural Women in South-West Nigeria." *African Journal for the Psychological Study of Social Issues* 20, no. 1 (2017): 119–31.

Akinsipe, Felix, and Bunmi Babarinde-Hall. "Dance in the Yoruba Family Rites of Birth, Marriage and Death." *International Journal of Integrative Humanism* 9, no. 1 (June 2018): 117–23.

Akintunde, Dorcas Olu. *The Lukan Narratives about Women: With Reference to Women's Role in Aladura Churches*. Ibadan: African Association for the Study of Religion, 2005.

Akinyemi, Akintunde. "Art, Culture, and Creativity: The Representation of Ifá in Yorùbá Video Films." In *Ifá Divination, Knowledge, Power, and Performance*, edited by Jacob K. Olupona and Rowland O. Abiodun, 340–58. Bloomington: Indiana University Press, 2016.

———. "Deities: The Òrìṣà." In *Encyclopedia of the Yorùbá*, edited by Tóyìn Fálọlá and Akíntúndé Akínyẹmí, 84–85. Bloomington: Indiana University Press, 2016.

Aluko, J. O. *Osomalo: The Early Exploits of the Ijesa Entrepreneur*. Ibadan: African Book Builders, 1993.

A Nun's Life Ministry. "What Is the Difference between a Sister and a Nun?" Accessed June 5, 2020. https://anunslife.org.

Apter, Andrew. "The Embodiment of Paradox: Yoruba Kingship and Female Power." *Cultural Anthropology* 6, no. 2 (May 1991): 212–29.

———. "Recasting Ifá: Historicity and Recursive Recollection in Ifá Divination Texts." In *Ifá Divination, Knowledge, Power, and Performance*, edited by Jacob K. Olupona and Rowland O. Abiodun, 43–49. Bloomington: Indiana University Press, 2016.

Arewa, Ojo, and Kerry Stroup. "The Ogboni Cult Group (Nigeria): Analysis and Interpretation of the Communicative Events Which Constitute the Behavior of Its Members." *Anthropos* 72, nos. 1–2 (1977): 274–87.

Aṣẹ Ire. "About Iya Funlayo." Accessed July 7, 2020. https://aseire.com.
Ashcraft-Eason, Lillian, Denise C. Martin, and Oyeronke Olademo, eds. *Women and New and Africana Religions*. Santa Barbara, CA: ABC-CLIO, 2010.
Awe, Bolanle, ed. *Nigerian Women in Historical Perspective*. Lagos: Sankore, 1992.
———. "Yoruba Women in History." *Gangan: A Magazine of Oyo State, Nigeria* 8 (October 1979): 14–15.
Awolalu, J. Omosade, and P. Adelumo Dopamu. *West African Traditional Religion*. Ibadan: Onibonje, 1979.
Awoniyi, Timothy A. "'*Omoluwabi*': The Fundamental Basis of Yoruba Traditional Education." In *Yoruba Oral Tradition: Poetry in Music, Dance and Drama*, edited by Wande Abimbola, 357–88. Ile-Ife: Department of African Languages and Literature, 1975.
Ayegboyin, Deji. "'. . . But Deliver Us from Evil . . .': The Riposte of the MFM and Its Implications for the 'Reverse in Mission.'" *Orita: Ibadan Journal of Religious Studies* 37, nos. 1–2 (June–December 2005): 33–64.
———. "Women in the Nigerian Baptist Convention: The Pace-Setter for Men in Missions." In *Women, Culture and Theological Education: Proceedings of West African Association of Theological Institutions (WAATI) Conference, Ilishan-Remo, Ogun State, Nigeria, 28 July–3 August, 1996*, edited by Protus O. Kemdirin and Mercy A. Oduyoye, 139–59. Enugu, Nigeria: West African Association of Theological Institutions, 1998.
Badejo, Diedre. *Ọ̀ṣun Ṣẹ̀ẹ̀gẹ̀sí: The Elegant Deity of Wealth, Power, and Femininity*. Trenton, NJ: Africa World, 1996.
Balogum, Santero. "Orisha Oshun—(Ochun)." YouTube, posted June 9, 2015. www.youtube.com/watch?v=bzeKIHDprCA.
Barber, Karin. *I Could Speak until Tomorrow: Oriki, Women, and the Past in a Yoruba Town*. Washington, DC: Smithsonian Institution Press, 1991.
Bascom, William R. *The Yoruba of Southwestern Nigeria*. New York: Holt, Rinehart and Winston, 1969.
Beliso-De Jesús, Aisha M. "Contentious Diasporas: Gender, Sexuality, and Heteronationalisms in the Cuban Iyanifa Debate." *Signs: Journal of Women in Culture and Society* 40, no. 4 (2015): 817–39.
Bhagwati, Jagdish. *In Defense of Globalization*. New York: Oxford University Press, 2004.
Bibbs, Susheel. "Vodou: A Heritage of Power." In *Women and New and Africana Religions*, edited by Lillian Ashcraft-Eason, Denise C. Martin, and Oyeronke Olademo, 75–97. Santa Barbara, CA: ABC-CLIO, 2010.
Brown, Karen McCarthy. *Mama Lola: A Vodou Priestess in Brooklyn*. 1991. Updated and exp. ed. Berkeley: University of California Press, 2001.
Caldwell, John C., I. O. Orubuloye, and Pat Caldwell. "The Destabilization of the Traditional Yoruba Sexual System." *Population and Development Review* 17, no. 2 (June 1991): 229–62.
"Call of Their Own, A: The Role of Deacons in the Church." *U.S. Catholic* 79, no. 6 (June 2014): 24–28. www.uscatholic.org.

Canaan Ministries. "Focus." Accessed June 5, 2020. www.canaanministriesintl.org.

Clark, Mary Ann. *Where Men Are Wives and Mothers Rule: Santería Ritual Practices and their Gender Implications*. Gainesville: University Press of Florida, 2005.

Clark, Peter B. *West Africa and Islam: A Study of Religious Development from the 8th to the 20th Century*. London: Edward Arnold, 1982.

Clarke, Kamari Maxine. "Ritual Change and the Changing Canon: Divinatory Legitimization of Yorùbá Ancestral Roots in Ọ̀yọ́túnjí African Village." In *Òrìṣà Devotion as World Religion: The Globalization of Yorùbá Religious Culture*, edited by Jacob K. Olupona and Terry Rey, 286–319. Madison: University of Wisconsin Press, 2008.

Clarke, Lynda. "Women in Islam." In *Women and Religious Traditions*, 3rd ed., edited by Leona M. Anderson and Pamela Dickey Young, 213–30. Don Mills, ON: Oxford University Press, 2015.

Cole, Patrick. *Modern and Traditional Elites in the Politics of Lagos*. Cambridge: Cambridge University Press, 1975.

Connor, Randy P., and David Hatfield Sparks. *Queering Creole Spiritual Traditions: Lesbian, Gay, Bisexual, and Transgender Participation in African-Inspired Traditions in the Americas*. New York: Routledge, 2013/2004.

Countries of the World. "Nigeria People 2020." Accessed May 12, 2020. https://theodora.com.

Crumbley, Deidre Helen. "Impurity and Power: Women in Aladura Churches." *Africa* 62, no. 4 (October 1992): 505–22.

Daniel, Komolafe. "Alaafin of Oyo Declares Ifa Priests Wanted, Sues them for Giving Oyinbo (Europeans) Titles." *Naija News*, June 24, 2017. www.naijaloaded.com.ng.

Diakite, Dianne M. Stewart. "Orisha Traditions in the West." In *African Indigenous Religious Traditions in Local and Global Context*, edited by David O. Ogungbile, 333–52. Lagos: Malthouse, 2015.

Drewal, Henry. "Art and the Perception of Women in Yorùbá Cultures." *Cahiers d'Études Africaines* 17, no. 68 (1977): 545–67.

———. "Yoruba Gelede Masquerade." *Art and Life in Africa*. University of Iowa Stanley Museum of Art. Accessed June 20, 2017. https://africa.uima.uiowa.edu.

Drewal, Henry John, and Margaret Thompson Drewal. *Gẹlẹdẹ: Art and Female Power among the Yoruba*. Bloomington: Indiana University Press, 1983.

Eboiyebi, Friday A. "Convicted without Evidence: Elderly Women and Witchcraft Accusations in Contemporary Nigeria." *Journal of International Women's Studies* 18, no. 4 (August 2017): 247–65.

Eltis, David. "The Diaspora of Yoruba Speakers, 1650–1865: Dimensions and Implications." In *The Yoruba Diaspora in the Atlantic World*, edited by Toyin Falola and Matt D. Childs, 17–39. Bloomington: Indiana University Press, 2004.

Epprecht, Marc. "Religion and Same Sex Relations in Africa." In *The Wiley-Blackwell Companion to African Religions*, edited by Elias Kifon Bongmba, 515–28. Oxford: Wiley-Blackwell, 2012.

"Erinle." *Ifamatters* (blog). Accessed July 27, 2020. https://ifamatters.wordpress.com.

Fabunmi, M. A. *Ife: The Genesis of Yoruba Race*. Lagos: John West, 1995.
Fadipe, N. A. *The Sociology of the Yoruba*. Ibadan: Ibadan University Press, 1970.
Fahm, AbdulGafar Olawale. "Muslim Women and Social Responsibility in Nigeria: Contributions of Muslim Women's Associations in Nigeria (FOMWAN)." *Alternation* 19 (2017): 175–91.
Falola, Toyin, and Matthew M. Heaton. *A History of Nigeria*. Cambridge: Cambridge University Press, 2008.
Falola, Toyin, and Matt D. Childs, eds. *The Yoruba Diaspora in the Atlantic World*. Bloomington: Indiana University Press, 2004.
Feast of Esther. "About Feast of Esther." Accessed December 27, 2018. www.feastofestherna.org.
Friedl, Ernestine. *Women and Men: An Anthropologist's View*. Prospect Heights, IL: Waveland, 1975.
"Funmilayo Ransome-Kuti: Nigerian Feminist and Political Leader." *Encyclopædia Britannica Online*. Accessed May 11, 2020. www.britannica.com.
Gates, Henry Louis, Jr. "How Many Slaves Landed in the U.S.?" *The African Americans: Many Rivers to Cross*. PBS. Accessed January 1, 2019.www.pbs.org.
Gbadamodsi, T. G. O. *The Growth of Islam among the Yoruba: 1841–1908*. London: Longman, 1978.
Glatz, Carol. "Pope Francis: More Must Be Done to Include Women in Church Bodies." Catholic News Service, November 18, 2019. www.ncronline.org.
Golebiewski, Daniel. "Religion and Globalization: New Possibilities, Furthering Changes." E-International Relations, July 16, 2014, 1–11. www.e-ir.info.
Griffith, R. Marie, and Barbara Dianne Savage, eds. *Women and Religion in the African Diaspora: Knowledge, Power, and Performance*. Baltimore: John Hopkins University Press, 2006.
Hallen, Barry, and J. Olubi Sodipo. "A Comparison of the Western 'Witch' with the Yoruba 'Aje': Spiritual Powers or Personality Types?" *Ife: Annals of the Institute of Cultural Studies* 1 (1986): 1–7.
Hayes, Kelly E. "Serving the Spirits, Healing the Person: Women in Afro-Brazilian Religions." In *Women and New and Africana Religions*, edited by Lillian Ashcraft-Eason, Denise C. Martin, and Oyeronke Olademo, 101–22. Santa Barbara, CA: ABC-CLIO, 2010.
Hiskett, Mervyn. *The Development of Islam in West Africa*. New York: Longman, 1984.
Hoad, Neville Wallace. *African Intimacies: Race, Homosexuality and Globalization*. Minneapolis: University of Minnesota Press, 2007.
Hucks, Tracey E. "From Cuban Santería to African Yorùbá: Evolutions in African American Òrìṣà History, 1959–1970." In *Òrìṣà Devotion as World Religion: The Globalization of Yorùbá Religious Culture*, edited by Jacob K. Olupona and Terry Rey, 337–54. Madison: University of Wisconsin Press, 2008.
———. "'I Smoothed the Way, I Opened the Doors': Women in the Yoruba-Orisha Tradition of Trinidad." In *Women and Religion in the African Diaspora: Knowledge,*

Power, and Performance, edited by R. Marie Griffith and Barbara Dianne Savage, 19–36. Baltimore: Johns Hopkins University Press, 2006.

———. *Yoruba Traditions and African American Religious Nationalism*. Albuquerque: University of New Mexico Press, 2012.

Hunt, Carl. *Oyotunji Village: The Yoruba Movement in America*. Washington, DC: University Press of America, 1979.

Ibrahim, Ahmadu. "The Impact of Globalization on Africa." *International Journal of Humanities and Social Science* 3, no. 15 (August 2013): 85–93.

Idowu, Bolaji E. *Olódùmarè: God in Yorùbá Belief*. London: Longman, 1962.

Igenoza, Andrew O. *Polygamy and the African Churches: A Biblical Appraisal of an African Marriage System*. Ibadan, Nigeria: African Association for the Study of Religions Publication Bureau, 2003.

Ilesanmi, Oluwatoyin Olatundun. "Efunsetan Aniwura: A Psycho-Historical Exploration of Women's Psychopathology." *International Journal of Information and Education Technology* 4, no. 2 (April 2014): 147–50.

Ilesanmi, T. M. *Ipa ti awon Obinrin nko Lawujo Yoruba laye Atijo bo ti han ninu Litereso Atenudenu*. Lagos: Department of African Languages and Literature, University of Lagos, 1987.

"It's Tough Carrying Out Rituals in US, Europe—Ifa Priests." *NigerianEye*, January 2014. www.nigerianeye.com.

Johnson, Samuel. *The History of the Yorubas: From the Earliest Times to the Beginning of the British Protectorate*. 1921. Edited by Obadiah Johnson. Cambridge: Cambridge University Press, 2010.

Kalu, Ogbu. *Christianity in West Africa: The Nigerian Story*. Ibadan: Daystar, 1978.

Kandala, Ngianga-Bakwin, Glory Atilola, Chibuzor Christopher Nnanatu, Emmanuel Ogundimu, Lubanzadio Mavatikua, Paul Komba, Zhuzhi Moore, and Dennis Matanda. "Female Genital Mutilation/Cutting in Nigeria: Is the Practice Declining? A Descriptive Analysis of Successive Demographic and Health Surveys and Multiple Indicator Cluster Surveys (2003–2017): Evidence to End FGM/C: Research to Help Girls and Women Thrive." Working Paper, February 2020, Population Council, New York, 2020. www.popcouncil.org.

Kasongo, Alphonse. "Impact of Globalization on Traditional African Religion and Cultural Conflict." *Journal of Alternative Perspectives in the Social Sciences* 2, no. 1 (2010): 308–22.

Kerr, David A. "Islamic *Da'wa* and Christian Mission: Towards a Comparative Analysis." *International Review of Mission* 89, no. 353 (April 2000): 150–71.

Lawal, Babatunde. *The Gẹ̀lẹ̀dẹ́ Spectacle: Art, Gender, and Social Harmony in an African Culture*. Seattle: University of Washington Press, 1997.

Lawuyi, O. B. "The Obatala Factor in Yoruba History." *History in Africa* 19 (1992): 369–75.

Lehmann, David. "Religion and Globalization." In *Religions in the Modern World: Traditions and Transformations*, 2nd ed., edited by Linda Woodhead, Paul Fletcher, Hiroko Kawanami, and Christopher Partridge, 407–28. London: Routledge, 2009.

Logan, Linda. *From Women's Experience to Feminist Theology.* London: Bloomsbury Academic, 2016.
Lopes, Steven, and Helen Alvaré, eds. *Not Just Good, but Beautiful: The Complementary Relationship between Man and Woman.* Walden, NY: Plough, 2015.
Lovejoy, Paul. E. "The Yoruba Factor in the Trans-Atlantic Slave Trade." In *Yoruba Diaspora in the Atlantic World*, edited by Toyin Falola and Matt D. Childs, 40–55. Bloomington: Indiana University Press, 2004.
Mahmood, Saba. *Politics of Piety: The Islamic Revival and the Feminist Subject.* Princeton, NJ: Princeton University Press, 2005.
Matthew 280811. "Oshun Festival in Matura." YouTube, posted March 15, 2013. www.youtube.com/watch?v=5A26IM5Iihw.
Matory, J. Lorand. *Black Atlantic Religion: Tradition, Transnationalism and Matriarchy in the Afro-Brazilian Candomblé.* Princeton, NJ: Princeton University Press, 2005.
———. *Sex and the Empire That Is No More: Gender and the Politics of Metaphor in Oyo Yoruba Religion.* 1994. Reprint, New York: Berghahn Books, 2005.
McElwee, Joshua J. "Francis Creates New Women Deacons Commission, Naming Entirely Different Membership." *National Catholic Reporter*, April 8, 2020. www.ncronline.org.
———. "Francis Officially Creates Catholic Ministry of Catechist, Open to Men and Women." *National Catholic Reporter*, May 11, 2021. www.ncronline.org.
McKenzie, Peter Rutherford. *Hail Orisha! A Phenomenology of a West African Religion in Mid-Nineteenth Century.* New York: Brill, 1997.
Mernissi, Fatima. *Beyond the Veil: Male–Female Dynamics in Muslim Society.* Cambridge, MA: Schenkman, 1975.
———. *Women's Rebellion and Islamic Memory.* London: ZED Books, 1996.
Mohammed, Jadé. Introduction to *Education for All (Islamic Perspectives): Being a Compilation of FOMWAN Education Workshop/Lecture Series, January 2000–June 2010, in Honour of Alhaja Lateefa M. Okunnu*, edited by Lateefah M. Durosinmi and Jadé Mohammed, 1–4. Utako, Abuja, Nigeria: FOMWAN National Education Committee, 2010.
Morton-Williams, Peter. "The Àtíngà Cult among the Southwestern Yoruba: A Sociological Analysis of a Witch-Finding Movement." *Bulletin de l'Institut Français d'Afrique Noire, Série B Sciences Humaines* 18 (1956): 315–34.
Murdock, Heather. "Nigerians Applaud Anti-gay Law as Islamic Court Hands Out 20 Lashes." *Christian Science Monitor*, January 17, 2014. www.csmonitor.com.
Murphy, Joseph M., and Mei-Mei Sanford. Introduction to *Ọṣun across the Waters: A Yoruba Goddess in Africa and the Americas*, edited by Joseph M. Murphy and Mei-Mei Sanford, 1–9. Bloomington: Indiana University Press, 2001.
Nigerian Baptist Convention. "Highlights on History." Accessed June 6, 2020. www.nigerianbaptist.org.
Obanifa, Babalawo. "Obi Divination: Facts on Obi Dida (Obi Divination)." Babalawo Obanifa's blog, April 2017. www.babalawoobanifa.com.

O'Connell, Gerard, and Colleen Dulle. "Pope Francis Has Set Up a New Commission to Study Women Deacons." *America: The Jesuit Review*, April 8, 2020. www.americamagazine.org.

Oduyoye, Mercy Amba. *Daughters of Anowa: African Women and Patriarchy*. New York: Orbis Books, 1999.

Oduyoye, Mercy Amba, and Musimbi R. A. Kanyoro, eds. *The Will to Arise: Women, Tradition, and the Church in Africa*. New York: Orbis Books, 1992.

Oduyoye, Modupe. *The Planting of Christianity in Yorubaland*. Ibadan, Nigeria: Day Star, 1969.

Ogungbile, David O., ed. *African Indigenous Religious Traditions in Local and Global Contexts: Perspectives on Nigeria*. Lagos: Malthouse, 2015.

———. "Ẹ́ẹ̀rìndínlógún: The Seeing Eyes of the Sacred Shells and Stones." In *Ọṣun across the Waters: A Yoruba Goddess in Africa and the Americas*, edited by Joseph M. Murphy and Mei-Mei Sanford, 189–212. Bloomington: Indiana University Press, 2001.

———. "Religious Experience and Women Leadership in Nigerian Islam." In *Islam in Africa South of the Sahara: Essays in Gender Relations and Political Reform*, edited by Pade Badru and Brigid Maa Sackey, 187–204. Lanham, MD: Scarecrow, 2013.

Ogunyemi, Chikwenye Okonjo. *Africa Wo/man Palava: The Nigerian Novel by Women*. Chicago: University of Chicago Press, 1996.

O'Hear, Ann. "The Enslavement of Yoruba." In *The Yoruba Diaspora in the Atlantic World*, edited by Toyin Falola and Matt D. Childs, 56–74. Bloomington: Indiana University Press, 2004.

Ojo, Akinloye A. "Yoruba Language Pedagogy in the United States of America: Retrospect, Prospects and Lessons for Nigeria." Unpublished paper, Institute of African Studies, University of Georgia, Athens, July 2015.

———. "Yorùbá Omo Odùduwà: Papers on Yoruba People, Language, and Culture by Yoruba Language Program Students." African Languages Program, University of Georgia, Athens, 1999. https://yorubafactfinder.files.wordpress.com.

Okure, Teresa. "Unwise Words in a Wise Word: Ephesians 5:21–33." In *Women in Religion and Culture: Essays in Honour of Constance Buchanan*, edited by Mercy Amba Oduyoye, 18–29. Ibadan, Nigeria: Sefer, 2007.

Olademo, Oyeronke. *Gender in Yoruba Oral Traditions*. Lagos: Centre for Black and African Arts and Civilization-CBAAC, 2009.

———. "New Dimensions in Nigerian Women's Pentecostal Experience: The Case of DODIM, Nigeria." *Journal of World Christianity* 5, no. 1 (2012): 62–74.

———. "The Paradox of Love: Women and Religion in Society." 136th Inaugural Lecture, University of Ilorin, June 27, 2013. Ilorin, Nigeria: The Library and Publications Committee, 2013. http://dowlv193zyfe6.cloudfront.net.

———. "Women in Yoruba and Igbo Spirituality." In *African Indigenous Religious Traditions in Local and Global Contexts: Perspectives on Nigeria*, edited by David O. Ogungbile, 303–12. Lagos: Malthouse, 2015.

Oladimeji, Debo. "The Barubas: One People, Two Countries." *The Guardian*, December 18, 2015. https://guardian.ng.

Olajubu, Oyeronke. "The Place of Susan Wenger's Art in Yoruba Religion: A Preliminary Survey." *IJELE: Art Journal of the African World* 5 (2002). www.africa knowledgeproject.org. Also available at https://studylib.net.

———. "Seeing from a Woman's Eye: Yoruba Religious Tradition and Gender Relations." *Journal of Feminist Studies in Religion* 20, no. 1 (2004): 41–60.

———. "A Socio-cultural Analysis of Celibacy among the Yoruba: Oyo Alafin's Servants as a Case Study." In *Celibacy and Religious Traditions*, edited by Carl Olson, 275–84. New York: Oxford University Press, 2008.

———. *Women in the Yoruba Religious Sphere*. New York: State University of New York Press, 2003.

Olanipekun, Shittu Tunde. "Women and Mosque Attendance in Islam." Accessed October 2, 2018. www.slideshare.net.

Olarinmoye, Adeyinka Wulemat. "The Images of Women in Yoruba Folktales." *International Journal of Humanities and Social Science* 3, no. 4 (February 2013): 138–49.

Olateju, Fola T., and Oladosu Olusegun. "Chieftancy Titles in Yorubaland (Nigeria, Africa) and Their Implication for the Growth and Tolerance among Christians and Muslims." *Asia Journal of Theology* 26, no. 2 (October 2012): 86–95.

Ologundudu, Dayo. *The Cradle of Yoruba Culture*. New York: Center for Spoken Words / Institute of Yorùbá Culture, 2008.

Olosun, Iyalorisa Melissa. "Candomblé Priesthood." Candomblé USA, June 8, 2008. https://candombleusa.wordpress.com.

Olúpònà, Jacob K. *City of 201 Gods: Ilé-Ifẹ̀ in Time, Space and the Imagination*. Berkeley: University of California Press, 2011.

———. Introduction to *African Spirituality: Forms, Meanings, and Expressions*, edited by Jacob K. Olupona, xv–xxxvi. New York: Crossroad, 2001.

———. "Yorùbá Goddesses and Sovereignty in Southwestern Nigeria." In *Goddesses Who Rule*, edited by Elisabeth Benard and Beverly Moon, 119–32. New York: Oxford University Press, 2000.

Olupona, Jacob K., and Rowland O. Abiodun, eds. *Ifá Divination, Knowledge, Power, and Performance*. Bloomington: Indiana University Press, 2016.

Olupona, Jacob K., and Rowland O. Abiodun with Niyi Afolabi. Introduction to *Ifá Divination, Knowledge, Power, and Performance*, edited by Jacob K. Olupona and Rowland O. Abiodun, 1–13. Bloomington: Indiana University Press, 2016.

Olúpònà, Jacob K., with Ṣọlá Ajíbádé. "*Ẹkún Ìyàwó*: Bridal Tears in Marriage Rites of Passage among the Ọ̀yọ́-Yorùbá of Nigeria." In *Holy Tears: Weeping in the Religious Imagination*, edited by Kimberly Christine Patton and John Statton Hawley, 165–72. Princeton, NJ: Princeton University Press, 2005.

Olupona, Jacob K., and Terry Rey. Introduction to *Òrìṣà Devotion as World Religion: The Globalization of Yorùbá Religious Culture*, edited by Jacob K. Olupona and Terry Rey, 3–28. Madison: University of Wisconsin Press, 2008.

———, eds. *Òrìṣà Devotion as World Religion: The Globalization of Yorùbá Religious Culture*. Madison: University of Wisconsin Press, 2008.

Omotoye, Rotimi William. *Christianity as a Catalyst for Socio-economic and Political Change in Yorubaland, Nigeria: An Account of a Church Historian*. 159th Inaugural Lecture of the University of Ilorin. Ilorin: University of Ilorin Press, 2015.

———. "Pentecostalism and the Yoruba Worldview: The Case of Mountain of Fire and Miracles Ministries, Nigeria." *International Journal of Religion and Spirituality in Society* 1, no. 2 (2011): 181–94.

Ọmọyajowo, Joseph Akinyẹle. *Cherubim and Seraphim: The History of an African Independent Church*. Lagos: NOK, 1982.

———. "The Role of Women in African Traditional Religion and among the Yoruba." In *African Traditional Religions in Contemporary Society*, edited by Jacob Kehinde Olupona, 73–80. St. Paul, MN: Paragon House, 1991.

Oni, Babatunde Adetunji. "Discriminatory Property Inheritance Rights under the Yoruba and Igbo Customary Law in Nigeria: The Need for Reforms." *IOSR Journal of Humanities and Social Science* 19, no. 2 (February 2014): 30–43.

Oni-Orisan, Adeola. "To Be Delivered: Pregnant and Born Again in Nigeria." PhD diss. University of California, San Francisco, 2018.

Onyeocha, Izu Marcel. "Formation of Character in Traditional Nigerian Moral Education." In *Identity and Change: Nigerian Philosophical Studies, I*, edited by Theophilus Okere, 70–91. Washington, DC: Council for Research in Values and Philosophy, 1996. www.crvp.org.

Oroge, E. Adeniyi. "Iwofa: An Historical Survey of the Yoruba Institution of Indenture." *African Economic History* 14 (1985): 75–106.

Orogun, Uvi. "The Feast of Esther—RCCG." YouTube, posted November 13, 2010. www.youtube.com/watch?v=tRqr_aYoPWY.

Oshun, Christopher Olubunmi. "Christ Apostolic Church of Nigeria: A Suggested Pentecostal Consideration of Its Historical, Organisational, and Theological Development, 1918–1978." PhD diss., Exeter College, University of Oxford, 1981.

Oyewole, Jadesola. "Humuani's Life Is a Pride to Muslims." *Vanguard* (Nigeria), February 28, 2014. www.vanguardngr.com.

Oyěwùmí, Oyèrónkẹ́. *The Invention of Women: Making African Sense of Western Gender Discourses*. Minneapolis: University of Minnesota Press, 1999.

———. *What Gender Is Motherhood? Changing Yorùbá Ideals of Power, Procreation, and Identity in the Age of Modernity*. New York: Palgrave Macmillan, 2016.

Parés, Luis Nicolau. "The Birth of the Yoruba Hegemony in Post-Abolition Candomblé." *Journal de la Société des Américanistes* 91, no. 1 (2005): 139–59.

Parfitt, Tudor. "The Construction of Jewish Identities in Africa." In *The Jews of Ethiopia: The Birth of an Elite*, edited by Tudor Parfitt and Emanuela Trevisan Semi, 11–24. New York: Routledge, 2005.

Pearce, Tola Olu. "She Will Not Be Listened To in Public: Perceptions among the Yoruba of Infertility and Childlessness in Women." *Reproductive Health Matters* 7, no. 13 (May 1999): 69–79.

Peel, J. D. Y. *Christianity, Islam, and Orișa Religion: Three Traditions in Comparison and Interaction*. Oakland: University of California Press, 2016.

———. *Religious Encounter and the Making of the Yoruba*. Bloomington: Indiana University Press, 2000.

Pessoa de Barros, José Flávio. "Myth, Memory, and History: Brazil's Sacred Music of Shango." Translated by Maria P. Junqueira. In *Òrìṣà Devotion as World Religion: The Globalization of Yorùbá Religious Culture*, edited by Jacob K. Olupona and Terry Rey, 400–415. Madison: University of Wisconsin Press, 2008.

Probst, Peter. *Osogbo and the Art of Heritage: Monuments, Deities and Money*. Bloomington: Indiana University Press, 2011.

Quadri, Y. A. "The Tijaniyyah in Nigeria." PhD diss., University of Ibadan, 1981.

Raju, M. Sreerama, and N. Udaya Bhaskar. "Impact of Globalization on Indian Higher Education and Universities Service Quality." In *Trends, Challenges & Innovations in Management*, vol. 2, edited by Ramesh Kumar Miryala and Ravi Aluvala, 109–18. Hyderabad, India: Zenon, 2015.

RCCG. "Thanksgiving Service—RCCG Holy Ghost Congress 2018—Glory Ahead." YouTube, streamed live December 9, 2018. www.youtube.com/watch?v=OnkUQL-FgwQ.

RCCG Solution Centre. "The School of Disciples (SOD): Department Overview." Accessed December 27, 2018. https://rccgsolutioncentre.org.

Redeemed Christian Church of God Victory Centre. "Good Women Fellowship." Accessed December 27, 2018. http://rccgvictorycentre.com.

Rhema Chapel International Churches Agege. "About Us." Accessed August 5, 2020. https://rhemachapelagege.org.

Richards, Kimberly. "History Has Been Made: Female Genital Mutilation Banned in Nigeria." *A Plus*, June 3, 2015. https://aplus.com.

Rodney, Walter. *How Europe Underdeveloped Africa*. London: Bogle-L'Ouverture, 1973.

Ruether, Rosemary Radford. "Christianity." In *Women in World Religions*, edited by Arvind Sharma, 207–33. Albany: State University of New York Press, 1987.

Rufai, Saheed Ahmad. "Rethinking the Proliferation of Muslim Chieftancy Titles in Contemporary Yorubaland (Southwestern Nigeria) for an Effective Administration of Muslim Affairs." *Journal Hadhari* 3, no. 1 (2011): 69–77.

Sabbah, Fatna A. *Woman in the Muslim Unconscious*. Translated by Mary Jo Lakeland. New York: Pergamon, 1984.

Sandoval, Mercedes Cros. *Worldview, the Orichas, and Santería: Africa to Cuba and Beyond*. Gainesville: University Press of Florida, 2006.

Schmidt, Bettina E. "The Discourse about 'Africa' in Religious Communities in Brazil: How Africa Becomes the Ultimate Source of Authenticity in Afro-Brazilian Religions." In *The Public Face of African New Religious Movements in Diaspora: Imagining the Religious "Other,"* edited by Afe Adogame, 29–45. New York: Routledge, 2014.

Shaarawi, Huda. *Harem Years: The Memoirs of an Egyptian Feminist (1879–1924)*. Translated by Margot Badran. New York: Feminist Press at City University of New York, 1987.
Solagberu, A. M. B. "An Historical Sketch of Sufi Orders in Ilorin, Nigeria." *Journal of Arabic and Religious Studies (JARS)* (Department of Religions, University of Ilorin) 14 (2000): 16–24.
Sudarkasa, Niara. *Where Women Work: A Study of Yoruba Women in the Marketplace and in the Home*. Ann Arbor: University of Michigan Press, 1973.
"3 Ifa Priests Turned Yahoo Boys Arrested for Selling Fake Yoruba Chieftancy to Americans." *NaijaGists.com*, June 11, 2017. http://naijagists.com.
Tirmithi, Muhammad. *Sunanu Tirmithi*. Vol. 4. Egypt: Albabi Alhalabi, 1975.
Topping, Alexandra. "Nigeria's Female Genital Mutilation Ban Is Important Precedent, Say Campaigners." *The Guardian*, May 29, 2015. www.theguardian.com.
Udobang, Wana. "How Nigeria's Millennial Priestess Is Revitalizing Spirituality." *Ozy*, February 11, 2018. www.ozy.com.
Ukah, Asonzeh. *A New Paradigm of Pentecostal Power: A Study of the Redeemed Christian Church of God in Nigeria*. Trenton, NJ: Africa World, 2008.
———. "Religion and Globalization." In *The Wiley-Blackwell Companion to African Religions*, edited by Elias Kifon Bongmba, 503–14. Oxford, UK: Wiley-Blackwell, 2012.
———. "Roots and Goals: Nigeria's Redeemed Christian Churches of God." Pulitzer Center, January 13, 2014. https://pulitzercenter.org.
Ukpong, Donatus Pius. *Nigerian Pentecostalism: Case, Diagnosis and Prescription*. Uyo, Nigeria: Fruities, 2008.
UNESCO. "Ifa Divination System." Accessed May 8, 2019. https://ich.unesco.org.
———. "Osun-Osogbo Sacred Grove." Accessed April 8, 2019. https://whc.unesco.org.
van Gennep, Arnold. *The Rites of Passage*. Chicago: University of Chicago Press, 1960.
Vasquez, Gina. "First Yoruba Egungun Festival in Mexico of Baba Olosun." www.youtube.com/watch?v=d6jwTngC7zo.
Vega, Martha Moreno. "The Dynamic Influence of Cubans, Puerto Ricans, and African Americans in the Growth of Ocha in New York City." In *Òrìṣà Devotion as World Religion: The Globalization of Yorùbá Religious Culture*, edited by Jacob K. Olupona and Terry Rey, 320–36. Madison: University of Wisconsin Press, 2008.
Wadud, Amina. *Qur'an and Woman: Rereading the Sacred Text from a Woman's Perspective*. New York: Oxford University Press, 1999.
Wallace, Ruth A. "Catholic Women and the Creation of a New Social Reality." *Gender and Society* 2, no. 1 (March 1988): 24–38.
———. "The Social Construction of a New Leadership Role: Catholic Women Pastors." *Sociology of Religion* 54, no. 1 (1993): 31–42.
Washington, Teresa N. *Our Mothers, Our Powers, Our Texts: Manifestations of Àjẹ́ in Africana Literature*. Orífín, Ilé Àjẹ́: Oya's Tornado, 2015.
Weber, Max. *The Theory of Economic and Social Organizations*. Edited and translated by A. M. Henderson and Talcott Parsons. New York: Free Press, 1964.

Wessinger, Catherine. *Theory of Women in Religions*. New York: New York University Press, 2020.
Willis, John Thabiti. *Masquerading Politics: Kinship, Gender, and Ethnicity in a Yoruba Town*. Bloomington: Indiana University Press, 2018.
Witte, Hans. "Fishes of the Earth: Mud Fish Symbolism in Yoruba Iconography." In *Visible Religion: Annual for Religious Iconography*, vol. 1, *Commemorative Figures*, edited by H. G. Kippenberg, 154–67. Leiden: Brill, 1982.
Yai, Olabiyi Babalola. "Yorùbá Religion and Globalization: Some Reflections." In *Òrìṣà Devotion as World Religion: The Globalization of Yorùbá Religious Culture*, edited by Jacob K. Olupona and Terry Rey, 233–46. Madison: University of Wisconsin Press, 2008.
"Yoruba." *Encyclopædia Britannica Online*. Accessed May 18, 2020. www.britannica.com.
"Yoruba Are 99.9% Identical to Igbos, Akan and Gaa-Adangbe—Study." *News Rescue*, November 20, 2016.

INTERVIEWS
Abiodun, Mrs. Fadeke. Abeokuta. July 12, 2019.
Abiona, Reverend Father Lawrence Adekunle. Principal. St. Joseph Centenary Catholic College, Ilorin, Kwara State, Nigeria. May 19, 2016, and May 17, 2021.
Abdulraheem, Dr. (Mrs.) Modinat. University of Ilorin, Ilorin, Kwara State, Nigeria. August 31, 2019.
Abubakar-Hamid, Dr. (Mrs.) Hassanat Funmilayo. Lecturer, Department of Arabic, University of Ilorin, Ilorin, Nigeria. August 31, 2019.
Adedayo, Pastor (Mrs.) Abigail. Minister of Counseling and Administration, and Associate Pastor. First Baptist Church, Abuja, Nigeria. May 25, 2016.
Adegboyega, Mohammed. Priest of Gelede termed Ogalagbo Onigelede (Ogalabo the carrier of Gelede) and an artisan. Abeokuta. June 15, 2016, and September 30, 2016.
Aderibigbe, Reverend (Mrs.) Olayemi Titilope. Church Pastor. Ijero Baptist Church, Apapa Road, Ebute-Meta, Lagos, Nigeria. May 19, 2016.
Adeyemi, Olori (Queen) Roheemat Olabimpe. The Iya Adinni, Anwarul Islam Society of Nigeria, Igboho branch, Oyo State. Department of Linguistics, University of Ilorin, Nigeria. August 25, 2019.
Adisa, Madam Ajiun Funke. Erinle orisa shrine (ojuba) in Agbole Bameke Ijaiye, Abeokuta. July 23, 2019.
Akanbi, Mrs. Wuraola. Abeokuta. July 12, 2019.
Anaeke, Reverend Sister Irene Mildred. Department of Religion and Human Values, University of Cape Coast, Ghana. May 6, 2016.
Ayano, Mrs. Tomilola. Ilorin, Kwara State. March 20, 2019.
Badru, Ibitooke Amoke. Iyalode Onisegun of Erunwon, Abeokuta. Abeokuta. June 12, 2016.
Balogun, Waheed. Jagunnailu ago-egun (Jagunna of egun [ancestral cult] cult) of Gelede and a retired footballer of the Abiola Super Babes. Abeokuta. June 16, 2016, and September 28, 2016.

Fashiku, Mr. John. Elder. Emmanuel Baptist Church, Ilorin, Nigeria. May 23, 2016.
Folorunsho, Mrs. Bose. Taiwo Road, Ilorin, Kwara State, Nigeria. March 20, 2019.
Ijaiya, Professor (Mrs.) Sidikat. Telephone conversation in Ilorin, Kwara State, Nigeria. August 11, 2019.
Ileuma, Associate Pastor (Mrs.) Julie. Redeemed Church of God, Abuja. June 4, 2016.
Irele, Iya Agan, Iya Oloya, Idayat. Oke-ipa Area, Lagos. December 5, 2015.
Mbamalu, Sister Cynthia. St. Thomas Aquinas Catholic chaplaincy, University of Ilorin, mini-campus. June 27, 2020.
Nwosu, Reverend Father Uchenna, PhD. St. Thomas Aquinas Catholic chaplaincy, University of Ilorin, mini-campus. June 27, 2020.
Obagbemiro, Doras. Prophetess in Cherubim and Seraphim Movement Church, Branch 6, Ilorin, Kwara State, Nigeria. February 16, 2021.
Obitosin, Osunfunke. Chief priestess at Ojuba Obatala, Ijemo Alape, Abeokuta. Abeokuta. June 12, 2016.
Ogunbiyi, Dr. Oyewole. Department of Religions, University of Ilorin. He is also Registrar, Orimolade Theological Institute, Ilorin, which is owned by Cherubim and Seraphim movement, Nigeria. June 27, 2020.
Ogungbile, Prof. David O. Department of Religious Studies, Obafemi Awolowo University, Ile-Ife, Nigeria. By telephone. June 30, 2020.
Ogunsanya, Aina. Ifa priest-babalawo. Abeokuta. June 16, 2016.
Olanrewaju, Mrs. Wulemat Motunrayo. The Atesinse Adinni, Asalatu Laola and Iya Adinni at Oke Aluko Street, Ilorin. August 22, 2019.
Olosun, Chief Adigun. Baba Osun of Osogbo and a babalawo. October 8, 2016. He has been living in Germany since 2004.
Olosun-Faniyi, Yeye Chief (Mrs.) Doyin. At the Susanne Wenger House, Ibokun Road, Osogbo, Nigeria. June 12, 2015, and January 4, 2017.
Oluwasanmi, Mrs. Shade. Abeokuta. July 12, 2019.
Omole, Mrs. Dupe Folashade. Catechist at St. Joseph Cathedral, Ilorin, Kwara State, Nigeria. May 17, 2021.
Osunibi, Mr. Saidi. An asogun at the ojuba Erinle Ijaiye, Abeokuta. August 12, 2016.
Oyelade, Agbaakin Sunday. Custodian of tradition at Itokun, Abeokuta. Abeokuta. June 15, 2016.
Raji, Dr. (Mrs.) Barakat. Faculty of Law, University of Ilorin. The current coordinator of University of Ilorin Muslim Ladies Circle. September 11, 2019.
Saliu, Alhaja Sikiratu. Clerk at the Faculty of Law, University of Ilorin. May 17, 2021.
Umeugo, Sister Josefa. St. Thomas Aquinas Catholic chaplaincy, University of Ilorin, mini-campus. June 27, 2020.
Wood-Menzies, Dr. Funlayo E. Postdoctoral scholar at the University of California, Santa Barbara, and scholar-priestess of Aṣẹ Ire. January 6, 2020.

WEBSITES AND SOCIAL MEDIA
African Studies Institute. Franklin College of Arts and Sciences, University of Georgia. Accessed January 2, 2019. http://afrstu.uga.edu.

Ansar ud Din Society of Nigeria, Washington, DC, Chapter. Accessed August 7, 2020. https://ansaruddeen-northamerica.com.
Aṣẹ Ire. Accessed July 7, 2020. https://aseire.com.
Bow Central Mosque. Accessed August 7, 2020. www.bowcentralmosque.co.uk.
Busola Olotu's Blog. Accessed October 3, 2018. https://busolaolotu.wordpress.com.
Daughters of Deborah International Ministry. Facebook page. Accessed October 3, 2018. www.facebook.com/Daughters-of-Deborah-Intl-Ministry-657452060932577/.
Esther Ajayi (Iya Adura). Facebook page. Accessed May 17, 2021. www.facebook.com/A.E.Ajayi.
love_of_christ_generation, Rev. Esther Ajayi. Instagram account. Accessed May 17, 2021.
MFM Women Foundation. Accessed May 20, 2016. www.mfmprovidence.org.
Nigerian Baptist Convention. Accessed June 6, 2020. www.nigerianbaptist.org.
The Noble Qur'an. Sahih International. Accessed October 9, 2021. https://quran.com.
Omniglot: The Online Encyclopedia of Writing Systems and Languages. Accessed September 3, 2018. www.omniglot.com.
Orisha Image (blog). Accessed April 9, 2019. www.orishaimage.com.
Orisha Marketplace. Accessed June 10, 2020. http://orishamarketplace.com.
Oyotunji African Village. Accessed January 10, 2019. www.oyotunji.org.
Owa African Market. Accessed July 10, 2020. www.owamarket.com.
Pastor (Mrs.) Foluke Adenike Adeboye. Accessed June 6, 2020. https://faadeboye.com.
Redeemed Christian Bible College. Accessed December 27, 2018. www.rcbc.edu.ng.
Redeemed Christian Church of God. Accessed June 5, 2020. http://rccg.org.
Trans-Atlantic Slave Trade Database. Accessed January 1, 2019. www.slavevoyages.org.
Yoruba Imports. Accessed July 10, 2020. https://yorubaimports.ecwid.com.

INDEX

Abdullahi, Amirah Biliqees, 99
Abeokuta Women's Union (AWU), 6
abiãs (in Candomblé), 114
Abiona, Reverend Father Lawrence Adekunle, 75
Abubakar-Hamid, Dr. Mrs. Hassanat, 89, 96
Adeboye, General Overseer Enoch Adejare, 66, 84–85
Adeboye, Pastor (Mrs.) Folu, 84
Adefunmi, Adelabu (Efuntola Osejiman Adelabu Adefunmi, born as Walter Eugene King), 110–11, 120
Adegboyega, Reverend Mrs. Bosun, 78
Adeoye, Alhaja Sheidat Mujidat, 101
Aderibigbe, Reverend Mrs. Olayemi Titilope, 78
àdìre eléko (indigo resist-dyed cotton cloth), 123
Adisa, Madam Ajiun Funke, 42
adoption, 10, 23, 138
adura, 91
African Studies Institute at the University of Georgia in Athens, Georgia, 118
agbára, 37
Ailara, Reverend (Mrs.), 80
Aimela, Prophetess, 80
Ajayi, Reverend Mother Esther Abimbola (Iya Adura), 125
àjẹ́, 2, 6, 8, 10, 21, 26, 42, 54–57, 58–62, 63, 138; *àjẹ́ funfun*, 55; *àjẹ́ dúdú* or *àjẹ́ pupa*, 55
Ajé, 46
akíkanjú, 43

Akindayomi, Pa Josaih Olufemi, 84
alabês (in Candomblé), 114
Aladura (Christ Apostolic Church) movement. *See* Christ Apostolic Church
Alaga, Alhaja Humuani, 90
alájàpà, 14, 94
Alakija, Folorunsho, 13
Alanamu Jamuiyat Istijabat Society of Nigeria (AJISON), 92
Alase-Arawole, Bimbo, 13
Alufa, 91
Amirah, 89, 98–99
ancestor veneration, 2, 28, 30–32, 116, 120
animal sacrifice, 120–21
Aniwura, Efunsetan, 13
Ansar-ud-Deen Society of Nigeria, 125
apètèbí, 124, 161n59
arugbá, 37, 51–52, 53
asalatu, 98
àṣẹ, 26–27, 35, 37, 38, 49, 54–57, 59, 62, 114, 140
Aṣẹ Ire, 104, 133
Asociación Cultural Yoruba de Cuba (ACYC; the Yoruba Cultural Association of Cuba), 113
aso-ebí ("the cloth of family members"), 19
asògún, 48, 50
awo, 53–54
àwọn ẹyẹ òru (the midnight birds), 61
àwọn Ìyà Mi (refers to powerful women), 42
Awo-opa, 52
axé (in Candomblé; Yoruba, àṣẹ), 114
axôguns (in Candomblé), 114

Aya Olua, 33
Ayo-Obiremi, Reverend Mrs. Olusola, 78

babalao (in Santería). See babaláwo
babaláwo, 23, 34–35, 52, *112–13*, *121*, *123–24*, 161n56; babaláwo elégán, 34; babaláwo olódù, 34
Babalola, Apostle Joseph Ayo, 71, 79
baba-òrìṣà (also baba-òòsà), 45
babaorixá (in Candomblé), 115
balance of male and female, 4, 7, 8, 37–38, 39, 40, 51, 62, 63, 80, 88, 113, 137. *See also* complementarity
Bamidele movement, 90
Bamidele, Shaykh 'Abd al-Salam, 90
Bible passages, 69, 72, 74, 80, 82
Bight of Benin, 16, 107
Bolaji, Pastor (Mrs.) Bosede, 83
Bolatan, Mary, 77
Bon Dje (in Haitian Vodou), 116
Bowen, Reverend Thomas Jefferson, 76
bride lamentation. See Ẹkún ìyàwó
bride wealth, 19–20
British colonialism, 6, 12, 16–17, 23
Buhari, Mrs. Aisha, 30

Candomblé, 1, 104, 108, 109–10, 112, 113–15, 117, 122, 123, 126, 131, 132, 140; *Candomblé jeje-nago, 113*
casa, 114
Casa Branca, 114
Casa de Yemanjá, 114
Catholic Church in Nigeria. *See* Roman Catholic Church
Celestial Church of Christ (CCC or Cele), 79, 80, 81
charisma, 43
charismatic churches. *See* Pentecostal/charismatic churches
chieftancies, 39, 40, 41, 44, 76, 80, 95–96, 102
Cherubim and Seraphim Church (C&S), 80–81, 124–25. *See also* Eternal Sacred Order of Cherubim and Seraphim (C&S)
childbirth, 54, 80–81
children, 5, 10, 17, 19, 21, 22–24, 55, 123, 130
Christ Apostolic Church (CAC), 71, 79, 80
Christianity, 1, 6, 19, 20, 21, 22, 30, 31, 63, 64, 65–88, 89, 90, 95, 103, 124–25, 134, 137–38, 139–40; African independent churches, 70, 71, 79–81, 87, 101, 124–25, 140; attitudes toward "witches," 57, 79, 83; commercialization in, 135; mission churches, 69, 70, 71–79, 87, 140; Pentecostal/charismatic churches, 65–67, 70, 71, 81–86, 87, 124, 140; women's ordination in, 70, 72, 73–74, 77–79, 83–84, 85, 87, 140; women's prophecy in, 65–67, 71, 79, 80, 81–82, 125, 140–41; women's roles in, 4, 6–7, 10, 12, 16, 65–88, 89, 95, 124–25, 137–41. *See also* Roman Catholic Church
Church of God Mission International, 71
Church Missionary Society, 6, 68
circumcision. *See* female genital mutilation; male circumcision
clothing, 18–19
colonialism, 6, 12, *16–17*, 23, 132. *See also* British colonialism
complementarity, Yorùbá concept of, 7, 8, 14, 26, 38, 42, 64, 68, 121, 137
cooking. *See* food preparation
cosmological narratives, 4, 7, 16, 26, 34, 36, 46, 54–55, 137

Daughters of Deborah International Ministry (DODIM), 66–67, 85–86
dálémosú, 22
da'wa, 98
Dáwóduù, 25
diaspora. *See* Yorùbá diaspora; Yorùbá religion, in diaspora
divination, 2, 11, 23, 26, 28, 34–37, 38, 41, 44–45, 47, 51–52, 58, 91, 103, 111, 113, 114, 117, 121, 126, 129, 132, 133, 134, 135, 140
divorce, 21–22, 100

INDEX | 181

ebo (sacrifice), 115
ebomin, 114
Ebora, 32
economic productivity, of Yorùbá women, 5, 7, 8–9, 10, 12, 13–14, 21, 22, 40, 41, 42, 63, 70, 76, 86, 87, 93, 94, 96, 97, 98, 102, 130, 133, 137, 138, 141
education, women's, 5, 11, 20, 21, 28, 29, 63, 68, 70, 75, 77, 79, 89, 90, 97, 99–100, 125, 139
eégún (plural, *egúngún*), 31, 120
Ẹẹ́rìndínlógún, 23, 34, 36, 43, 51–52
Èfẹ̀, 58, 60–61, 62
ẹgbẹ́, 12, 40, 69, 76, 80, 87, 88, 93, 97, 100–102, 137–38
ẹgbẹ́ alasalatu. *See* prayer groups, women's
Egúngún, 2, 31–32, 40, 67, 90, 120
èkejì, 115
Ẹkún ìyàwó, 27
Ẹla-isu, 48
Elédàá, 1
elégùn (mount), 33–34
eléri-ìpín, 36
Emanuel, Captain Christiana Abiodun Akinsowon, 71, 79
engagement ceremony, 19, 20
equedes (in Candomblé), 114
Erinlè, 34, 42, 45, 49–51, 63
ẹrú, 106
erù-òòsà, 50–51
ẹsẹ̀ Ifá, 34, 35
Èṣù, 35, 46, 52
Eternal Sacred Order of Cherubim and Seraphim (C&S), 71, 79. *See also* Cherubim and Seraphim Church
ẹyẹ, 42
Ewe people, 116, 126, 132
Ezili Danto, 116
Ezili Freda, 116

Fadillulah Muslim Mission, 101
family structure, 7, 9, 17, 24, 44

Federation of Muslim Women's Association in Nigeria (FOMWAN), 99–100
Federation of Nigeria Women's Societies (FNWS), 6
female circumcision. *See* female genital mutilation
female genital mutilation (*also called* female genital cutting), 28–30, 41
Festa de Iemanjá, 115
filho, 112. *See also* ọmọ
Fon people, 116, 126, 132
food, 18, 19, 21, 24, 42, 44, 46, 47, 51, 52, 58, 97–98, 104, 114, 115, 117, 118, 123
food preparation, 18, 28, 47, 97–98, 114, 117, 123, 124, 126
funerals. *See* ancestor veneration

Gèlèdé, 58–63; origins of festival, 58
gender roles, 2, 3, 4, 5, 6–9, 12, 13–14, 17–18, 21–22, 23–24, 26, 27–28, 38–41, 51, 63, 68, 69, 70, 72, 87–88, 91–94, 96–97, 100, 102, 111–13, 121–22, 137–39, 141
globalization, 70, 127–36, 139, 141. *See also* Yorùbá religion: globalization of
Good Women Fellowship, 85
gùn, 33–34, 44

hadith, 93, 94–95, 96
Haitian Vodou, 1, 108, 109, 116–17, 122, 126, 131, 132, 140
hijab, 89, 94
homosexuality, 44, 109, 112–13, 121–22, 154n7
horticulture, 2, 9, 14, 17–18
houngan, 116
houngan asogwe, 116
houngan sur pwen, 116

iabassé ("mother who cooks," in Candomblé), 114
ialorixá ("mother of orisa," in Candomblé; Yoruba: *iyá-òrìṣà*), 114, 115

INDEX

iaôs ("wives of the orixás" in Candomblé; Yoruba, *ìyàwó*), 114–15
ibó, 36
Idahosa, Archbishop Benson Andrew, 71
Ìdí Igi, 24–25
Ifá, 2, 4, 23, 26, 34–36, 38, 42, 43, 45, 50–52, 54, 58, 60, 91, 103, 110, 112–13, 117, 118, 121, 122, 123–24, 129, 132, 133, 139, 162n20
igbodu, 35
ìlàrí, 106
Ilẹ̀ (Earth goddess), 59
ilê (in Candomblé; Yoruba: *ilé*), 113–14, 119, 122, 126, 140
ilé, 17, 24, 55, 113, 119
Ilê Axé Opó Afonjá, 114
Ilé-Ifẹ̀, 16, 46–47, 59
ilé-kéwú, 90
imam, 95
infertility, 10, 22–23, 40, 84, 101, 128–29
inheritance, 24–26
initiation, 32–33, 34–35, 42, 43–44, 45, 48, 104, 111, 113, 115, 116, 119, 122, 123–24, 127, 135–36, 139, 140, 161n56
Isabatudeen Society, 90
Islam, 1, 6, 19, 20, 21, 22, 30, 31, 60, 63, 64, 65, 67, 89–102, 124–25, 137–38, 139–40, 141; commercialization in, 135; women's leadership in, 89, 95–97, 98–102, 125, 132, 134, 141; women's roles in, 4, 6–7, 10, 12, 89–102, 125, 137–38, 139–41
ìwòfà, 105–06
ìwo-gbódù, 123–24
ìyá, 9
Ìyá, 23
Ìyá Àdínì, 96, 102
Ìyá àgan, 31
Ìyá Ajé, 48–49
Ìyá Ìjo, 76, 80, 87. *See also* Òtún Ìyá Ìjo
iyakekere (in Candomblé). *See mãe pequena*
Ìyálóde, 40, 80, 90. *See also* Òtún Ìyálóde.
iyálóòsà. *See iyá-òrìṣà*

Ìyá Mi ("my mother," *also* "our mothers"), 5–6
Ìyà Mi (refers to powerful mothers, possibly malevolent), 5–6, 12, 21, 26–27, 54–57, 58–60, 62, 122, 138
Ìyámi Òṣòròngà, 59
iyánífá, 23, 34–35, 41, 52, 112–13, 124, 127, 133, 139
iyanifá (in Santería). *See iyánífá*
Ìyá Nlá, 58–60, 62, 63
Iya-Oloya, Iya Agan Idayat Irele Oke-Ipa, 52–54, 155n27
iyá-oómo, 48
iyá-òrìṣà (also *iyálóòsà*), 45, 48, 134
Iya Sonta, 127, 161n3
iyawo (in Santería). *See ìyàwó*
ìyàwó, 33, 45, 111, 115

Jeje-Nagô, 113
Jeje-Nagô Ilê, 114

keferi, 91
khatib, 95
Kongo people, 116

La Regla de Ocha. *See* Santería
Lasyrenn, 116
LGBTQ persons, 8, 109, 121–22
Lucumí. *See* Santería
Lukumí dialect, 111
lwa (in Haitian Vodou), 116

mãe-de-santo (Portuguese: "mother of saint," in Candomblé), 114
Mãe Filhinha, 114
mãe pequena ("small mother," *iyakekere*, in Candomblé), 114
Mãe Stella de Oxossi, 114
male circumcision, 28–29
mambo, 116–17
mambo asogwe, 116, 126
mambo si pwen (or *mambo sur point*), 116
Mama Keke, 110

marriage, 5, 19–22, 27, 28, 45, 48–49, 83, 87, 111–12. *See also* polygyny
Matory, J. Lorand, 7, 33, 44, 112
menstruation, 37, 49, 51, 54, 63, 69, 80, 95, 96, 140
MFM Women Foundation, 83
monogamy, 21, 22, 68
Moore, Audley (Queen Mother Moore, Iyaluwa), 110
Mora, Babaláwo Pancho (Ifá Moroti), 110
Moremi Book Store, 110
motherhood, 4, 5–6, 9–10, 12, 22–24, 28, 30, 37, 40, 54–57, 58–62, 69, 75, 86, 89, 96, 97–98, 112, 122, 134, 138
Mountain of Fire and Miracles (MFM), 82–84, 124; women in, 82–84, 124
Muallimaat, 98

Nasrul-lahi-li Fathi Society of Nigeria (NASFA), 125
National Council of Catholic Women Organizations (NCCWO), 76
Nigerian Baptist Convention, 70, 76–79; women in, 76–79
Nigerian Women's Union (NWU), 6
Nwosu, Reverend Father Patrick, 75

Òbà, 40, 52, 54
Obagbemiro, Prophetess Dorcas, 125
Ọbàìṣà (Obatala), 54
Ọbàtálá (also Òrìṣà Nla), 34, 36, 45, 46–49, 52, 54, 58, 63, 103, 107, 111, 118, 122, 133, 154n9
Obì, 34, 37
Ochún (in Santería). *See* Ọṣun
Odù (goddess), 34, 42, 44–45, 59
Òduà, 16, 56, 59
odù Ifá, 34, 35, 124
Odùduwà, 16, 47, 154n9
Odù Ìmàle, 132
odún, 119
Odun Ifa festival, 52, 120
Odun Isese, 52, 163n28

Òfósí, 32
ògán, 115
ogãs (in Candomblé), 114
Ògbóni, 5, 40, 52–53, 59
Ògún, 46, 54, 103, 107, 110
ojúbà, 51, 123
oko, 33
Oliana, Christopher, 111
Olódùmarè, 1–2, 26, 36, 37, 38, 43, 46–47, 54–55
Olókun, 59
Ọlórun, 1
olórí-ebí, 17
Olórí-ebí, 39
olórìṣà, 33, 36
Olosun, Chief Adigun, 160n44
Olosun-Faniyi, Yeye Chief (Mrs.) Doyin, 127–29
Olotu, Pastor (Mrs.) Busola, 65–67, 86
Olukoya, Dr. Daniel Kolawole, 82–83
Olukoya, Pastor (Dr.) Mrs. Shade, 83
Olúsarùn, 33
ọmọ, 112
Omole, Mrs. Dupe Folashade, 75
omolúàbí, 38
omo-òòsà, 127, 129, 134
omo-òrìṣà, 44–45, 48, 52
oògùn, 37
ọpèlè, 35
ọpọ́n-Ifá, 35
oral genres, 3–4, 16, 24, 26–28, 34, 41, 42, 68, 86, 91, 109, 117, 119, 126, 139, 140; and women, 27–28, 117, 127, 138, 140
Order of Damballah Hwedo, 110
ordination. *See* Christianity: women's ordination in
orí, 52
orichá (in Santería). *See òrìṣà*
oríkì, 4, 16, 27–28, 42, 46, 123, 138; Bridal Crying (*Ẹkún Ìyàwó*), 4, 27; Lineage Praise Poetry (*Oríkì ìdílé*), 27
Oríkì Ìdílé, 27
Orí Òju Orí, 25

òrìṣà, 2–3, 7, 8, 27, 28, 32–34, 35, 36, 38, 42–56, 58–63, 91, 103–5, 107, 108–9, 110–15, 117–22, 133, 137–38, 140, 154n9
Òrìṣà Nla. See Ọbàtálá
òrìṣà parapọ̀, 128–29
òrìṣà worship, 27–28, 32–34, 42–56, 58–59, 63, 104–5, 107, 108–9, 110–15, 117–22, 133, 137–38, 140
orixá (in Candomblé; Yoruba, òrìṣà), 114, 115
Orisha Marketplace, 133
Orisha (Shango) in Trinidad and Tobago, 108, 119, 132
Orò, 3
Orúnla. See Ọ̀rúnmìlà
Ọ̀rúnmìlà (Orula in Santería), 2, 34, 36, 113
Ọsanyìn, 46
òṣè, 117
Oshoffa, Reverend Samuel Bilewu Joseph, 79
Ọṣun (Ochún in Santería), 2, 26–27, 34, 35, 36, 42, 44–45, 46, 50, 52, 53, 54, 59, 67, 90, 103, 107, 110, 118, 119, 122, 127
Osun Osogbo festival, 50, 53
Osun-Osogbo Sacred Grove, 124, 127, 133, 162n20
Òtúnba, 39
Òtún Ìyá Ìjo, 80, 87
Òtún Ìyálóde, 80, 90
Owa Afrikan Market, 133
Ọya (Oyá in Santería), 2, 46, 52, 59, 107, 111, 120
Oyedeji, Deaconess Mrs. Rachel Morawo, 18
Oyewumi, Oyeronke, 8, 23, 145
Ọ̀yọ́ kingdom (empire), 16, 33, 106
Ọ̀yọ́túnjí African Village, 110, 119, 120

pai-de-santo (Portuguese: "father of saint," in Candomblé), 114
patriarchy, 8–9
Pentecostal churches. See Christianity: Pentecostal/charismatic churches
polygyny, 5, 20–21, 30, 40, 42, 55, 68, 87, 91
possession, 32–34, 41, 44–45, 47, 48, 50, 112, 113, 117, 119, 122
power, concept of, 5–6, 17, 21, 24, 26–27, 37, 38, 40, 42, 49, 53–57, 59, 62, 121, 122, 140, 141
prayer groups, women's, 69, 85–86, 88, 97–99, 100–102, 125, 138, 140–41; Christian, 69, 85–86, 88, 138, 140; Muslim, 97–99, 100–102, 125, 138, 140–41
pregnancy, 24, 37
priestesses (cultic functionaries), 2, 32–34, 36, 41, 42–56, 57, 63, 103–04, 109, 111–12, 117, 118, 119, 123, 124, 125–26, 127–29, 131, 132–33, 135, 140
priests (cultic functionaries), 32–34, 36, 43, 44, 45, 112, 117, 119, 123, 131, 132, 135
property rights, women's, 24–26
purdah, 90

Qur'an passages, 91–92, 93–94, 97

Ransome-Kuti, Funmilayo, 6, 151n11
rárí, 43
Redeemed Christian Church of God (RCCG), 65–66, 82, 84–85, 124; women in, 65–66, 82, 84–85, 124
reincarnation, 31
resources for the equality of women, and resources for the subordination of women, 4–5, 12
rites of passage, 28–32, 41
Roman Catholic Church, 70, 72, 107; women in, 72–76
rulers, 38–40, 41, 44, 47, 54, 56; female rulers, 5, 39–40, 41

salat al-istikhara, 91
Sàngó, 7, 33–34, 36, 44, 45, 46, 107, 110, 117, 118, 124
santera, 111, 126
Santería, 1, 104, 107–8, 109–13, 117, 122, 123, 126, 131, 132, 139, 140

secrecy, 38, 55
Serrano, Sunta (Asunsión Rodriguez Serrano), 111, 161n3
serviteurs, 116
sexual orientation, 121–22
Shagaya, Hajia Bola, 13
Shango Temple in Harlem, New York City, 111
Sinha, Ekedy, 114
Slave Coast. *See* Bight of Benin
slave trade, among Yoruba, 105–7. *See also* transatlantic slave trade
syncretism, 131

taboos, 24, 42, 46, 47, 52, 63, 103, 115, 123
taqwā, 91
Teish, Yeye Luisah, 103
terreiro (Portuguese: "yard"), 114
Townsend, Reverend Henry, 68
transatlantic slave trade, 1, 3, 12, 14, 16, 105–8, 117, 119, 122, 125, 132, 140
Tunolase, Moses Orimolade, 71, 79

virginity, 20
Violence Against Persons (Prohibition) Act (2015), 29
Vodou. *See* Haitian Vodou
Vodun, 126

websites, 124, 131, 133, 141
wedding, 20, 28
Wenger, Susanne (Adunni Olorisa), 127–28
widow, 25, 28

Winners Chapel International, 124
witchcraft accusations against women, 54–55, 57, 83
Woli, 91
Women Missionary Union (WMU) of Nigeria, 77
Women of Faith, 86
women's ordination. *See* Christianity: women's ordination in
Wood-Menzies, Dr. Funlayo Easter (Iya Funlayo), 103–5, 133

Yemọja, or Yemọnja, or Yemanjá (Yemayá in Santería), 58–59, 107, 111, 118, 119, 120, 122
yèyé, 161n1
Yoruba Civil War, 16
Yorùbá diaspora, 1, 3, 12, 103–9, 113, 117–26, 129–36, 138, 140, 141
Yoruba Imports, 133
Yorùbá people, 1, 14, 16, 116, 125
Yorùbá language, vii-viii, 118, 123, 136, 162n25
Yorubaland, 1, 14–15, 16
Yorùbá religion, 1–6, 9, 12, 20, 26–38, 42–64, 67, 68, 72, 90, 101–2, 103–26, 127–36, 137–38, 140, 141; commercialization, 129, 133–35, 141; in diaspora, 103–26, 129, 132–36, 138, 140, 141; globalization of, 3, 12, 127–36, 141; and social media, 3, 124, 135; women in, 26–38, 40–41, 42–64, 103–26, 127–30, 133–36, 137–38, 140–41
Yorùbá Temple in Harlem, New York City, 110–11

ABOUT THE AUTHOR

OYÈRÓNKÉ OLÁDÉMỌ is Professor of Comparative Religious Studies, Department of Religions, University of Ilorin, Nigeria. She is the author of *Women in the Yoruba Religious Sphere* (2003) and *Gender in Yoruba Oral Traditions* (2009) and coauthor, with David Ogungbile, of *Religion, Environment and Sustainable Development in Africa* (2020).

www.ingramcontent.com/pod-product-compliance
Lightning Source LLC
Chambersburg PA
CBHW020411080526
44584CB00014B/1276